Mapping Gay L.A.

In the series *American Subjects*,
edited by Robert Dawidoff

Mapping Gay L.A.

The Intersection of Place and Politics

Moira Rachel Kenney

Temple University Press
PHILADELPHIA

Temple University Press, Philadelphia 19122

Published 2001
Printed in the United States of America

♾ The paper used in this publication meets the requirements of the American National Standard for Information Sciences—Permanence of Paper for Printed Library Materials, ANSI Z39.48–1984.

Library of Congress Cataloging-in-Publication Data

Kenney, Moira Rachel.
Mapping gay L.A. : the intersection of place and politics / Moira Rachel Kenney.
p. cm. — (American subjects)
Includes bibliographical references and index.
ISBN 1-56639-883-5 (cloth : alk. paper) — ISBN 1-56639-884-3 (pbk. : alk. paper)
1. Gay activists—California—Los Angeles Metropolitan Area.
2. Gay liberation movement—United States—Los Angeles Metropolitan Area.
3. Gay communities—United States—Los Angeles Metropolitan Area.
4. Lesbian communities—United States—Los Angeles Metropolitan Area.
I. Title. II. Series.

HQ76.8.U5 K466 2001
306.76'6'0979494—dc21 00–053676

Contents

List of Maps

Foreword

Moira Kenney's *Mapping Gay L.A.* does just that. It locates the sexual minority's history and presence in the geographically sprawling and culturally confusing city of Los Angeles. Drawing on her own background in urban planning, Kenney has developed an original and practical way of thinking about history and activism. Her book makes a cogent argument for the importance of Los Angeles as a site of modern American gay and urban history. *Mapping Gay L.A.* is a readable, scholarly, and comprehensive recent history of lesbians and gay men in Los Angeles and also suggests new directions for studies and activism in contemporary multicultural cities. This is a book that has much to add to our understanding of Los Angeles and its part in U.S. urban history, although Kenney rejects the intentional and haphazard Los Angeles exceptionalism that has characterized so much writing on the subject.

The familiar narrative and myths of gay history do not include Los Angeles. New York, Boston, San Francisco, even Paris, have seemed to be the cities where American lesbian and gay history happened, where homosexual Americans ended up. Los Angeles, the site of the homophile movement and other significant origins and institutionalizations of American lesbian and gay culture, has been comparatively neglected. Its distinctive version of a city, geographically, sociopolitically, and culturally, hosted an influential and distinct gay response to its conditions and to the general conditions of the sexual minority in modern America.

For Kenney mapping is a process joining "strands of geography, planning, and environmental psychology that allow for the reading of the city both as space and as text. Mapping—the daily and unconscious practice of negotiating the city—produces what geographers have termed the mental (or cognitive) map, an individual's own image of the city." Mapping informs Kenney's account of the "strategic visibility" of lesbians and gay men in various configurations of felt and built individual and community city spaces. It connects the rhetorical strategy of this lively and clearly presented study with the actual experiences and decisions of the people who lived and thus created "gay L.A." as a network of residential and commercial neighborhoods and communities of geography and interest.

Gay urban experience fashions activism out of circumstance, and Kenney shows how lesbians and gay men made Los Angeles a safer gay place and a safer home. These twin themes of coming out and coming home are common to most of her chapters She discusses several instances of place claiming: "the appropriation of physical, social, and mental spaces by marginalized groups" including studies of "gay" neighborhoods, social service institutions, lesbian responses to gay male dominated institutions and the alternatives they created, and a revealing history of L.A. public activism. One reason Kenney's book is so clear and so convincing is that her use of "mapping" makes the thought processes of activism and those of people who happen to live in Los Angeles and happen to be gay easier to compare. Individuals and groups alike "map" their cities and alike share the propensity for action taken in the course of and in response to their lives. Gay lives are more likely than many others to become political because they "map" in ways that cause politics and require activism.

Mapping Gay L.A. helps me to understand how I have mapped my own life as a gay man and sometime activist in Los Angeles. West Hollywood was first a destination and is now a neighborhood for me. Kenney captures its landmarks and character as I have experienced them. I recognize the neighborhoods and institutions of the lesbian and gay Los Angeles she describes. I remember the 1993 demonstrations against Governor Wilson's veto of a gay rights bill he had promised to sign, which forms so vivid a part of Kenney's story. Those street protests transformed my own sense of Los Angeles and my role as a gay activist within it. It was as a result of participating in those demonstrations that Michael Nava and I decided to write a book about gay civil rights. I see my own life and those of my friends and acquaintances reflected in these pages but transformed by Kenney's understanding beyond the personal into a shared lesbian and gay experience of city life.

The inevitable subject of *Mapping Gay L.A.* is activism, because Kenney understands that living as a lesbian or gay man is itself a kind of activism. Urbanity is equally her subject, because she understands the connection between the sexual minority and the city's places that make gays and lesbians archetypally urban citizens. In a book as direct and clearly written as it is exceptionally well informed and just plain smart, Moira Kenney remaps engaged gay activism in ways that surely apply to other groups and even beyond the city. She starts with two assumptions: "First, place and the city have importance for culture and politics; and second, place is created and altered through our interactions in and with it." Each episode in this action-packed book reflects them and "illustrates collective political action in a spatial context." The book takes place in a particular Los Angeles setting, but its readers can live anywhere. *Mapping Gay L.A.* gives a good way to map past and present into acceptable future.

ROBERT DAWIDOFF

Acknowledgments

This book's arrival proves, if such proof were needed, the generosity, kindness, and persistence of many. The joys I experienced while researching and writing this book prove this even more.

The project began as a doctoral dissertation at the Graduate School of Architecture and Urban Planning at UCLA, under the direction of Professor John Friedmann. His truly unique commitment to pushing the boundaries of our discipline and to bring new voices into the field meant that I was able to conceive of such a project. His generous advice and critique was critical for the project's completion. Also at UCLA, Edward Soja created the climate for taking on the intricacies and complexities of Los Angeles. At crucial moments, Carole Pateman and Anastasia Loukaitou-Sideris provided guidance to the project as well. At UCLA, colleagues whose own interest in the city and in my work carried this project through included Amy Anderson, Barbara Hooper, Eric Lee, Geoff DiGirolamo, Gail Sansbury, Demosthenes Peterson, and Eric Reyes.

The transition from dissertation to book could not have happened without the intellectual and emotional support of Professor Robert Dawidoff at Claremont Graduate University. His curiosity about my work rescued it from its postdissertation oblivion, and his enthusiasm for its publication guided it through this long process. Most importantly, he provided the first critique from a gay academic and activist. Because of his own work in the field, his comments carry special weight and meaning.

In many ways, this book is the product of the city it explores, and there are many Angelenos to thank. Dana Cuff and Michael Dear are among those whose work has guided mine. Among the many gays and lesbians I interviewed, Morris Kight remains for me the best indication that Los Angeles is a city of activists. His decades-long commitment to justice and human rights has set a proud standard for gay and lesbian activism.

This book was completed while I had the great pleasure to work at the Getty Research Institute, with colleagues and friends whose own interest in the city's public life encouraged me in many ways. With the support and guidance of Josephine Ramirez, Karen Stokes, Mario Ontiveros, and Michael Roth, I was able to look deeper into the intricacies of Los Angeles and add to the story I have told here.

My family has provided the intellectual, emotional, and at times financial support that has made me a writer. My parents, Michael and Sara, are tough editors and good listeners. My brother Padraic has been my guide throughout my academic life. My sister Shelagh helped make Los Angeles a real home.

Finally, this book is dedicated to my friend, Darcy Buerkle. She reminds me why there are writers in this world, and what are our responsibilities.

1 Locating the Politics of Difference

The popular narrative of the gay and lesbian movement in the United States tends to be a tale of two cities, centering on New York and San Francisco. Seen as models of freedom and sophistication, these cities are accepted as uniquely enabling gay and lesbian community formation and as models for communities in other cities. Their enclaves—Greenwich Village and the Castro—are celebrated as offering the best of gay and lesbian community life, and these cities as well as their satellite neighborhoods are similarly cosmopolitan. Like most popular narratives, this one ignores complexity. My purpose is not to deny that the promise of these two historical poles has made possible generations of gay and lesbian cultural and political achievements, but only to suggest that it enshrines a permanence of place and a constancy of behavior that is exceptional, even for post-liberation gays and lesbians. Gays, lesbians, and bisexuals living elsewhere more often experience their cities in ways that would be more familiar to their counterparts in Los Angeles than those in New York or San Francisco. Although Greenwich Village or the Castro captures the imagination of gays and lesbians, their movement owes as much to Los Angeles, where the struggle has largely been one of being present and visible within the urban whole, rather than in designated enclaves. For fifty years community building has followed several trajectories in Los Angeles, with moments of public achievement against a backdrop of smaller, more mundane gains. The evidence of these struggles is embedded in the city

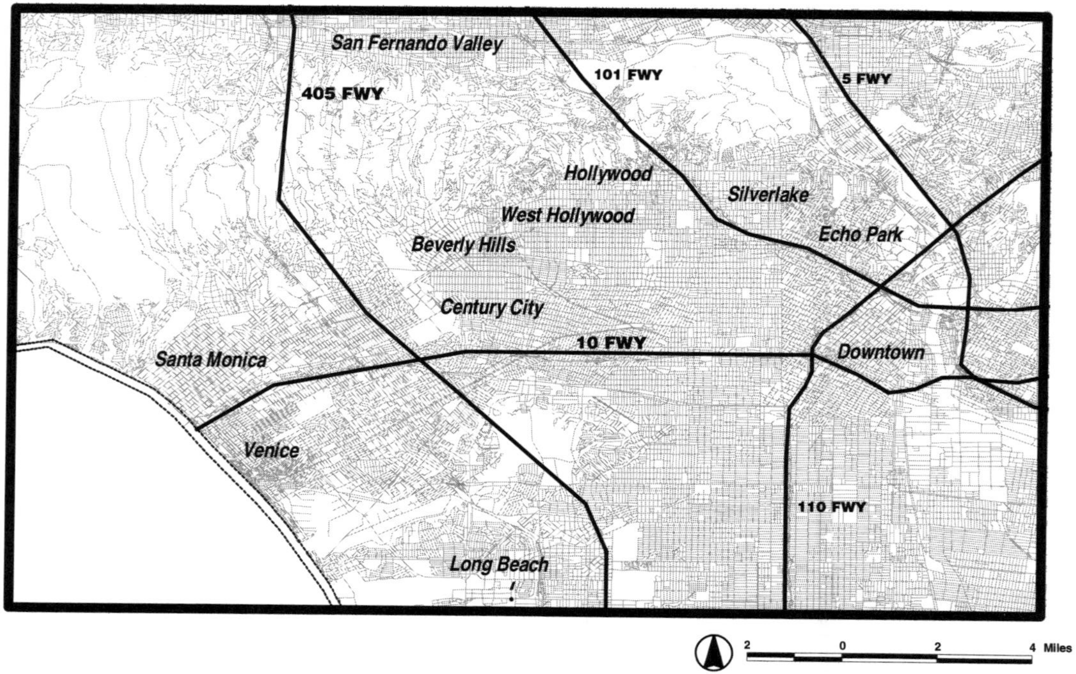

Map 1. The Los Angeles Area

map, and its very lack of visibility makes it more representative of the lived reality of gays and lesbians across the United States.

Setting the story of the gay and lesbian urban experience in Los Angeles goes against the grain. The mythic migration of gays leaving their homelands to live in Greenwich Village or the Castro has tended to obscure the importance of the development of both the movement and a broader gay culture elsewhere. What makes it more difficult to compare Los Angeles with New York and San Francisco is the problem of reading Los Angeles itself. Contemporary urban studies also have seen Los Angeles as an exception, strange and often unrecognizable. The differences within Los Angeles's gay and lesbian community, combined with the apparent differences between Los Angeles and other American cities, have contributed to the oversight of its urban history.

Since the 1920s, the possibilities of modern urbanity—freedom, anonymity, and community—have allowed for new expressions of homosexuality. The search for a community, friendship, and love in an environment at once hostile and forgiving has required an often-revolutionary appropriation of public and private places. Now, the collective celebration of gay and lesbian life in the city intertwines with the social, political, and cultural transformations of the urban at a pace and level of complexity not possible in suburban or rural America. At pride parades and protest marches, in residential and commercial neighborhood developments, gays and lesbians have entered public life, not just as community leaders, but more simply as community builders. The social diversity, economic opportunity, and political exchange characteristic of modern American cities support both individual and collective growth, as well as the development of urban subcultures. Thus, the history of homosexuality and the development of the city in the United States are intertwined phenomena.

The multiple formulations of gay and lesbian community—homophile, homosexual, liberationist, feminist, queer—respond to and emerge from the changing political and social particularities of the urban experience (as has been well described in standard gay and lesbian histories). My interest encompasses both the social and the physical aspects of this interchange, examining the effect of the gay and lesbian movement on place in urban America.

The diversity within gay and lesbian communities and differences between communities across the country reflect the individuality of the movement in disparate urban settings. The story of Los Angeles epitomizes this entanglement of place and community. In many ways, modern Los Angeles is as new as the gay and lesbian movement itself. The early twentieth century saw Los Angeles emerge from its Spanish colonial beginnings and gradually develop an urban character that both fostered a multicultural growth and at the same time secured the power of the dominant Anglo culture. Only in the midcentury, as the homophile movement was emerging, did the city begin to acknowledge and at times encourage the richness of its political and cultural difference. Since the midfifties, the engine of the city's growth evolved from the expansionary dictates of a select group of industrial and commercial leaders to one fed by innumerable communities and cultures. The political organizing in the ethnic communities central to this new expansion have intersected the gay and lesbian experience, drawing from and adding to its particular Angeleno character.

Recent attention to the cultural, political, and social landscapes of Los Angeles has raised the questions of the city's fit within broad analyses of urban phenomena. The debate over Los Angeles's relevance—either as "an exceptional case, a persistently peculiar and irreproducible type of city or as an exemplary, if not paradigmatic, illustration of the essential and generalizable features of late-twentieth-century urbanization"[1]—has become, unfortunately, the lens through which Los Angeles is viewed. Thus, studies of Los Angeles have been particularly polarized, showing Los Angeles to be either a paradise of the American dream or an unlivable tangle of freeways and smog. However, this history of Los Angeles is best understood apart from any notion of exceptionalism. The major commonality of the Los Angeles experience is the promise it has held for the waves of arrivals, for whom the combination of employment and sunshine outweighs, at least initially, the many complications of life in Los Angeles. Similarly, gays and lesbians continue to migrate to Los Angeles for both the financial and personal opportunity it promises. More than any other city, Los Angeles is seen as an alternative to the rest of country. In this way, gays and lesbians arriving in Los Angeles share certain characteristics with their contemporaries arriving from other places and epitomize one of the central motivations for the growth of this city. Understanding their motivations, aspirations, and achievements may well shed light on the peculiar dynamic of community building in this city.

The enigma of Los Angeles begins with the geographic. Manhattan and San Francisco together cover less area than central Los Angeles. The size and sprawl of the city necessitates a mobility of daily life that scatters ethnic, racial, religious, and other culturally defined communities, reducing the possibilities of the kind of geographic concentrations of community landmarks that characterize enclaves like Greenwich Village or the Castro. Across the Los Angeles region, gay and lesbian communities exist at all scales and levels of visibility. Most obviously, West Hollywood in the center of the city and Silverlake northwest of downtown support the most recognizable markers of gay public life—bars and community organizations. Lesbians, however, have gravitated toward a number of smaller neighborhoods in Long Beach and the San Fernando Valley where they remain less visible. Reflecting the affluence of the gay community, resort destinations such as Laguna Beach (to the south) and Palm Springs (to the east) also have become major centers for both residents and the weekend getaway crowd. This multicentered geography results from the region's own character—the combined populations of Manhattan and San Francisco roughly equal that of Los Angeles. The sheer numbers and density of the gay and lesbian communities in these other cities are primary engines of their community's peculiar visibility; simply put, the complexity of Los Angeles's social and physical geography is the basis for a different narrative.

The same idyllic dream that propelled the settlement of the city (primarily but not exclusively by Anglos)—from the oranges in the street promised by city boosters in the early 1900s to the suburban solidity of the post–World War II boom and the entrepreneurial expansion of recent years—has inspired the gay and lesbian community as well. Although a celebration of the city's physical charms—beaches, weather, artificially green suburbs—is often mocked by those chronicling the city, these do play a significant role in the making of the city and explain much of its character. Gays and lesbians may be drawn to New York or San Francisco by images of political triumphs, such as the election of Harvey Milk in San Francisco or the inspiring images of ACT UP protests in New York, but such signal events rarely occur in Los Angeles. The drive for political visibility and separatist culture that typifies enclave development in other cities runs directly counter to the desire, in Los Angeles, to find individual fulfillment within the safety and support of the community.

Two questions emerge when we look at the geography of Los Angeles as it relates to the strategy of gay and lesbian community building: First, how can the city as used and understood by the gay and lesbian communities of Los Angeles be mapped; and second, how do activists reshape the city through their actions and associations? These emphatically spatial concerns require that we look at the physical constitution of communities as well as the techniques used to map physical, social, and political places in the city. Physical manifestations of abstract ideas such as community, safety, legality, and pride can be located, as can the particular actions through which gays and lesbians make these abstract ideas into concrete reality. Together, these approaches constitute and create a new consciousness about place and activism.

Los Angeles is the greatest hidden chapter in American gay and lesbian history. Despite the acceptance within the community of the characterization of their attitudes as apolitical, Los Angeles has provided the setting for many important chapters in the struggle for gay and lesbian community, visibility, and civil rights. Despite the relatively low level of activism of Angelenos in creating the city through other traditional urban movements, gay and lesbian Angelenos have both benefited from and been at the forefront of the national struggle since the early 1950s.

The landmark achievements of Los Angeles's early gay and lesbian community and activists are impressive. The first long-running national gay organization, the Mattachine Society, was founded by a group of leftist men (some members of the Communist Party) in a small house in the Silverlake district. There, Harry Hay and others, including Bob Hill, Chuck Rowland, and Dale Jennings, conceptualized the "modern homosexual," freeing the term from both criminal and degenerate connotations through their actions and manifestoes. The ONE Institute and *ONE* magazine developed out of the early Mattachine group and evolved into a national institution that fostered early gay scholarship. Lisa Ben (her anagrammatic pseudonym) stole time from her secretarial job in Hollywood to write and publish *Vice-Versa*, the first lesbian publication circulated in the United States, on the office typewriter and mimeograph machine. Reverend Troy Perry founded the Metropolitan Community Church, the first gay and lesbian religious organization and the first gay and lesbian organization to publicly own property in the United States. All of these events predate the riots at Stonewall Inn, a gay bar in New York City's West Village, in June 1969.[2]

The public education and community outreach of the Mattachine and other successor organizations attracted a critical mass of gays and lesbians committed to civil rights in Los Angeles beginning in the late 1950s and early 1960s. Following a model for assimilationist organizing established in the Mattachine, gay men (and some lesbians) worked to challenge the harassment enshrined in city code and ruthlessly carried out by the Los Angeles Police Department. One milestone, in early 1952, was the trial of Dale Jennings, charged with soliciting a police officer. Although Jennings denied the charge, he took the unusual step of publicly admitting his sexuality and defending the rights of homosexuals, writing in the first issue of *ONE* that "even if I had done all the things which the prosecution claimed . . . I would have been guilty of no unusual act, only an illegal one in this society."[3] Represented by a Mattachine lawyer, Jennings was acquitted by eleven members of the jury, and the city dismissed the charges.

As the movement grew, it diversified, spurring breakaway factions and the intracommunity tensions that have persisted over time. Friction among activists, however, did not dampen the growth of the community, and outreach efforts and publications created a culture of understanding within the larger gay and lesbian community that drew others into the movement. Even those whose participation in the community was limited to frequenting the bars knew of these activities and had, perhaps, seen some of the early literature put out by the homophile movement. Equally important was that these efforts made city officials aware of the concerns of the emerging homosexual consciousness, laying the groundwork for the negotiations to follow.

Although these early efforts created the foundation for gay and lesbian activism and politics, only with the liberation movement of the 1970s did the city truly engage with the struggles of gays and lesbians as a recognizable group. It would be decades before either the city or the mainstream movement recognized the diversity within this group. During the 1970s, gay liberation and the women's movement changed the political language of the gay movement, transforming it first into a movement for liberation, one challenging the assumptions and norms of American culture, rather than seeking acceptance within these norms. Soon after, the women's movement provided the vocabulary for separate (and separatist) lesbian theories and strategies. These liberationist agendas led to the creation of the first social services for gays and lesbians in the city—in some cases in the United States—and of alternative spaces, including coffeehouses, art galleries, performance spaces, and separatist communes.

In the 1980s, a new intensity of organizing in Los Angeles and across the country emerged out of the depths of the AIDS epidemic, creating new pressures on existing community organizations that necessitated a reevaluation of the meaning of community and the differences within the movement. As in other cities across the country, the community responded by establishing new organizations to combat AIDS. In Los Angeles, however, the AIDS battle was peculiarly shaped by the emergence of a new open relationship between the Hollywood movie industry elite and the gay and lesbian movement, which substantially increased the funds available for community projects. Overlapping with the city's redevelopment schemes, the movement emerged as a player in city politics, enabling the development of landmark social services for the gay and lesbian community (both general and AIDS related) with city support. With AIDS in the foreground, the City of West Hollywood emerged as a pioneer of civic empowerment and responsibility. The city, incorporated in 1984, supported a rapid expansion of gay commerce but this commitment at times threatened to divide the community along class and race lines. All of this transformed the community as gays and lesbians struggled with the issues of diversity and multiculturalism central to contemporary Los Angeles politics.

As the meaning and dimensions of the AIDS epidemic

changed in the 1990s, new issues and agendas appeared, returning in large part to the broader call for civil rights. In Los Angeles, the movement turned to the state and federal governments for action, with local issues giving way to the pursuit of agendas (job protection, equal access to housing, and gay marriage) within mainstream politics.

The continued transformation of the movement and the increasing diversification of its political and social agendas have demanded changes in the way gays, lesbians, and bisexuals in Los Angeles interact with the city. The decentralized community living within an even more decentralized city has continually had to develop different strategies to deal with the unique, changing character. Understanding the nature of the movement in Los Angeles means understanding the city itself.

Mapping, Activism, and Place Claiming

Gays and lesbians live in cities they have mapped for their own purposes: neighborhoods discreetly appropriated in forgotten zones, street corners where kisses can be exchanged proudly, and community centers to provide safe space for coming-out or mobilizing activists. And then there are the places where none of these things can happen, where gay bashing and subtler forms of heterosexism are expected and feared. The experience of being part of, and subject to, the life of the city, combined with the search for specific spaces that permit and affirm one's own way of being, are the key elements in such maps. Although maps are easily understood as concrete translations of the city with practical value, mapping is a process that marks the specific ways individuals navigate their urban environment. Mapping begins with the physical geography and adds intangible and conceptual evaluations of specific places within the city. Physical spaces become imbued with value based on personal need and desire and the experience of inclusion or exclusion from chosen places. These interpretations of the city's physicality begin with the individual but occur as well at the collective levels, as groups create and dismantle the segregation inherent in city form and structure.

As a tool for understanding people's actions in relation to specific environments, mapping brings together strands of geography, planning, and environmental psychology that allow for the reading of the city both as space and as text. Mapping—the daily and unconscious practice of negotiating the city—produces what geographers have termed the mental (or cognitive) map, an individual's own image of the city.

> Cognitive mapping is a process composed of a series of psychological transformations by which an individual acquires, codes, stores, recalls and decodes information about the relative locations and attributes of phenomena in his everyday spatial environment.[4]

Mental maps spatially organize the pictures we carry around in our heads of the environment we inhabit, incorporating the world as experienced and the world as desired. Together, experience and desire are reflected in the unconscious cartography of our daily lives. Beginning with an individual's practical spatial knowledge—including key locations and landmarks (as well as boundaries of safety and danger) the mental map connects the exploration of the individual experience in relation to a larger spatial collective. The resulting map reflects one's understanding of the city not simply as a physical place but also as a social construction that sustains certain social, cultural, and economic boundaries. These mental maps are in one sense highly personal, selective, and abstract. Although each person carries around his or her own mental map, these maps reflect as well shared knowledge, experiences, and boundaries. The idea of a map that reflects all our actions is powerful, suggesting a key to our behavior and our preferences for certain environments. By drawing attention to and arising from the details of our lives, a cognitive map is more than a theoretical construct; it becomes a real part of our spatial negotiation. Thus, mapping is a narrative process that incorporates both autobiography and cultural history.

Although most attention has been paid to the way observers can use maps to understand others and to plan in response to community needs, it is the daily construction of one's own map that helps to explain the development of communities and movements, including those built by gays and lesbians. The often overemphasized individual nature of these maps—assuming that each of us operates from a unique image of the city—belies the more powerful collective meaning of these maps as shared among groups and neighbors. Traditionally, geographers have used mental maps primarily to construct an individualist picture of the city that turns away from the commonalities of experience that underlie life in the city. Collecting these individual depictions of the city into a whole reveals the nature of community, the meaning of otherness in the city, and the context for place claiming by marginalized groups. The experiential knowledge collected and circulated through communication and codes forms a collective unconscious about the connection between the physical space of the city and the possibility of gay and lesbian empowerment. This knowledge, written on streets and in neighborhoods, constitutes a map that is used practically and strategically. Each encounter with the city leaves its impression, marking the city with clues for future generations.

Attention to the collective is also necessary for marginalized people in forming their identity. Identity, as lived on the margins, is neither static nor independent, but the result of a complex interplay between place, community, and politics. To understand identity, then, is to take account of this interplay, and the means by which specific groups, marked by race, class, gender, religion, or sexuality, claim and are denied places to live, work, and make their own. Notions of biological determinism aside, our attempts to understand lesbian and gay identities have been helping to answer questions about the meaning of community, the opportunity for politics, and the specificity of these definitions in spatial contexts.

A systematic charting of the spaces of gay and lesbian communities in use at a specific time and in a specific context can therefore become the basis for a deeper understanding of sexual identity at that same time and place. In addition, these maps may help to explain the city as a whole, the way it is accessed by groups, transformed over time, and negotiated at the street level.

To understand the strategies and tactics of contemporary activists, we must examine their maps. The new cultural politics of identity creates a framework for looking at communities and difference and uses the vocabulary of place metaphorically in discussions on positioning, location, and situated knowledge. Charting the sites of community building uncovers the day-to-day, street-level decisions that activists make. The narratives of Los Angeles's gay and lesbian activists challenge traditional notions of the boundaries, dimensions, and uses of the urban landscape.

Because the experiences of gays and lesbians reflect the specific social and political conditions of their time, their maps are not static. Combating homophobia, oppression, and violence while demanding respect for difference leads gays and lesbians into a dynamic relationship with the city. As they confront the city, they seek to change it, to make it reflect their experience, desires, and needs. These strategies define the gay and lesbian experience in the city—one characterized by the shared desires and demands of a marginalized people. These individual efforts acknowledge and reveal the truth of sexual otherness; in the aggregate they become collective responses to discrimination and isolation. Personal risks make possible the activist interventions of the whole. Mapping, then, activates the city.

Politically, gays and lesbians struggle for visibility on the streets and in other public places, representation at city halls and in Washington, and recognition in the courts. Economically, entrepreneurs establish new strongholds—in the form of cooperatives, businesses, or bars to "recycle dollars" within the community and claim economic self-sufficiency. Socially, groups and individuals appropriate and establish churches, schools, or community centers, using space in both customary and transgressive ways. All of these practices constitute activist strategies that can be examined in the context of both political goals and cultural expression.

Lacking in theoretical explorations of recent social movements is reference to the grounds on which these battles for rights and visibility are fought. What does the map (in Los Angeles or elsewhere) of gay and lesbian activism look like? What distances must activists travel to meet and act? Are the places of residence the place of struggle? What public places are available for gathering and protest? Mapping these places and tracing the processes of mapping deepens our understanding of social activism. Looking at the physical and social dimensions of a social movement thus leads to a more visceral level of understanding than allowed by attention to movement ideology alone. Current literature that emphasizes identity as an organizing principle for social movements fails to capture the experience of social activism or the central role of strategy in movement building. The focus on identity and difference that has been proposed by both social movement theorists and, more generally, within cultural studies is only the first step in understanding contemporary activism, a foundation upon which I want to build.

Activism, the political and social efforts to win civil rights, access to social goods, acceptance, and equal opportunity, constitutes the crucial link between the individual and the community, and politics and place. For gays and lesbians, activism begins with the very personal act of coming out and continues with the unending efforts to assert both presence and rights in the city. Routine choices—whether to live in a gay-identified neighborhood, where to go with friends and lovers, how to perform (or make public) one's sexuality—define the boundaries of the urban gay and lesbian experience. These routine, even pedestrian, aspects of gay and lesbian experience fuel the generation of a more organized and recognizable activist practice.

The very nature of gay and lesbian life in the city begins with activism. In response to the isolation of the closet, the individual becomes collectivized. As individuals, gays and lesbians have the choice to be out or not, and the spatial decisions—where to live, work, or socialize—may result from many factors, some perhaps distinct from the implications of one's sexuality. However, when the city—rather than personal space—becomes the backdrop for the validation of one's self, identity, rights, and responsibilities, then visibility and risk are inevitable. Visibility, in the context of gay and lesbian activism, has been at the center of collective attempts to confront the risk. Gay and lesbian activists working together, sharing knowledge to create common agendas and strategies make visible the daily strategic decisions of individuals living in the city.

The concept of place, as a physical reality, metaphoric goal, and political right, reflects these challenges and offers a new and more dynamic way of reading the strategies of contemporary activists. Place encompasses both the physical landmarks of a community within which social relations are constructed, the political legitimacy of territories, and the metaphorical and strategic uses of community. Place works both as a physical and social site of resistance and as a manifestation of shared meaning in specific contexts and communities. In this way, place carries the emotional resonance created through the continued interplay between people and their surroundings and provides tangible evidence of a community's history and experiences.[5]

Certain sites become imbued with symbolic value that reflects the pride of collective struggle and the pain of oppression. The geography of gay and lesbian protests, like the geography of social and political protest in general, has not been well researched. Although it is clear that protests add to the meaning of the places they occupy, geographers and planners have not specifically looked at the varied locations where protests occur or the connections between the choice of places and the activist agenda. In the case of gay activism, however, there is a very direct link between the types of protests used by activists, the places where these protests occur, and the overall strategy of the movement at a particular time. The earliest gay rights demonstrations in Los Angeles were a series of small marches outside the few prominent gay bars to protest police activities. Later, during the gay liberation movement, protests were much more diffuse, taking place across the city, often at sites with no particular gay resonance. Since the late 1980s, however, and the development of ACT UP (AIDS Coalition to Unleash Power) and other direct-action movements, gay and lesbian protests have become highly specialized, focused, and symbolic. Specific sites with lasting or temporal significance become the scenes of targeted campaigns, and the locations become part of the demonstration.

As the gay movement agenda has shifted from assimilation to confrontation, so has the geography of protest, with gay visibility across the city exploited and challenged. Demonstrations across the city at malls (Century City), local hospitals (County-USC Medical Center), and government offices (the County Administration Building) are used strategically, with tactics and messages tailored to specific audiences and for specific demands. This intersection of the map of gay protest with zones of safety and legality marks the movement's evolution.

But gays and lesbians have not taken to the streets only in protest. A hallmark of gay liberation in the 1970s, which has become an institution in cities around the world, is the gay pride parade, typically held in the end of June to commemorate the Stonewall Riots of 1969.[6] This celebration is important not only because it aims to challenge mainstream conceptions of community and sexuality but also because it confronts the idea of public space as off-limits to gays and lesbians.

Pride parades have been sanctioned officially since the early 1980s in many cities (including Los Angeles where the first pride parade was held in 1970). Because the pride parade magnifies the community's visibility, it provides not only an opportunity to show the "arrival" of the gay community but also serves as a platform for articulating civil rights struggles. One of the recurrent debates within the movement, however, is the extent to which these events have been co-opted, diluted by the passage of time and the increasing assimilation of gay cultural mores into straight norms. During the height of gay liberation, marches often were held without permits and followed a route out of the gay enclaves, down major avenues, and into public parks for rallies. In contrast, by the mid-1980s, many parades had been rerouted to stay within the confines of gay neighborhoods, thus losing much of their disruptive character. Douglas Crimp describes the reversal of the route in New York City: "We walked downtown, into the confines of the gay ghetto, where instead of attending a rally, we could drink, eat, dance, and spend money to enrich Mafia-owned, gay-run businesses."[7]

In describing the shift from protest to a celebration, Crimp emphasizes the loss felt by more radical activists. In Los Angeles, by contrast, these moments of celebration, of being activists simply by being visible, hold greater importance, and are, in fact, central to what the map of the movement looks like. In Los Angeles, the movement started in a living room, not outside a bar in a crowded street—not simply because Angelenos are less confrontational, but also because in Los Angeles crowds are rarely spontaneous and are not easily assembled. To read this map is to understand that the living room can be a public place, and that visibility is more subtly obtained.

Place Claiming

How can we explain the strategies of a movement as diverse and contradictory as that sustained by contemporary gays and lesbians? With activists simultaneously calling for civil rights, equality, the transformation of society, and the right to establish distinct and separate societies, is there a way to draw some meaningful and perhaps unifying conclusions about their strategies and goals?

To understand the role of activism, in its broadest sense, in the making of the gay and lesbian city, the relationship between place and political strategy must be foregrounded. Place claiming—the appropriation of physical, social, and mental spaces by marginalized groups—defines this link and is the central strategic mechanism of social movements.

Not only are these place-claiming strategies an important and unexplored way of understanding activism in the urban context, they also define aspects of gay and lesbian activism.[8] The city is not a clean slate upon which to build something new, but a thing constructed, upon which activists and communities layer new meanings. A theory of place claiming provides a framework for understanding, at the macrolevel, the relationship between place and politics in gay and lesbian activism. This framework considers the following: the brokering of contradictory claims to place by marginalized communities, the city bureaucracy, the media, and others; the social production of space; the disjunction and connections between place and community; and, given these changing notions of place and identity, the appropriation of place by gays and lesbians.

Looking at gay and lesbian activism as a process of place claiming leads to a deeper understanding of the particularities of the movement as it has changed over time, in different geographies, and under different notions of politics. These strategies draw not from a sourcebook shared across movements, but emerge from the particular histories of oppression, attempts at assimilation, and practices of resistance developed within marginalized societies. They mix cultural practices, individual innovations, and immediate responses to particular needs. This does not deny the possibility for and experience of learning from other movements. In fact, as the experience of the gay and lesbian movement suggests, social movements are continually borrowing from other sources, in part because most members of the gay and lesbian community are simultaneously members of other oppressed groups. Activists and social theorists alike cite these links between radical discourses as an important aspect of the contemporary struggle.

Highlighting place-claiming strategies introduces the discussion of the physical, social, and symbolic construction of the city into the analysis of social movements. Although the theories discussed above are useful for understanding ideology, collective identities, and the connection between strategy and action at the macrolevel, the specifics of social movements—in particular the geography of these movements—are generally ignored. In contrast, a mapping of the places used by activists and the subsequent adoption of these places for use by the wider gay and lesbian communities deepens our understanding of activism. This theory provides the opportunity for a critical discussion of the relationship between the gay and lesbian movement and the places marked as specifically occupied by gays and lesbians.

Contemporary gay and lesbian place claiming reflects a specific set of opportunities and obstacles that like gay and lesbian life both reflects and counters contemporary notions of community. Proscriptions against homosexuality have restricted gays and lesbians from developing community identity within the family. Similarly, gays and lesbians often encounter resistance at other typical places for identity formation—school, religious center, and workplace. Thus, for people whose first contact with community has been limited to social outlets (such as bars or clubs), the very notion of community building can seem foreign. The histories of gay and lesbian culture in the United States attest to the fear of discrimination and prosecution that limited the development of community within the context of traditional social institutions. Community centers serving people living with HIV and AIDS, teenagers on the streets, gay and lesbian parents, and activists of all agendas constitute a parallel social network for gays and lesbians who have no use for, or have been shut out of, mainstream social institutions. For gays and lesbians, the notion of community remains problematic, as gays and lesbians attempt to restructure socially ingrained notions of community (and its connections to home and family) in light of these barriers. Given the tension between the desire for community and the claim of individual nonconformity, challenging the ideal community characterizes much of gay and lesbian movement building since the emergence of gay liberation.

Only a mapping that makes central these collectivized struggles for personal freedom and safety can describe the particulars of the gay and lesbian movement in Los Angeles, a city whose long-overlooked place in the history of gay and lesbian struggles exemplifies the inadequacy of previous analyses. Just as the city itself defies common understandings of the urban, so does the experience of its diverse communities. The primarily decentralized geography of the city, the relative absence of distinct gentrified neighborhoods, the disconnections between progressive politics across the city, and the rapid pace of demographic change all contribute to the specificity of the Los Angeles experience as one based in the daily enactment of the personal.

To understand the complexity of gay and lesbian place claiming as distinct from more general notions of the gay and lesbian "experience," we must look beyond simple notions of community. Even when we pay careful attention to the diversity within community, the term still evokes a certain social construct that erases the very real limitations of place and difference. A conceptual shift from the "ideal of community" (which strives for unity and suppresses difference) to the "real life of the city" lies at the heart of a politics of difference. Community, as an ideal or goal, carries complicated associations and confinements, not only for those on the margin but also for society at large. Iris Marion Young writes,

> The ideal of community fails to offer an appropriate vision of a democratic polity. . . . The ideal of community denies and represses social difference, the fact that the polity cannot be thought of as a unity in which all participants share a common experience and common values. In its privileging of face-to-face relations, moreover, the ideal of community denies difference in the form of the temporal and spatial distancing that characterizes social process.[9]

This ideal of community celebrates a lack of conflict and an absence of the unexpected. In community, writes Young, "persons cease to be other, opaque, not understood, and instead become mutually sympathetic, understanding one another as they understand themselves fused."[10] Members of an idealized community continually reaffirm identity without critical distance or engagement with others.

Group identity, like the city itself, does not remain static. Instead, the substance of the collective evolves materially, culturally, and socially over time and across regions. This change is initiated through an American engagement with others through the filters of its histories, both individual and collective. As individuals, activists, and groups confront the city, they remake it. Connecting this analysis to the experience of gays and lesbians in the city acknowledges that much of gay organizing in the late twentieth century has been in part a valorization of community, with gay and lesbian activism rooted in efforts to create acceptance within the norms of straight culture. As gays and lesbians struggled to make the first inroads against the heterosexism of our culture, community—as a safe space with known boundaries and entrances—was the goal, while community building was the method. More recently, the direct-action movements of the late 1980s and early 1990s open up the possibility of rejecting the community ideal and acknowledging the difference within activist movements.

Contemporary gay and lesbian activism exemplifies the radical openness of a politics of difference. On the street level, this difference is played out in the varied landscapes of contemporary struggles—the neighborhood, protests spaces, and the locations marginalized groups (including gays and lesbians) inhabit in the environments of the center.

These commonplace strategies of being out and visible across the city are in themselves political and as such are the basis for gay and lesbian activism. The geography of these strategies reveals, then, the emergence of a politically effective movement and development of an activist gay and lesbian presence in the city. Focusing on the spatial diversity of the gay and lesbian movements, the meaning of particular sites of resistance and confrontation, and the very real boundaries which signify danger, celebration, and power for gay and lesbian communities, illustrates the importance of place as a generating force of community and as an objective reality of social movements.

At the most basic level, the mapping of gays and lesbians in any city begins with the boundaries between safe and dangerous places. Despite the increased visibility of gays and lesbians and the mainstreaming of gay and lesbian concerns, safety remains a critical issue, even for those living in cities such as Los Angeles. In 1999, the State of California reported nearly two thousand hate crimes, of which 22 percent were "motivated by sexual orientation bias."[11] Within these 436 sexual orientation hate crimes, 78 percent were directed at gay men and 15 percent were directed at lesbians. Nearly all these crimes involved individual victims rather than institutions per se. By contrast a greater percentage of race and religion bias crimes are property crimes. According to these state reports, Los Angeles County accounts for 40 percent of all hate crimes reported to the state.

The most recent Los Angeles County Human Relations Commission annual report, issued in 1997, showed a 25 percent increase for all hate crimes over the previous year for Los Angeles county alone and a 43 percent increase in crimes against gays, lesbians and bisexuals. Fifty-four percent of all reported crimes in Los Angeles were racially or ethnically motivated while 34 percent were classified as "sexual orientation motivated." The report also indicated that these hate crimes were clustered around new locations: Hollywood and Long Beach.[12] Only six hate crimes were reported in West Hollywood in the 1999 California data.

The statistics on hate crimes, however, reveal little of the complexity of these assaults. These statistics cannot be separated from the context of reporting. As the Human Relations Commission insists each year, the continued rise in the numbers of hate crime incidents they receive is more likely because victims are more willing to report and police are more receptive to the reports. More importantly, however, these statistics are limited by problems in classifying reports, such as a lack of complete disclosure, confusion within law enforcement concerning the classifications of hate crimes, and, with sexual orientation crimes in particular, a certain invisibility of the crime, reflecting the invisibility of the community in general.

The statistical charting of hate crimes only begins to define the changing boundaries of safe and unsafe places for the community over time. Historically, gay space in the city was defined primarily by its lack of safety; in many ways this legacy remains. Legal codes and social mores relegated gay and lesbian bars to the urban periphery—warehouse districts, red-light districts, and other transitional neighborhoods. Not only were gays targets of attacks within the bars (particularly from police who enforced archaic laws in brutal and indiscriminate ways), but also as they left after closing. In Los Angeles, bars were first concentrated downtown, near the bus station and in the middle of a red-light district. By the 1950s, most bars moved to Sunset Boulevard in West Hollywood, an area known for lighter police control.

Place claiming, in this context, was always temporary and subject to the whims of police and the profit margin of nongay owners who exploited their "captive" market. In the introduction to his history of the police raid on the Stonewall Inn, Martin Duberman wrote of the unstable character of gay bars in premovement days:

> When I moved to New York in 1963, there were maybe five or six gay male bars and perhaps one lesbian bar. Even though few in number, these were not what we would today call "safe havens" from the oppression of heterosexist society. My own bar of choice rapidly became Stonewall. But in that bar no one was ever sure whether or not he or she would end the night by being arrested and thrown in jail.[13]

Safety and safe spaces, however, are about more than freedom from crime and harassment (police or otherwise). As developed in the context of the women's movement, the notion of safe space implies a certain license to speak and act freely, form collective strength, and generate strategies for resistance. Although bars represent one type of space—a momentary respite from oppression—the women's movement sought to create a radically different sort of place, one where the energy and collective effort to create place were the defining features. Safe space, in the women's movement, was a means rather than an end and not only a physical space but also a space created by the coming together of women searching for community. Kathy Sarachild, a founder of New York Radical Women (an early 1970s radical feminist organization) describes the most enduring of these safe spaces, the consciousness-raising group:

> The purpose of hearing people's feelings and experience was not therapy. . . . The importance of listening to a woman's feelings was collectively to analyze the situation of women, not to analyze her. The idea was not to change women, not to make "internal" changes except in the sense of knowing more. It was and is the conditions women face, it's male supremacy, we want to change.[14]

But even safe space can become the place for conflict. One

of the most contentious issues in gay and lesbian activisı recent years has been the perception that gay and lesbian activist organizations are engaged in bitter infighting and attacks from within the community, which threaten both the movement and the sense that these groups provide "safe space." Racism, sexism, internalized homophobia, the degaying of community-based AIDS organizations that now serve the broader HIV-infected community all threaten the stability of the movement.

The discussion of safe space is more about the forces that create and threaten this safety, its nature, and the ground rules upon which it is constructed. In looking at organizations, institutions, and other places (including open spaces) that function as safe space for lesbians and gay men in Los Angeles, I will emphasize these structural elements of internal division and conflict.

Theorizing Place Claiming

Each of these terms and concepts—mapping, activism, and place claiming—has been used by others to describe and interpret the city. Recent attempts to understand the city as used by gays, lesbians, and other marginalized groups have increasingly turned to the images of the city as drawn and imagined by individuals and groups. This history of gay and lesbian activism in Los Angeles builds upon this method for creating a narrative of the city. Maps, however, can be more than the reflections of daily life. Mapping is, in fact, an integral part of the activist experience itself; it is the way the experiences of place claiming become the collective practice of a community. These earlier projects, however, both inform and highlight particular aspects of the work here.

Critical spatial theory, a reaction against the depoliticized nature of most urban geography, has allowed identity and difference questions to be introduced into the discussion of place.

Its attention to the intersection of social struggles in space has opened geographical questions to the arguments of contemporary social critiques, drawing connections for social theorists that have been obscured by disciplinary lines. Critical spatial theory highlights identity as an important aspect that simultaneously draws these interdisciplinary connections and suggests new ways of mapping and reading the city. Key to the question of urban activism here is that space, as a set of physical arrangements, can be viewed not only as the product of social relations but also as the "arena for the reproduction of social relations and as itself such a [set of social] relations."[15]

This notion of the city as a socially constructed form rather than a collection and organization of neutral physical objects implicitly affirms the presence of politically and socially excluded groups in the city and allows for an investigation into the nature of their access to the city. Gays and lesbians personify this connection between identity and place.

However, the focus of these geographic investigations is not on place in the traditional sense (that of landmarks and other tangible markers of a community's presence), but on the intersections between the real (place) and the imagined (perception). Although these imagined places are an important addition to our theoretical maps of our experiences, there remains a need to see, in practice, how this imaginary is discovered and comprehended at the ground level. For marginalized and activist groups, the search for place carries great risk, and these struggles, if effective, ultimately lie not in the imaginary, but in the real. Despite its usefulness in expanding geographical analysis, then, this new theoretical discourse on space and difference only partially accommodates the experiences and practices of marginalized communities. Tracing the origin and meaning of our vocabulary of place, I emphasize and distinguish between metaphors of place, theoretical constructions of place, and the everyday experience of place in its physical, social, and mental dimensions.

Some of the ambiguity of critical spatial theory is addressed in the recent attempts to define queer space, which seeks to explore the particular power relationships of sexual difference as spatially produced and experienced, and to uncover "the ways in which the spatial and the sexual constitute one another."[16] Despite numerous much-needed case studies of the experience of gays and lesbians in cities, the regional and local specificities of place often are overlooked, as certain motifs of queer life in the city (usually those based on the example of New York or San Francisco) are inscribed.[17] Surprisingly, given their ostensibly geographic orientation, these essays, like most other work under the queer space rubric, are interested in place only as an afterthought or a context, rather than as the actual stuff of investigation. The very term, "queer space," with its obvious roots in critical spatial theory, repeats some of the practices of the more general work, again leaving the urgency and activist basis for gay and lesbian life behind. As explained in one recent collection of essays, "The phrase [queers in space] connotes being 'out there floating,' disconnected and separated from the planet. Although people who experience marginalization might like to be more 'grounded,' inequity in access to public space continues. At least in terms of visibility, most of us remain 'out there,' constrained by marginalization."[18] However, despite this interesting notion of an invisible and unlocated space, the evidence of physicalized, locatable places remains crucial even to the notion of sexual difference itself. Certainly, gays and lesbians have not always enjoyed equal access to certain public places. However, this inequity cannot so easily be equated to a lack of visibility without completely denying a person's own agency in identifying as gay, lesbian, or bisexual. As has been true for other marginalized groups, discrimination on the basis of race, class, or gender does not leave one "disconnected and separated from the planet." Discrimination, per se, does not preclude the fundamental practice of creating places in which to perform and present sexual difference.

Despite these qualifications, this recent work on sexuality and space (like the new spatial analyses) goes well beyond traditional geographical work in marking the difference within spatial parameters. Although these analyses do not fully explore the development and maintenance of marginalized spaces, they do provide a framework with which to illuminate the existence of gays and lesbians (or other marginalized communities) within spatial parameters.

The Particularities of Gay and Lesbian Politics

Gay and lesbian politics exemplify the notion of place claiming as an activist strategy. First, because the discrimination experienced by gays and lesbians has been predicated on notions of public and private behavior and the heterosexual public's fears of infection (or contamination) through contact with hidden degeneracy, gay and lesbian activism has been practically focused on undoing these boundaries between public and private. These structures have in turn fostered a number of counterstrategies that lay claim to certain places, landscapes, and discourses.

Gay and lesbian political movements are a particularly appropriate context for this investigation of place and place claiming because of their efforts to create connections with other social movements—both past and present. Gay and lesbian politics use place-claiming strategies learned from the women's movement, the civil rights movement, and the labor movement. In turn some of these movements now are looking to the strategies of gay and lesbian politics for answers. Direct-action techniques, learned on the front lines of other movements then refined and extended by AIDS activists, have been borrowed back by many of the new movements, as evidenced by the unpredicted success of the World Trade Organization protests of 1999 and 2000.

Today, there are affinities between the gay and lesbian

movement and others, primarily those calling for a renewed attention to questions of civil rights. The gay and lesbian movement, in turn, shares both ideological and organizational characteristics with these movements. A new politics of place that centralizes questions of community, territory, the urban environment, and the conflicts over public and private space defines much of this recent activism.

Recent attempts to write the history of the gay and lesbian movement are commonly marked by numerous obstacles. These studies largely overlook the fact that the gay and lesbian movement has not always been a movement for civil rights, nor has it always been a movement for all gays and lesbians. Although the most public and vocal periods of the movement have been those concerning the civil rights of gays and lesbians, the twists and turns of the movement resist such easy interpretation. Speaking of, or writing about, gay and lesbian politics leads one necessarily to the dilemma of activism itself. How do we bring together the varied competing strands of the communities that make up the gay and lesbian population in the United States, many with their multiple allegiances and politics, and how do we isolate those aspects of the movement's history that have had lasting impact on the course of the struggle?[19]

My answer focuses on the belief that the complexity of gay and lesbian activism can be understood by looking at place and the connection between place, community, and politics. How are contradictory claims to place brokered—by marginalized communities, the city bureaucracy, the media, and others? How, specifically, does this process of allocating place shift as groups collectively realize their marginality and acquire the power needed to redress inequality at a local or national level? The liberal tradition uses a public/private divide to distinguish between the orderly and the disorderly; relegating to the private sphere differences of gender, ethnicity, and other identity markers that might be considered dangerous to the political order. Contemporary feminist theory looks for social change in the rediscovery of the public identity of marginalized groups (especially women). Thus, this new understanding of place becomes the groundwork for a new formulation of citizenship, participation, and the political process.[20]

The Book in Brief

The case study research focuses on four crucial developments in the gay and lesbian communities of Los Angeles in the last three decades. West Hollywood, the most visible gay and lesbian neighborhood in Los Angeles, is the focus of Chapter 2. The particularities of its development, including the creation of a political coalition to secure cityhood, the opportunities for gay and lesbian entrepreneurs, and the positive and negative connotations of West Hollywood's symbolic role for gays and lesbians in Los Angeles, are critical aspects to their stability and growing stature.

Chapter 3 explores the role of gay and lesbian and AIDS social service organizations in the redevelopment of Hollywood Boulevard and the realignment of a traditional growth coalition to include gays and lesbians. The geographic decision-making processes that led to the relocation of these agencies beyond the boundaries of West Hollywood is discussed, particularly in relation to the concerns and expectations raised by both staff and clients. The needs of specific client populations of these community organizations (people with AIDS, youth, and other marginalized groups) are specifically addressed, as are the impacts of this geographic shift of community organizations to Hollywood.

In Chapter 4 I look more carefully at the role and meaning of difference within the gay and lesbian movement, looking at the twenty-year struggle to create lesbian spaces in the city. Using the key examples of the Woman's Building, a major and innovative women's art space in downtown Los Angeles, and Connexxus, the lesbian community center created in opposition to the male-dominated Gay Services Center, this chapter examines the political arguments for separate spaces for lesbians and the meaning of this separateness.

In Chapter 5 I trace the history of gay and lesbian street protests in Los Angeles from the gay liberation movement actions in the 1970s to the present. The strategies and locations of street protest in Los Angeles are discussed, with particular attention to the constraints on street protest created by the geography of the city. Los Angeles, in comparison to other cities with strong gay and lesbian movements, is notable for the relatively minor influence of direct-action organizing on the movement, particular with respect to the efforts of ACT UP and the Gay Liberation Front. The only major example of gay and lesbian street protest in recent Los Angeles history—the 1991 marches to protest Governor Wilson's veto of crucial job protection legislation—offers an opportunity to examine the particular impediments to street protest in Los Angeles.

The final chapter reconsiders the mapping of the contemporary gay and lesbian movement in Los Angeles and extrapolates the central themes about the relationship between place and activism in the city. This project is motivated by a belief that the appropriation of public places and the construction of new places at different scales (from the body to the city) are an integral part of this struggle. Because gays and lesbians have been discriminated against, are expected to remain invisible, and in the past have had only limited recourse to the strategies of community organizing used by other social movements, the history of organizing in these communities reveals innovative strategies to claim and label space. These strategies challenge and deconstruct accepted notions of public and private, personal and communal, and accessible and remote.

Ultimately, however, the true map of gay and lesbian Los Angeles, even as created by the collective, remains often private and privileged, shifting and ephemeral. Telling this story and drawing this map inevitably entails some loss of crucial details and the richness of the mapping process. Writing and mapping the connections between identity, politics, and place blends the individual with the collective, the personal with the observed, the writer with the subject. The maps that follow are informed by my own experiences of Los Angeles as it has transformed during the years that I have lived here. I have used this way of seeing the city—as an intersection between the personal and the collective—as a method of understanding my own practices.

But to describe this map, I start with two assumptions: First, place and the city have importance for culture and politics; and second, place is created and altered through our interactions in and with it. From this beginning, a process of mapping ties together place and specific perceptions of that place, locating the actions that transform these places. In this context, mapping refers both to the process of uncovering these interactions with place and the users' own unconscious decisions in relation to place. This process of mapping, which emphasizes the experiences of individuals as members of a community, is a powerful tool for a deeper understanding of gay and lesbian uses of the city. The growth and change in gay and lesbian communities, via activism, can be read in the physical spaces of the city, as gays and lesbians code them. I draw and reveal these physical associations and thus detail the boundaries and lines, which have been drawn and redrawn by the visible presence of gays and lesbians in the city. The cases presented here include the development of community centers in both overtly gay and unmarked neighborhoods, the transformation of a small gay neighborhood into a gay-identified city, and the use of the streets and other public spaces for protest. Each of these examples illustrates collective political action in a spatial context.

2 Inclusion and Exclusion in West Hollywood

West Hollywood sits in the center of Los Angeles County, at the edge of the City of Los Angeles's wealthy Westside, nestled between Hollywood to the north and east and Beverly Hills to the west. Covering less than two square miles, West Hollywood is well known as the hub of the interior design industry. "To the trade" showrooms occupy the blocks surrounding the city's most notable architectural landmark, the Cesar Pelli–designed Pacific Design Center, known colloquially as "the big blue whale." West Hollywood is also home to the Sunset Strip, a one-mile stretch of trendy nightclubs and restaurants in a constant cycle of boom and bust. In the early 1980s, West Hollywood became a major destination for émigré Jews from the Soviet Union—an influx reflected in the Russian language signs and Jewish community centers that dominate the eastern half of the city. More recently, however, there has been evidence that gentrification and city redevelopment plans may be driving the Russian immigrants out of the neighborhood.

On the west end of Santa Monica Boulevard, the major thoroughfare bisecting the city, is the area known (either affectionately or derogatorily) as Boystown, which contains a dense concentration of gay bars and clubs, specialty shopping, and a few community institutions, most notably the headquarters of the Metropolitan Community Church. Gays and lesbians throughout Southern California recognize this upscale section of town as the most visible concentration of gay culture and power in the region.

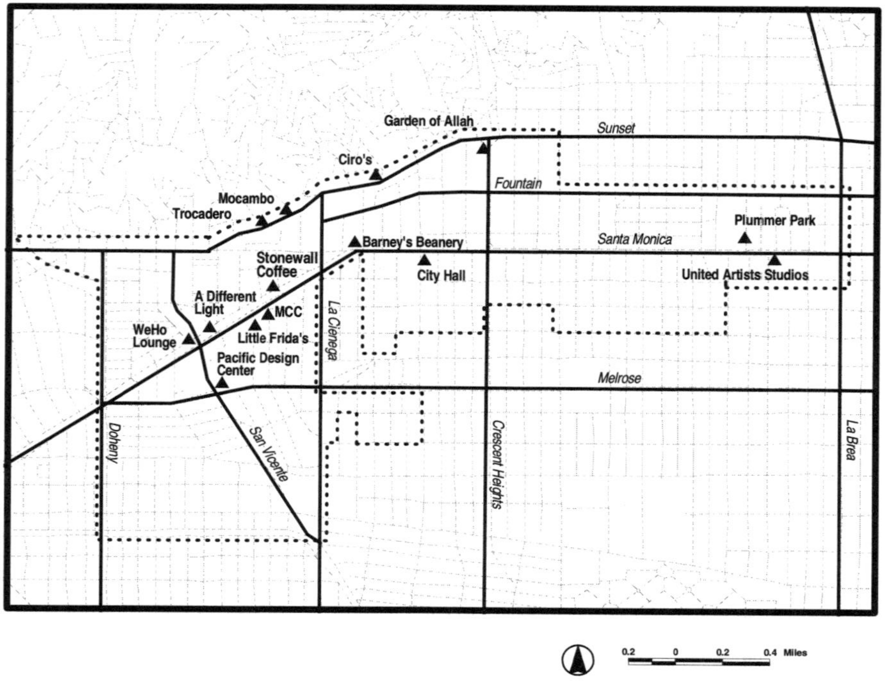

Map 2. The City of West Hollywood

West Hollywood symbolizes gay and lesbian political strength as well, with its progressive city government leading the process of institutionalizing gay and lesbian rights in Southern California and continuing at the forefront of gay political mobilization. Since becoming an independent city in 1985, West Hollywood has been a magnet for gay businesses, and the city government has become a nationally recognized example of progressive policies. At the same time, the labeling of the area as "the gay city" by locals and the media carries multiple meanings, not all of them positive. As long as West Hollywood's image remains predominantly one of healthy, middle-class, white gay men, it is likely that the rest of the community, including lesbians, bisexuals, and people of color, will continue to view the area with suspicion. For those marginalized by the movement, West Hollywood has come to symbolize all that is problematic about the construction of sexual identity in a postliberation era: a focus on capital accumulation, conspicuous consumption, and appearance, rather than on civil rights. Activists and apolitical gays and lesbians alike continue to debate West Hollywood's role as both a political and cultural center of the community, with the alternately welcoming or discriminatory nature of the Boystown nightlife fiercely contested. At the extreme, critics argue whether West Hollywood's status as an independent city has aided or constrained the political agendas of gays and lesbians in Los Angeles.

More than any other single location in the Los Angeles region, West Hollywood has been both the product of and constraint on the place-claiming strategies of the lesbian and gay movement. West Hollywood, like other gay enclaves in major cities, has emerged as a center for gay and lesbian business, politics, and culture because of an imperative to create a place where gay visibility is the norm rather than a daily struggle. Its presence, in turn, has shaped the access to and use of other gay and lesbian places outside the city's boundaries. The experience of building West Hollywood continues to shape place-claiming strategies and decisions around the region.

What sets West Hollywood apart from similar enclaves is the political independence of the neighborhood that in turn makes the gay political governance synonymous with a gay activist presence. This chapter frames the myths of West Hollywood and its usefulness as a point of reference for the gay or lesbian culture in the context of their activist efforts in Los Angeles. West Hollywood mirrors the complexities of Southern California urbanization as much as it reflects the processes of gay neighborhood building in other cities such as New York or San Francisco. Although West Hollywood is more residential and more suburban than these other gay enclaves, by Los Angeles standards the city is atypically dense and street oriented, with mixed commercial and residential areas. Reflecting the residential segregation of Los Angeles, however, West Hollywood—like most two-square-mile neighborhoods in the county and the city—remains ethnically and racially homogeneous. West Hollywood's development has closely followed the general patterns of Southern California's economic and urban growth, drawing its strength from the presence of the film industry with its emphasis on service jobs, many of them temporary. These regional characteristics, along with the specific history of the gay and lesbian movement in Los Angeles, have shaped the place-claiming strategies in West Hollywood.

Preincorporation West Hollywood

Ironically, West Hollywood's rise as a gay mecca rests only partly on the success of its much-heralded incorporation drive in the mid-1980s. Equally important is the earlier unincorporated status of the city, which was an overlooked and relatively ungoverned area in the middle of the county. In the first years of the twentieth century, Moses Sherman, one of Los Angeles's many railroad entrepreneurs, expanded his Pacific Railway

Company into what is now West Hollywood, establishing a terminal at San Vicente and Santa Monica Boulevards (now the site of the Pacific Design Center). Although this development did not significantly transform the area, it did foreshadow the continuing use of West Hollywood as a place where the wealthier Westside could put less attractive businesses and industry.

As an unincorporated area of Los Angeles County, West Hollywood languished under government indifference for thirty years after a social heyday in the 1920s, 1930s, and 1940s. During the 1920s, when much of West Hollywood was still onion fields, the Sunset Strip emerged as a fashionable nightclub and residential district for the Hollywood silent screen crowd. This early Hollywood scene centered on the Garden of Allah, a residential hotel and bungalow colony on Sunset at Crescent Heights (now a mini mall). Russian-born silent film star Alla Nazimova built the Garden as a private residence but turned it into a hotel as the silent film industry (and her screen career) collapsed. In its earliest days, the Garden was home to many of Nazimova's fellow silent film stars, including Greta Garbo, Ramon Navarro, Errol Flynn, and John Barrymore. Later, the Garden became the West Coast retreat for New York's literary circle known as the Algonquin Table, most notably Robert Benchley, Lillian Hellman, and Dorothy Parker. Known within certain circles as a place that welcomed unmarried guests, the Garden also earned a reputation as a place for parties and was eventually targeted by early anti-Communist witch-hunts. Elsewhere in West Hollywood, the film industry expanded its influence, building numerous studios, including the headquarters of United Artists on Santa Monica at the eastern edge of the city.

At the same time, the nightclub scene along the Sunset Strip reached its heyday; the Trocadero and Ciro's (both opened by William Wilkerson, founder of the *Hollywood Reporter*), and the Mocambo all flourished in the 1940s. Money from Hollywood and the Las Vegas mob built many of the establishments, which attracted a cast of characters slightly more mainstream (and perhaps wealthier) than those at the Garden. Unlike the Garden, the nightclubs attracted tourists, oil and industry millionaires, and others outside Hollywood, creating a name for the area beyond the relatively tight Hollywood community. This shift in clientele likely affected the gay presence on the Strip, as more underground gay-only nightclubs and bars, such as the Eagle, began to open down the hill on Santa Monica Boulevard. These establishments were rarely gay owned, and were often funded by the same money (particularly organized crime) that funded the Sunset Strip clubs.

After the war, as the club scene on Sunset Strip waned (the victim of the collapse of the wartime economy and the rise of the television and other "home entertainment" industries) the upscale nightlife declined as clubs were closed and eventually torn down. In the 1960s, West Hollywood became a center of the counterculture, with the hippie movement and the rock scene moving into the clubs that the Hollywood stars had abandoned. Many of the lesbians and gay men who would later form the heart of the gay liberation movement of the early 1970s also gravitated to West Hollywood. The *Los Angeles Free Press,* which served as an unofficial headquarters for the alternative scene in Los Angeles from its offices on Sunset, was also an early site for gay organizing. The new rock scene transformed the area into a center for music publishing and sparked economic revitalization. As the Sunset Strip transformed from a relatively ritzy nightclub area to the center of the new youth culture and rock scene culture, the division between Sunset Boulevard and Santa Monica Boulevard became more distinct. Although gays were certainly part of this new incarnation, the more overt gay presence on Santa Monica Boulevard fostered an open, rather than assimilated, gay culture. Today, West Hollywood reflects all of these preincorporation cultures—hippie, rock, Hollywood star, and gay.

During the 1970s, as the Los Angeles Police Department

(LAPD) stepped up attacks against gay establishments and the growing gay liberation movement brought increasing numbers of lesbians and gays out of the closet, West Hollywood gradually emerged as the visible center of this new gay presence. The unincorporated status kept the streets and bars out of the reach of LAPD while the county's disinvestment in the area created a reservoir of cheap apartments and empty storefronts that were slowly filled by gay entrepreneurs and residents.[1] The depressed real estate market of West Hollywood was crucial to the early development of the gay neighborhood. In looking at West Hollywood, the long history of real estate development and disinvestment reveal important clues about the opportunities for gay commercial and residential occupation.[2]

In this way, preincorporation West Hollywood resembled the model of the gay enclave—an area of the city abandoned by "legitimate" businesses that has attracted an agglomeration of gay businesses, bars, and other institutional organizations. In his now-classic paper on "gay ghettos," Martin Levine reported that, in the mid-1970s, 78 percent of all gay institutions in Los Angeles were located within 3 percent of the metropolitan region, in an area centered along West Hollywood's Santa Monica Boulevard. Levine describes the development of a gay ghetto in marginalized areas:

> At first gay institutions and cruising places spring up in urban districts known to accept variant behavior, resulting in a concentration of such places in specific sections of the city. . . . This concentration attracts a large number of homosexuals, causing a centralization of gay culture traits, turning the districts into homosexual culture areas. Tolerance coupled with institutional concentration make the areas desirable residential districts for gays. Many homosexuals, especially those publicly labeled as gay or open about their orientation, settle in these areas. At this point, the areas have become partially developed gay ghettos.[3]

In each of the areas Levine describes—West Hollywood, San Francisco's Castro district, New York's Greenwich Village, and Boston's South End—the clustering of shops, bars, and restaurants catering to a gay clientele accounts as much as residential growth in the emergence of a gay neighborhood. Levine acknowledges that these areas are highly temporal, swelling on the weekends and after work with gays who have "passed" (appeared to be straight) outside the "ghetto" during the workday. This freedom of movement and fluidity of the borders glaringly differentiates the gay neighborhood from the traditional notion of the ghetto used to describe neighborhoods of nineteenth-century Jews and twentieth-century African Americans. Finally, of course, the gentrification of these neighborhoods as they became more openly gay also distinguished them from their namesakes.

Levine describes a West Hollywood in the mid-1970s of men walking hand in hand down Santa Monica Boulevard, teenage hustlers, and gays flaunting their "look," whether it be leather, western, athlete, or drag. This daring, revolutionary behavior transformed the Boulevard into a showcase for nascent gay culture.

The term "ghettos" is used and misused often by those trying to understand the dynamics of gay geographies, and this misunderstanding underlies the need to map the boundaries and meanings of these neighborhoods with greater specificity. Esther Newton, in her history of the Cherry Grove community on Long Island, wrestles with the metaphors and uses of the term ghetto. Her attempt to define the term points to the ambivalence gays and lesbians have often voiced about the word's use:

> If Cherry Grove was a beacon towards which gays were drawn by possibility, it was also a ghetto into which they were pushed by the hatred and intolerance of straight society. . . . Founded in affluence rather than poverty, Cherry Grove is not exactly comparable to urban slums, but the exclusion underlying its existence is just as violent, if somewhat less effective. It has become common among younger gays in America, uneasy about

> an emerging model of the gay community as a minority analogous to ethnic and racial groups, to denounce the existence of gay ghettos. . . . Part of the feeling against "ghettoization" arises from the AIDS epidemic. . . . The gay meccas have become maelstroms of loss and magnets for homophobic hatred. It is not surprising that there has been a reaction against them within the gay community.[4]

As Newton obliquely suggests, the gay use of the term "ghetto" to indicate a concentration of gay businesses is counter to the more established American usage of the word to signify a high-poverty, residential concentration and place of limited mobility where ethnic and racial groups become the targets for economic and social discrimination. This is very different from the gay and lesbian experience in West Hollywood, since at least the 1970s and perhaps before. More recently, of course, this gay and lesbian use of the term has gained greater resonance as AIDS discrimination and hysteria forced gays and lesbians to reconsider their status within the majority. Most often, however, West Hollywood represents more a place to escape to than a place to escape from.

As with a whole host of terms in white urban gay lexicons, the use of "ghetto" to describe areas with high gay concentrations is not meant simply to signify connection with the oppression experienced by African Americans or Jews in their respective ghetto histories (although there may be some measure of similarity implied), but rather (often derogatorily) particular subcultures within the gay community. In this case, living in a "gay ghetto" has also come to be a way for gays and lesbians living in nongay environments to refer to the surreal quality of life in a neighborhood where there is a higher level of public comfort and awareness. Those living within an enclave such as West Hollywood are often seen as having an easier—and narrower—life than those integrated into predominantly heterosexual neighborhoods.

Perhaps the most obvious markers of the transformation of

gay and lesbian communities have been the growth of clearly marked residential zones. Mickey Lauria and Lawrence Knopp's landmark article on gay community development cited the development of gay neighborhoods as a primary spatial response to gay oppression made possible by the relative openness of urban dwellers to interact with "alien groups."[5] The development of visible gay neighborhoods often begins in the context of the simultaneous process of gentrification and urban redevelopment made possible by service sector job growth in downtown districts. They tie the spatial processes of urban change to the social dynamics of gay communities with access to the capital (through service sector employment) necessary to participate in this renaissance.

> Gays have done more with space than simply use it as a base for political power. They continually transform and use it in such a way as to reflect gay cultural values and serve the special needs of individual gays vis-à-vis society at large. . . . In the context of a rapid commodification of space, the optimal strategy for gays with respect to the development of political and economic power is to participate in the revalorization of physical structures in a neighborhood—in other words, to emphasize exchange value.[6]

The growth of these communities has had a lasting effect on their cities, in a sense expanding gay life well beyond circumscribed boundaries. For those with adequate resources, residential neighborhoods serve as the ultimate safe space, particularly to the extent that visibility as homeowners "committed to improving their neighborhoods" translates into political power. Lauria and Knopp cite eight cities (including Washington, DC; Boston; Philadelphia; Denver; and Houston) where the gay vote was mobilized out of these gentrified neighborhoods in sufficient number to elect a gay-sympathetic straight mayor.

For the most part, this participation in the gentrification of urban neighborhoods has been a white male phenomenon. Theorist Manuel Castells, trying to make a broader argument about cultural participation in urban transformations, explains that lesbians do not participate as much because men have an innate territorial imperative, whereas lesbians, in general, have a greater "radical political agenda."[7] His argument, based on the early transformation of the Castro neighborhood, certainly reflects a general theme in the gentrification literature as planners and geographers have tried to understand the complexities of gay efforts to overcome societal disapprobation through place claiming. However, urban lesbians often do not have the residential choices of gay white males because they are poorer, are more attuned to physical danger, and are less mobile. Similarly, gays and lesbians of color have been found to place greater importance on the development of residential communities within communities of color, choosing to live outside those gay residential enclaves that exist in large cities.[8]

Not all residential enclaves, however, are easily identified. Recent research questions the ways in which the existence of a gay or lesbian neighborhood is measured, suggesting that some neighborhoods have been overlooked in the search for the gay-gentrification connection. As Sy Adler and Johanna Brenner have found in San Francisco, "there is a spatial concentration of lesbians, a neighborhood that many people know about and move into to be with other lesbians. But the neighborhood has a quasi-underground character; it is enfolded in a broader countercultural milieu and does not have its own public subculture and territory."[9]

In Los Angeles gays and lesbians recognize a number of neighborhoods as "gay or lesbian friendly" that are not immediately apparent from the outside, neighborhoods like Venice that have few openly gay or lesbian establishments and no community centers. In addition, gay enclaves within communities of color need to be understood on their own terms, as efforts to strengthen ties within ethnic neighborhoods.

Upscale commercial zones with a distinct gay or lesbian character have grown as well. Like the residential neighborhoods they abut, these commercial areas also prove important to the expansion of political capital, especially because they bring in new sources of sales tax and tourism revenue. They also indicate the changing boundaries of gay and lesbian influence. The recent development of the West Hollywood commercial strip, like the development of the Castro district in the mid 1970s, marked a shift of the center of the gay community away from earlier strongholds. As with the discussion of residential neighborhoods, however, there are questions of access here as well, because gay commercial zones are largely white and male.

Neighborhood place claiming in the 1970s, before the emergence of the AIDS epidemic, was more explicitly public and recreational than is the case today. Although businesses and bars catering to gays dominated Santa Monica Boulevard, many of these establishments were still owned by people outside the gay community, and therefore were not locations for political or community organizing. Edmund White, whose 1979 travelogue, *States of Desire,* chronicles many of the newly emergent gay enclaves, describes the Los Angeles scene as a mix of pleasure seekers and community activists:

> Hedonism is the governing philosophy of gay Los Angeles. With the collapse of traditional values, hedonism seems as workable as any other available code. And, since Angeleans are so career-minded, their aspirations structure their love of pleasure into long-range hedonism, always more satisfying than the melancholy search for instant sensations.[10]

White describes the other side of the West Hollywood scene as "the most active and civic minded gay movement in the country," with charity benefits, the Municipal Election Committee (to support gay candidates), the gay Metropolitan Community Church (founded in Los Angeles in 1969 by Reverend Troy Perry), and the Gay Community Services Center, which, in the late 1970s, far surpassed community centers in other cities in terms of services, size, and outreach.

Both hedonistic and civic-minded, West Hollywood was, to outsiders like Levine and White, impossible to categorize. As Edmund White writes, gay male Los Angeles, for the most part, bypassed the gay ghetto phenomenon, moving from scattered and isolated locations to a network of neighborhoods across the city, with no one location reaching the density or intensity of the Castro or the West Village:

> The main gay neighborhoods are West Hollywood ("Boystown") and the Hollywood Hills ("the Swish Alps"), where even little houses are in such demand they're selling for $80,000. The "Sycamore Sissies" live in Spanish Revival mansions along Sycamore Street—large cool chambers with tile floors and wrought-iron balconies overlooking tinkling fountains in shaded patios; the rents there vary between $500 and $900. Silver Lake [*sic*], where the rents are lower, is the leather and Western neighborhood. Los Feliz, with its 1920s mansions, is becoming the Beverly Hills for gays. The nearby beach community is Venice. But Angeleans can live anywhere; the car and the freeway made the idea of the neighborhood obsolete.[11]

Here, White describes one of the enduring characteristics of gay and lesbian community life in Los Angeles. Although Angelenos identify West Hollywood as a central location, perhaps the hub of gay culture and place making, it is sustained far less by a local resident population (who might engender a more neighborhood atmosphere) than by a transient nightlife pulled from smaller gay and nongay neighborhoods around Southern California.

Political-Territorial Strategies in the Incorporation of West Hollywood

West Hollywood is important, not only because it helps us understand the transformation of Los Angeles, but also because it signals an important new strategy for gay political empowerment. West Hollywood marks the evolution of Los

Angeles's gay movement from one focused on short-term responses to crises within the community to one of creating and sustaining community institutions through alliances with other local constituent groups and residents. Along the way, West Hollywood became a place that supported a broader range of gay identities—from the engaged activist to the weekend club-goer to the closeted retiree. The history of West Hollywood's incorporation, however, is not just the popular tale of gay men creating a self-affirming culture, a "gay city," but of a popular struggle on behalf of a broad and unlikely coalition of liberal activists. By most accounts, the successful incorporation drive was a campaign against the county's neglect and overdevelopment of the area rather than a crusade for a "gay city." The independence that unincorporated status had provided to West Hollywood in the 1930s and 1940s had, by the 1980s, resulted in some of the highest residential densities in the city. The cheap apartments built by speculative developers made West Hollywood a pocket of affordability as compared with its more affluent neighbors—Beverly Hills, Bel Air, the Hollywood Hills, and Santa Monica. Seniors and others on limited incomes, including intermittently employed actors and screenwriters, were drawn to these hastily built "dingbat" apartments.

In the early 1980s, a crisis involving the county's strong rent control ordinance brought to the brink a long-simmering distrust between liberal activists and local government. The county's existing rent control ordinance, passed in part through the efforts of well-organized West Hollywood senior citizen residents, was scheduled to expire at the end of 1984 and be terminated. In Los Angeles County, where the Board of Supervisors tended to reflect the wishes of homeowners on the outskirts of the city—in the San Fernando Valley and wealthy enclaves on the Westside—West Hollywood was an anomaly, with one survey showing that nearly 90 percent of all residents were renters. As an area that had managed to remain off major developers' radar screens until the early 1970s, West Hollywood was, to many observers, in danger of rapidly losing its unique character and stability.

Because residents of West Hollywood were living in an unincorporated area, this collection of neighborhoods had no locally elected governing body to press for intervention. Furthermore, the political representation West Hollywood did have was extremely fragmented, with the area divided between two U.S. Congress representatives, two state senators, and two state assembly representatives. Ron Stone, a local gay activist and founder of the 1984 incorporation drive, captured this anxiety in an *LA Weekly* article written as the campaign got underway:

> All this sub-dividing and separation makes West Hollywood a prime target for development. With no local government to turn to or take control of, citizens of the area who want to retain the village-like characteristics that attracted them in the first place have had a difficult time of it.[12]

In part because it was understood that the legacy of county indifference was useful to the gay community, the gay and lesbian leadership in West Hollywood initially opposed the idea of another incorporation drive. Both the Stonewall Gay and Lesbian Democratic Club and the Harvey Milk Lesbian and Gay Democratic Club rebuffed Ron Stone's early outreach efforts. However, when Bob Craig, publisher of the local gay magazine *Frontiers,* became convinced that supporting cityhood might be a way to increase circulation, he established himself as a vocal spokesperson for the campaign. *Frontiers,* best known for its calendar of gay nightlife and social events (and for its sexually explicit dating and phone sex ads), became an important vehicle for publicizing the campaign. Stories in *Frontiers* on a regular basis attracted the attention of both the Stonewall and Harvey Milk clubs, and incorporation slowly became identified as a "gay cause."[13] Bob Craig made one of the more catalytic statements about the new city in a speech a few weeks before the cityhood election, calling West Hollywood "a gay Camelot on the horizon."[14]

The two other groups driving the cityhood campaign—seniors and renters—were brought to the table via the Coalition for Economic Survival (CES), a tenants' rights group that had long been active in West Hollywood politics. In 1980, CES led the successful battle for the county's rent control ordinance and later tried unsuccessfully to pass a countywide proposition that would have strengthened and extended the term of the law. Although the measure failed countywide, it won in West Hollywood by a five-to-one majority. With the coalition of gays, seniors, and renters forged, a West Hollywood Incorporation Committee was formed to do the actual work for cityhood required by the county and the state.[15]

For the gay establishment in West Hollywood, a major shift in thinking was needed before they could endorse the idea of cityhood. For the most part, the gay community in West Hollywood considered Ed Edelman, their County Supervisor, to be a friend of the community—a politician generally tolerant of gays and lesbians and concerned about the area. In 1974, when Edelman was first elected, he appointed a committee to draft a general zoning plan for West Hollywood aimed at controlling run-away development. After a slow start, the committee did manage to present a draft plan to the public in 1981. The plan set limits for building heights for every street, preserved the two remaining neighborhoods of single-story houses, closed many Santa Monica Boulevard intersections to reduce traffic, and encouraged construction of off-street parking areas by local businesses. Although many residents felt that the nine years it took for the plan to reach final approval ruined most of the area forever, Edelman was seen as their only ally. Moreover, as Adam Moos (a participant in the incorporation drive) notes in his analysis of the cityhood effort, the success of behind-the-scenes politicking by the gay community was not something the gay leadership wished to jeopardize. Many feared a backlash from Edelman if the cityhood vote failed. Only when the incorporation measure was approved for the 1984 ballot did the gay leadership become more directly involved. As Moos noted,

> Now, the gay community saw that it had the potential to elect openly gay and lesbian candidates to seats of power. The question at this point was no longer one of turning the community's back on its friend, Edelman, but one of "this is our chance to determine our own fate." In this sense, the question for the gay community became one of local control—control of issues that affected and concerned gays—and having a direct voice in how those issues would be handled.[16]

Throughout the campaign the question of gay control of city politics had been a contentious issue. The anticityhood forces were attacked as being homophobic, in part for circulating a survey to senior citizens that referred to cityhood as a means to effect a "gay takeover of the city." As the cityhood measure moved to the ballot the implications of its success for gays and lesbians became more obvious. Of the forty candidates for the new city council, nineteen were openly gay or lesbian. Because each of the candidates varied widely on their support of rent control, development, and other cityhood issues, their gay or lesbian identity quickly became a background issue. However, sensitive to the possibility of an antigay backlash, supporters continued to paint the incorporation campaign as one driven by economic, rather than cultural, demands. An endorsement editorial in the *West Hollywood Post* reflected the argument that cityhood was more about long-term viability and fiscal responsibility than a gay agenda:

> A city is a unique business. Money—financial statements, long-range planning, cost effective decisions, understanding the profit and loss potential—That's the bottom line. . . . What are we going to get for our money? . . . A lot has been said about the sexual preference of the candidates. That is of no importance.[17]

Perhaps because of the many agendas at work in the incorporation drive—including rent control, slowing growth, gay and lesbian rights, as well as seniors' issues—there was never a single gay platform for the campaign. Instead, gay and lesbian candidates for the new city council included, to varying degrees, each of these other agendas. Some gay candidates allied themselves directly with the rent control proponents, whereas others campaigned on the message that a "gay city" was necessary on its own merits. As Moos and others have argued, this unique situation of having enough gay or lesbian candidates to split the gay vote became a source of strength (in that sexuality was not viewed as a negative factor in the race) and a source of weakness for the new city (in that no gay slate was possible).[18] In the election, a gay/lesbian majority was elected to the council with three members—John Heilman, Valerie Terrigno, and Steve Schulte—openly identified as gay or lesbian. Of the five elected, only Schulte was not endorsed by the CES.

Although a gay or lesbian agenda had not been a centerpiece of the cityhood campaign, immediately after the election, lesbian and gay issues defined early city politics. The first official act of the city council was to pass an ordinance banning discrimination against lesbians and gays. One of the now-mythical episodes in West Hollywood's short history is the march of the entire city council and meeting audience to a local bikers hangout that sported at the entrance an antigay sign:

> The crowd stood to applaud. Some cried. Wielding this new law, council members later trooped to a restaurant [Barney's Beanery]—with news cameras in tow—to remove a sign that had long infuriated gays: "Fagots Stay Out" [*sic*].[19]

As participants themselves quickly noted, this gesture was largely symbolic. Few accounts of actual discrimination at Barney's Beanery had been filed with the sheriff's office or reported in the media. However, this symbolic act set a tone for governance in the city—one where policies and actions were often pursued for their community-building value in establishing West Hollywood as a place of tolerance and respect.

Profiling West Hollywood

Since incorporation, the central questions for the City of West Hollywood have been the following: To what extent has a gay city been established? On what grounds? For whom? Do demographics alone constitute a city where gays predominate, or does a city (rather than a neighborhood) require some other attributes that would mark it as gay or lesbian?

More than 36,000 people live in the less than two square miles that constitutes West Hollywood. According to the 1990 census, more than half the population was between twenty-five and forty-nine years old, with a median age of just over thirty-eight. Nearly 90 percent of the residents are white, and 12 percent of the population is Russian-speaking. West Hollywood is more highly educated (with one out of three people holding a college diploma) and wealthier (average household income at roughly $53,000) than the rest of Los Angeles County. Although 32 percent of residents earn less than $25,000 per year, this figure is much lower than the county average of 42 percent. Nearly the entire city is developed, with 70 percent dedicated to residential dwellings.

West Hollywood in many ways exemplifies the image of the Westside of Los Angeles as racially homogeneous. Whites account for 90 percent of West Hollywood's residents, compared with 57 percent of Los Angeles County as a whole. However, according to the 1990 census (which generally confirms the demographic estimates from the city's own surveys), West Hollywood has a much larger percentage of elderly residents (18 percent over the age of 65) than does the county as a whole (with only 10 percent elderly residents). In addition, roughly 9 percent of the county's elderly are reported by the census to be living in poverty, while fully 11 percent of the city's elderly are considered to be living in poverty.[20]

However, attitudes toward the city and its government are more telling than demographics. According to the city's own surveys of residents, conducted every five years, West Hollywood city government and city services inspire high levels of satisfaction. This stands in contrast to public perceptions of other local municipalities, including the City of Los Angeles itself, where secessionist movements have become a regular part of the political landscape.

A sense of strong connection to the city resounds throughout the 1993 and 1998 West Hollywood Community Needs Assessment surveys by residents.[21] As the 1993 study reported, city inhabitants expressed "widespread deep affection for the City, and strong attachment to local institutions that are open to all, and that serve the needs of residents for public interactions and use of their City space."[22] These comments reflect this visceral connection between the physical space of the city and the development of the city government since incorporation. Similarly, when interviewed, local officials, activists, and business people say they want to constantly improve city life and count on the city government to be an integral part of these changes. Survey respondents stress the interconnections between government and civil society, the diversity of the city, and a strong sense of community as reasons to live in West Hollywood. Most importantly for an understanding of place claiming, gay and lesbian respondents in particular indicate they view the gay community in West Hollywood as a prime factor in the development of West Hollywood since incorporation. They also see the continued importance of the lesbian and gay community to the health of the city.

As described by the survey, the population of West Hollywood consists of three significant population groups—gay men, senior citizens (especially women), and recent immigrants from the former Soviet Union. The majority of residents live in apartments, on their own. Most likely as a result of the city's proximity to Hollywood and Burbank, rates of employment are high, with a significant proportion of workers in the entertainment industry.

Of course, most surveys of lesbians and gays in the United States and, indeed, most attempts to chart gays and lesbians demographically, are fraught with complications and inaccuracies, not the least of which are doubts about the confidentiality of the data, conflicts about labels and terms for gay men and lesbians (which may affect a respondent's participation or self-identification), and bias in sample selection.[23] Although these concerns are valid for the West Hollywood Community Needs Assessment as well, the surveys reveal information about the community that appears more interesting and potentially more accurate than similar surveys. First, West Hollywood has established itself as a gay-friendly location, something that each West Hollywood resident can be reasonably expected to acknowledge. Second, this higher degree of comfort provided by West Hollywood's openness toward gays and lesbians might have mitigated some of the issues about self-identification. Nevertheless, 16 percent of the survey respondents in 1998 refused to self-identify as gay, lesbian, bisexual, or straight, indicating the limitations of demographic research on sexuality even within an exceptionally "safe" environment.[24] Unfortunately, the Needs Assessment does not give the race or gender characteristics of those declining to respond to the sexuality question. This information would be particularly useful in understanding the dimensions of this underreporting problem. Of those who did reveal their sexual identity on the survey form, 56 percent answered heterosexual, 35 percent answered gay, 6 percent answered bisexual, and only 3 percent self-identified as lesbian. Although anecdotal evidence also suggests that far fewer lesbians than gay men live in West Hollywood, this small number of lesbians does raise questions about the completeness of the survey.

The 1998 Needs Assessment shows that there are proportionately fewer lesbians living in West Hollywood than in 1993. Although gays, lesbians, and bisexuals constitute 44 percent of the total survey population (up from 34 percent in 1993), gay men outnumber lesbians by a ratio of eleven to one (up from a ratio of seven to one five years earlier). If these numbers are indeed accurate, they suggest a reversal of a previous trend in which the ratio of gay men to lesbians had been declining throughout the years since incorporation.

As with other well-publicized surveys of gays and lesbians that have been conducted at specific venues (such as the 1993 March on Washington) or through specific channels (such as national gay and lesbians marketing campaigns), the West Hollywood survey can be reasonably expected to be biased toward upper-income consumers. Because this survey targeted a gay and lesbian population that has chosen to live in West Hollywood, a relatively small geographical area, its results cannot be extrapolated to reflect the attitudes of gays and lesbians or bisexuals in Los Angeles as a whole. As a result, they represent a particularly enfranchised group that is not excluded (in reality or in perception) by questions of access. The attitudes of gays and lesbians of color who do not live in West Hollywood (and are therefore not potential survey respondents) will be discussed further below.

Only a few marked differences appeared between the lesbian and gay population and the total population. The gay male population of the city tends to be younger and wealthier than the total residential population. A greater percentage of gay men own their houses or apartments and have completed college or graduate education. There is little overlap between the Russian and gay populations, with very few gays reporting immigrant status. Not surprisingly, the distribution of AIDS in West Hollywood (accounting for 12 percent of the city's population) centers in the gay population.

The Community Needs Assessment offers much more than

a demographic analysis. The study also seeks to understand the expectations of residents concerning the growth and cultural life of the city. Many of these concerns confirm that, for residents, the physical space of the city ranks as one of the most important reasons to live in West Hollywood. During focus group discussions aimed at eliciting residents' attitudes about the city, several themes ranked high for gay men. These included the success of the city as a clearly gay space and the "gay-friendly atmosphere" of the city. One typical gay respondent characterized the positive aspects of West Hollywood life in the following way: "Small village feel, liberal views, safe for gay people, location."[25]

Gays and Lesbians as Neighborhood Activists

Because there are no exhaustive directories of West Hollywood's gay scene available for the years prior to incorporation, it is difficult to chart the concrete effect of cityhood on the number of gay businesses or residences. That the mainstream press gave attention to the gay involvement in the cityhood drive probably drew as many gays to the area as the city policies themselves. For Jodi Curlee, former director of the social services department at the City of West Hollywood and an activist in the community since the 1970s, the incorporation of West Hollywood was perfectly timed to take advantage of a new generation willing to work together and challenge discrimination with a new energy. According to Curlee, "West Hollywood emerged at a time when the movement was transforming itself and was ready to try a new kind of integration that was more about coexistence and less about hiding."[26]

As a result, the early years of incorporated West Hollywood were very much about challenging the kind of discrimination that gays and lesbians had long endured, even in that city. Gays and lesbians sought and secured representation on city boards and at city hall. In 1988 the city convened a gay and lesbian task force to review city policy, survey gay and lesbian residents, and make recommendations for community outreach and education. The task force made crucial recommendations: to create a permanent gay and lesbian advisory council to review city policy and make recommendations concerning services; coordinate with the sheriff's department to discuss active gay and lesbian recruitment in the sheriff's department; address problems with harassment and recruitment; arrange sensitivity training for city workers and the West Hollywood Marketing Corporation (an innovative public-private group responsible for city marketing) on gay and lesbian issues; include gays and lesbians in all descriptions of the city's population; develop a gay and lesbian community profile in the human services element of the city's general plan; and dedicate space for gay and lesbian community organizations.[27] Many of these concerns are echoed in the 1998 Community Needs Assessment, in particular the continued pressure on the sheriff's department concerning gay bashing.[28]

The place-claiming implications of these key recommendations underlie the feeling of security cityhood offered to gays and lesbians. The emphasis on the sheriff's department reflects the heightened attention to police harassment or unwillingness to report hate crimes that has become a central issue for the movement nationally. The emphasis on recruitment indicates a desire on the part of the community to challenge a dominant police culture and to allow for the possibility that law enforcement might be a useful ally.

The recommendations for a progay marketing strategy and greater recognition of gays, lesbians, and bisexuals in descriptions of the city's population point to a perception of the community's invisibility even in a city commonly referred to as "the gay city."

Beyond attention to specific requests and occasional friction between the gay community and other residents, the West Hollywood city government has distinguished itself with an attention to other progressive issues with no obvious reference to gays or lesbians. West Hollywood was one of the first local governments to press for sanctions on South Africa in the mid-1980s, enacted a landmark homeless services policy (which has since been replaced with a controversial anticamping ordinance that many felt reneged on the city's former commitment to the homeless and a backing away from its social justice stances), and worked to establish joint projects with African American neighborhoods following the 1992 civil unrest.

Although many of the achievements within West Hollywood have little or no relevance for those who live outside its boundaries, the city's landmark antidiscrimination policy, domestic partnership benefits for city employees, civil union registry, and close relationship with local law enforcement have become models for other cities and states. As gay and lesbian residents see that their rights are secure in West Hollywood, argues Curlee, "they can be involved in the bigger issues without fear that they are leaving their agenda behind."[29]

At the same time, however, Curlee describes an ongoing minority current of criticism against the visibility of gay issues on the city's agenda. Even while gay issues recede as priorities, some residents continue to level charges that the city favors its gay and lesbian population:

> Backlashers think that the city is a one issue city. This is so different from reality that it is scary. . . . They think that one queer equals one hundred queers and that is scary . . . as the population becomes more integrated and casual (this is who I am and you have to deal with it and it's not all I am) then the gays forget that that is how they are viewed by others. They don't even think about it when they are dealing with city issues but the others see it.[30]

As gays and lesbians in West Hollywood move beyond using city politics as a locus for their civil rights struggles primarily because they have succeeded, West Hollywood's role returns to one of creating a neighborhood for the gays and lesbians who live and visit there. In many ways, then, the question for the city is less how the government creates places for lesbians and gays than how the residents of West Hollywood have created a sense of community and the extent to which this enclave serves those living outside the city's borders. Since incorporation, West Hollywood has been a leader in providing services (from housing to health care) for people with HIV and AIDS. The annual gay pride parade is held in West Hollywood, and the only lesbian festival, Lesbian Visibility Week, is cosponsored with the Gay and Lesbian Center and funded by the city.

In addition to these annual events, which attract gays and lesbians across Los Angeles and emphasize the spectacle of gay and lesbian culture, the city continues to support the Lesbian and Gay Advisory Council, which serves as a shadow government to the city council, ensuring that gay and lesbian concerns are voiced and heard. The advisory council serves as a clearinghouse for events and issues in the community and coordinates with community institutions across the city and region. Thus, in recent years, the council has negotiated with the Gay and Lesbian Center to hold fund-raising events and celebrations, worked with local activists to obtain permits for demonstrations, and generally advocated the perception that West Hollywood is synonymous with gay and lesbian community and politics in Los Angeles. According to one member of the advisory council, the council acts as "the eyes and ears" of the city council members, "on the street and in the nightclubs. . . . We have become a sounding board for the gays and lesbians in the city, and we act as a buffer between the activist organizations and the city."[31]

The advisory council has been instrumental in the ongoing efforts of the city government to reform the attitudes of the sheriff's department toward lesbians and gays. As discussed earlier, police safety has been a constant issue in West Hollywood for gays and lesbians (as it is for gays and lesbians generally). In 1992, a ballot initiative to require the city to create an independent police force (rather than continuing to contract services from the county) was narrowly defeated after a vociferous campaign. According to one advisory council member, the police initiative provided an opportunity for a public debate on gay bashing and relations with the sheriff as well as a chance for the city to explain the measures it has instituted to improve these relations. Working with the advisory council, the city established a community board to work with the sheriff's department (to encourage gay and lesbian recruitment, provide sensitivity training, participate in a highly publicized sting operation, and monitor complaints). This community policing effort has become a model for improved community–police relations around the country, including for communities of color.

Eventually and perhaps inevitably, however, this proactive involvement of the city in these quality-of-life issues led some to argue that city hall is overinvolved in daily affairs. Although the city's policies and attitudes have contributed to the widespread perception (documented in the Needs Assessments) that its environment and lifestyle are the most important aspects of living in West Hollywood, this same engagement has some complaining that the city is overstructured. Like similarly progressive cities, West Hollywood has also been mocked by residents and the local press for its tendency to pass social justice ordinances that have little apparent effect on local life: declaring the city a nuclear-free, antiapartheid zone and opposing the military's antigay policy. As Thomas Crail, director of the Chamber of Commerce until his death in 1995 noted, "people expected mecca, but a less structured mecca" than exists today. For Crail, this backlash against the city government has to be understood in the context of gay and lesbian life outside West Hollywood:

> The question [our ambivalence about city government] begs is, Can queer culture exist in a structure like that? The interesting

> flip side is when queers get power we overstructure. . . . Suddenly we are in this position where we are in control and we have never been in control of anything in our lives. . . . We can do something, so we do everything.[32]

This backlash also comes from straight residents, many of whom blame the city's problems on the visible gay culture. In the mid-1990s, a highly publicized conflict between the gay and Russian Jewish émigré communities erupted, first over the use of Plummer Park, which includes a community center, on the east side of town. While gay residents charged that many of the park users (particularly the younger Russians) were harassing gays and lesbians and attempting to drive them out of the park (which is used by a number of gay organizations for meetings), the Russians countered that the gays and lesbians were equally intolerant and deliberately offended them with their visibility. Russian community leaders explained to city officials (including members of the Gay and Lesbian Community Advisory Council) that many older Russians were shocked simply by the gays passing them as they went to meetings, rather than by any overt actions or confrontations. The younger Russians, many of whom lived in the city from an early age, appeared to be motivated by a more traditional American homophobia. Attempts at negotiation have been largely successful, with many gays and lesbians involved in the negotiations admitting ignorance of the Soviet oppression from which the Russians fled and under which gay and lesbian behavior was completely unknown. Partly as a result of these new tensions, the city has embarked on a process of reevaluating the distribution of city services and the percentage of funding earmarked for gay and lesbian community uses.

Internal Conflicts

Lesbians give many reasons why they do not live in West Hollywood in the same concentration as gay men. Many lesbians view West Hollywood as a high-rent district welcoming only professionals. And many lesbians are uncomfortable about becoming pioneers in West Hollywood. Finally, they feel excluded because they believe that most businesses and services cater exclusively to gay men. The city and local businesses both assert that more lesbians are coming to West Hollywood on weekends, but they are not moving there. Since the mid-1990s, the number of lesbian clubs has increased. These "floating" clubs rent spaces once or twice a week from gay groups and target a young, racially diverse crowd. Rita Boyadjian, one of a new generation of lesbian entrepreneurs in West Hollywood, epitomizes the attitude of a younger generation that views this phenomenon without reference to decades of struggle and invisibility. For her, the arrival of lesbians onto the West Hollywood scene is inevitable:

> I think that there has been a commitment by lesbian entrepreneurs to create spaces for women and to create events for women in this city and that's the major change. A lot of women promoters were just sick of having their events in these "cheesy-chivy" places and why not do it in West Hollywood? The boys have their spaces, so why not create spaces for women?[33]

Despite this interest, however, the success of lesbian spaces in Boystown has been inconsistent. Only the Palms, the lesbian bar owned by two gay men, has endured since before incorporation. Little Frida's—a coffeehouse alternative a few blocks away—has gone through at least three changes in ownership and two locations since it opened. Boyadjian recognizes that West Hollywood remains a gay male place and that lesbians in Los Angeles are not necessarily looking to develop such a place: "I don't think lesbians go out as much as gay men. They find someone and they stay home; they become condo bound." Boyadjian's goal is clear: "If more lesbians lived in West Hollywood, there would certainly be more support of lesbian retail businesses that are open seven days a week."[34]

For gays and lesbians of color, West Hollywood presents a

similar paradox. Although the nightclub scene attracts a mixed crowd (and, according to many observers, grows more diverse every year), West Hollywood's racially coded atmosphere has not abated. Eric Reyes, in his master's thesis, "Queer Spaces: The Geography of Lesbians and Gay Men of Color in Los Angeles," presents diagrams and maps drawn by local activists (primarily young and all people of color) of their own understanding and use of public space.[35] Although no one he interviewed lived in West Hollywood, most of them identified the city as a key place on their maps. Compared with the positive comments in the Community Needs Assessment about West Hollywood's "spirit of togetherness," and "small town feel," or the attention of the city council to issues of access, equality, and discrimination, the attitudes expressed by self-identified queers of color are distinctly more qualified:

> West Hollywood is not an everything, just because it exists is not a reason to sing hallelujahs.[36]
>
> I don't really like West Hollywood. But it is one of the places where everyone is out. It's sort of like a little white boy's town, and I'm neither. . . . I guess West Hollywood is a token gay space.[37]
>
> West Hollywood is considered white, I feel no connection. It's too alien, foreign to me, like going to another country and I can't speak their language. . . . I am not free there and I choose not to deal with the comments, the looks, and everything.[38]

Despite these criticisms, West Hollywood was "mapped" by nearly all of Reyes's respondents, not solely as a place of estrangement, but also as a place to relax and meet other queers. Reyes argues that racial and ethnic experiences of discrimination complicate and bias the discussion of physical space with gays and lesbians of color. For many of his respondents, the social and mental spaces of their queer lives (represented by community networks, self-development and awareness, spaces created through temporary occupation) rank much higher than the physical spaces (in West Hollywood or elsewhere).

Reyes's work places this ambivalence about West Hollywood in the context of a white male privileging of physical space. He writes that "West Hollywood is a white-coded gay male place and to assign physical space as the only determinant of existence is to render queers of color invisible."[39] Reyes implies that the relative permanence of these physical spaces magnifies the disparity in power and access between the West Hollywood majority and communities of color. As such, these spaces are suspect. As one of Reyes's respondents described, West Hollywood reflects the norms and values of straight, rather than queer, culture: "West Hollywood is definitely not queer, it's gay. West Hollywood's gayness draws its validation from straight culture by appropriating norms, presentation, propriety and culture. The norms of society are not challenged—a normalized and assimilated gay."[40]

The Future of West Hollywood

Fifteen years after incorporation, many gays and lesbians moving to the city (and most using the city as a social escape) today know little if anything about the early struggles to create place in the city. How, then, does West Hollywood continue to assert its identity as a gay mecca beyond the attraction of the bars on Santa Monica Boulevard? Thomas Crail posed a set of three questions that reach the heart of a potential West Hollywood transformation:

> I wonder if West Hollywood is losing its queerness; and if it is losing its queerness what does it mean, A; and B, why is it happening; and C, is this good or bad? I don't know the answer to any of these three questions, but I think that they are valid questions that need to be addressed.[41]

Many city businesses contend that the changing demographics of the weekend crowd indicates a shift away from

West Hollywood, with the social scene increasingly dominated by younger gays, most of whom do not live in West Hollywood. Although this has increased the numbers of people on West Hollywood's streets and therefore revenue for the bars and similar businesses, this emphasis on the younger, more transient crowd reflects short-term hype rather than long-term stability. As Crail explains, "It's not the same thing as having a real base that is a queer community."[42] The transient nature of the club scene, with new venues opening every few months and others losing favor and folding, creates a boom and bust atmosphere that does little to strengthen business ties to the community at large. Increasingly, these clubs, like gay organizations, are relocating to Hollywood, drawn by cheaper space and better parking.

The dynamics of diversity that have challenged the gay and lesbian movement in the past five years seem to be more critical to the future of West Hollywood than the economics of gay business. As lesbians and people of color become more visible actors in the movement, their absence in West Hollywood becomes more glaring. As long as the movement was led and staffed by white men, the demographics of West Hollywood were not necessarily surprising. As long as the movement was led and staffed by white men, the homogeneity of the city's gay population was not a public issue. Throughout the 1990s, however, a more diverse community has emerged, led in part by activists of color, and the whiteness of West Hollywood has become something of a political liability for those activists trying to broaden the movement. Initially, community institutions moved to Hollywood to find cheaper and larger spaces, but soon after new organizations located elsewhere in response to demands that the movement recognize the diversity—demographic and geographic—of the community. One of the mainstays of the Santa Monica Boulevard throughout this transition has been the local bookstore, A Different Light. After moving to West Hollywood from its original location in

Silverlake, the bookstore has worked to offer literature that reflects the broader community and programs than attract people who would not otherwise visit the boulevard.

The feeling that there is a lack of community feeding the boulevard also affects the activist agenda in the city, and across local gay and lesbian politics. With little success, a few businesses (primarily coffeehouses) have opened with the intention, in part, of creating in West Hollywood a neighborhood atmosphere that would make the city more than a place to cruise on Friday night. One short-lived effort, the Six Gallery, aimed to be a community space by offering gallery space for artists and a back room for readings and meetings. During a series of massive street marches to protest the 1993 veto of a gay rights bill by the California governor, the Gallery transformed itself into an outpost of the Gay and Lesbian Center, serving as the semiofficial information central. Carter Bravmann, a founder of the Six Gallery, discovered, however, that even these popular cafes did not always benefit from the activity on the street, and that bars and clubs still defined the Boystown environment. These bars, many of which are still not gay owned and have few ties to the community, tend to be lax with the age restriction, thus encouraging the deterioration of the boulevard:

> The Boulevard has that reputation of being loud. . . . Women don't want to go down there, it is not women's town, girls' town, or men's town, it is known as "Boystown" and that is exactly what it is. . . . The average age is probably twenty-three.[43]

Following the example set by the Six Gallery (and many similar efforts since the 1970s), new coffeehouses have opened that combine social activist agendas and aggressive outreach to the typical Boystown regulars. As chains—like Starbucks—try to cash in on the gentrification and tourist development of the city, other gay-owned establishments such as Stonewall Coffee have begun as a conscious effort to counter any mainstreaming by offering specifically gay or lesbian events, including comedy evenings to benefit local gay organizations and coffee give-aways at local gay, lesbian, and AIDS events. The first franchise is owned by Gay and Lesbian Adolescent Social Services, which provides group homes and foster care placement of gay youth as well as foster care and adoption placement for gay and lesbian families. A second store is located inside the Gay and Lesbian Center's newest location.

Even more community entrenched is WeHo Lounge, a cafe run by the AIDS Healthcare Foundation (AHF). The coffee shop designs its outreach efforts (including HIV tests) for gay men between the ages of sixteen and 21, one of the hardest-to-reach at-risk groups. The cafe, funded at start-up with a pharmaceutical company grant, also offers information about clinical trials and support groups. "It's a very in-your-face thing," said AHF president Michael Weinstein in a 1997 interview for the *Advocate*. "We share a common wall with Mickey's, one of the biggest discos in Los Angeles. We have more foot traffic on this street than anywhere west of the Mississippi."[44] Moreover, he says, the location and casual approach of the cafe aims to counter the gap between an older population accustomed to safe-sex programs and messages and younger gays who may feel ostracized from more mainstream social service locations. "Younger people are not comfortable going into official places to be tested. But people are really comfortable coming into a community establishment." The outreach to the younger generation also has attracted a crowd that is more ethnically diverse and may have otherwise seen West Hollywood as unwelcoming.

Added to these difficulties with the culture of Boystown, the physical space of the area also seems to inhibit a community ethos. The other major obstacle to the generation of community life along Santa Monica Boulevard that goes beyond barhopping is the physical layout of the area and the design impediments typical of Southern California and Los Angeles.

Bravmann described the lack of community on the Strip as resulting not only from the transient nature of the bar crowd, but also from the rigidity of the public space of Boystown:

> Physically, it just doesn't support it. Compared to the Castro, which on a day like today would be paradise, with people walking around, a community feeling, and a mix of residential and commercial. . . . The public infrastructure cannot support more development because the Boulevard is filled up.[45]

From an urban design standpoint, the layout of the Santa Monica strip is difficult to improve. Along the busiest section of the Boulevard, across from the bookstore and a dense row of clubs and bars, is a walled-off zone containing a regional bus depot and the sheriff's substation. Together, they create a four-block obstruction to further commercial development. The sidewalks are extremely narrow, in part because Santa Monica Boulevard is a state highway, which prevents the city from widening the sidewalks that would improve pedestrian use. With four lanes of traffic, complicated intersections, and buses pulling in and out of traffic, the Boulevard has always been the most prominent feature of the neighborhood's landscape. One of the city's first major urban design projects after incorporation was the purchase of the median strip down the center of the Boulevard (a former trolley car right-of-way) to prevent the state from further widening the Boulevard. The median was lined with flagpoles flying the rainbow lambda flag. After years of planning and negotiation, the city finally undertook a major reconstruction, aiming to redesign the median and intersections to enhance city services and pedestrian safety.

The transient nature of the gay scene, however, remains the greatest obstacle to real transformation in the area. The expansion of weekend clubs on the eastern edge of Hollywood Boulevard and the emergence of new clubs in more diverse areas of the city aimed at young Latinos, Asians, and African American have shifted the geography of the community further away from West Hollywood. Some local observers believe that the city should be concerned about this shift given the financial impact on the city's economy. The current attitude toward the gay businesses, which has been described as one of "benign neglect," is exemplified by the willingness with which the city watched the community institutions move to Hollywood. "I think," explained one local business leader, "we have had the attitude that we are the center of it all. The city gets a little arrogant about that and in the meantime your community institutions are being pulled off into other space."[46]

This concern about neglect obviously contrasts sharply with the earlier argument that the city is "overinvolved" in its residents' lives. West Hollywood's role for gays and lesbians across the larger Los Angeles area has clearly evolved. First, with incorporation came the possibility that the region could support, on its own terms, a place to rival the Castro or the West Village—a place openly committed to the needs and desires of gay men and lesbians. However, the increasing visibility of lesbians and gay men of color and the diversity of the community in Los Angeles as a whole means that no one district can hold a monopoly on gay and lesbian space. Places as ostensibly straight as East Los Angeles or the San Fernando Valley once offered little more than a neighborhood bar. Now, as evidenced by listings in the gay press and the community yellow pages (a listing of gay and gay-friendly businesses), these neighborhoods host more visible enclaves. With the greater tolerance (if not acceptance) of gays and lesbians and the possibility of alternatives to West Hollywood, the city may lose some of the advantages that made it a mecca. Crail notes,

> You can't assume that because for 40 years or 50 years you have had a monopoly on queer space you are going to have that six months later. The fact is that we are successfully creating an alternative [to West Hollywood] by putting those institutions that are the heart of our community in Hollywood.[47]

Other gay and lesbian community institutions have searched for space elsewhere in recent years, and many have moved to areas of Los Angeles not previously coded as gay or lesbian. Most notably, the International Gay and Lesbian Archives recently acquired space at the University of Southern California to allow for an expansion of its operations. Although many institutions consider a location in West Hollywood to be desirable, the attraction of affordable and permanent space outside the city may well be impossible to resist. In the summer of 1998, the Gay and Lesbian Community Services Center expanded beyond its new building on Hollywood Boulevard to additional space for educational activities elsewhere in Hollywood. This new location also offers office space for struggling gay and lesbian community organizations, filling a need that, previously, only West Hollywood has acknowledged. Clearly, West Hollywood's reputation as the only safe place for community institutions is quickly fading.

Symbolically as well as practically, West Hollywood remains the central site for activism and community celebration. When President Clinton announced the "Don't Ask, Don't Tell" policy on gays and lesbians in the military, Barbara Boxer held a meeting for community leaders to try to control whatever reaction might come from the streets. The Gay and Lesbian Advisory Committee organized a town hall meeting (cosponsored by the Human Rights Campaign Fund, a national gay and lesbian legal rights group) and march in West Hollywood, which became, in part, an official response to the new policy. The Center's California AIDS Ride, which raises more than a million dollars for the Center's AIDS services, had, until 1998, concluded its route from San Francisco to West Hollywood with a massive celebration, speeches from community leaders and city officials from both West Hollywood and Los Angeles, further solidifying the niche West Hollywood has carved out for itself.

With the new understanding of its gay identity, the city has increasingly turned to development projects and social services that have less to do with gay and lesbian culture than with the city's insistence on serving residents in all categories (straight, gay, lesbian, senior, Russian, children) as well as supporting a diversified economic base. One case in point is the ongoing revitalization of the Sunset Strip through an intense planning process focusing on the use, design, and future of each building and lot on the street. Interests on the Strip range from those of the wealthy homeowners in the foothills north of Sunset Boulevard to the club owners and patrons that lend the Strip its signature character. Although there were fears of overcommercializing when the first plans appeared (including proposed celebrity statues), the plan for the area has evolved into one that balances economic development pressures and opportunities with the desires of the city's residents. At the same time, new developments on the Strip have been extraordinarily successful. This new approach to the Strip, of course, could not be more divergent from the first sixty years of development that rested on the lack of oversight and near lawlessness of the area between the 1920s and 1980s. In many ways, this approach to the area signifies one of the clearest signals coming from the gay majority city council: Overt and conscious participation in the city's development and character will have profound effects on the culture, economy, and design of the city. West Hollywood will finally achieve not just a gay enclave to rival Greenwich Village or the Castro, but also an integrated, diverse, and flourishing municipality that can be a model for cities, gay and straight, across the country.

This new burst of development has strengthened the role of gays (if not lesbians) in city government, after nearly a decade during which gays did not hold a majority of council seats. Mayor Steve Martin, the first openly gay candidate to be elected since the first election when he took his seat in 1994, sees the attention to the Sunset Strip as evidence that the city is now confident with itself as a place with a gay identity that it can now move on to other, less gay initiatives: "Developing the Strip during the 1980s was antithetical to what West Hollywood politics was all about then, and that was gay and lesbian rights, social services like AIDS information, and rent control."[48] Similarly, the revitalization of the eastern end of the city has also been a long-running attempt to improve the city's economic and cultural development. For years, the eastern edge of town languished while the westside boomed with gay development. Many of these improvements have been designed specifically for the Russian population or for the movie industry (such as postproduction houses). One consequence may well be a smoothing of relations between those who support Boystown expansion and those who feel that the city may have lost some of its original commitment to social services and livability.

In many ways, the enigma of West Hollywood is that, in an era where the focus is on national politics—from openly gay White House appointees to federal debates on gays in the military—the role of the local is not clear. Movement activists have declared that the new focus for gay and lesbian civil rights has relocated to the local level. By this they mean the cities and towns across America where the religious right is targeting gays and lesbians, not cities like West Hollywood where lesbians and gays live and work openly and without a high level of fear.

As the gay community decentralized, and the movement continues to broaden its agenda, the City of Los Angeles can claim to be responsive to gay and lesbian concerns and welcome their communities. In fact, Los Angeles increasingly steals the spotlight in the gay media with high-profile events and political accomplishments, such as the election of lesbian city councilwoman Jackie Goldberg or Mayor Riordan's public opposition to the antigay policies of fellow Republicans. But West Hollywood continues to balance its role as the gay mecca with its commitment to services for tenants, the elderly, and Russian immigrants, thus complicating the community model of identity politics. In the years since the gay "Camelot" was incorporated, one thing is clear; West Hollywood has not become a model for gay and lesbian local politics, nor is it the only platform for gay and lesbian politicians and activists. Instead, the city's influence may be waning, just as lesbians are beginning to be a visible (if small) part of the scene. The continuing challenge to the city's local gay elite from lesbians and people of color exemplifies the struggles of a community and a movement searching for a new politics and a new activism. For national gay and lesbian organizers, West Hollywood continues to represent a source of considerable wealth and power. But for those disengaged from these national politics, West Hollywood remains something much simpler—a place for escape. Like Hollywood Boulevard or Venice Beach, West Hollywood is a magnet for those seeking a version of the California myth, a place that cannot possibly deliver all that is expected. Perhaps, as suggested in the following observation, West Hollywood's most enduring lure will be the image that is created and circulated about the city, one that mingles the specific pleasures of the gay scene with the general pleasures of Southern California:

> For me, West Hollywood is an intense image that began before I arrived here—one of youthful, well-built men—a combination of surf, sand, and sun. It's our own city. It is a place where people can be open, obvious, and can be there in their gayness. It is a haven, a place to blow off the split in their lives.[49]

City officials appear to prefer to emphasize the "haven" aspect of the dream, downplaying the "sun and fun." The following description of West Hollywood, offered by the chair of the West Hollywood Lesbian and Gay Advisory Committee, expresses the heart of what the city and community leaders seek to provide and what the gay and lesbians who live in West Hollywood experience:

> It's a social base . . . our family, our community. . . . West Hollywood serves that purpose for [gays and lesbians]. Our

> population triples on weekends and it's not by error, it's consistently tripling as people come here to meet, to socialize. . . . It's validating to be among people who accept who you are, where you are safe.[50]

Critical for this perspective, however, is the often-simplistic assumption that many in the community make about what safety entails and how safety is constructed. Place claiming, for gays and lesbians in West Hollywood, has only recently begun to address these alternative visions and expectations. Although the past fifteen years of incorporation have created tangible opportunities for the most assimilated gays to build a local power base, the next decades will be a test of the flexibility of this power and the willingness of the city government and its residents to use this access for gays and lesbians outside the city's boundaries as well. For many gays and lesbians in Los Angeles, West Hollywood remains only a temporary weekend retreat. The following chapters look at the attempts of gays and lesbians without such open access to the government to claim corners of greater Los Angeles.

3 Beyond Gentrification

Social Services and the Redevelopment of Hollywood Boulevard

The exclusion by force of law or tacit disapproval of gay men and lesbians from participation in many community and service institutions has spurred one of the defining features of gay and lesbian community: alternative spaces for gathering and building community. The development of institutions to nurture identity formation and provide continuity for social support has been a critical element of community growth and a focus for activism by marginalized groups. This institutionalization of an activist agenda provides a sense of security and visibility that cannot be generated solely through the mass actions of activists and the diverse and sometimes disconnected actions of a dozen grassroots groups. The opportunity for these groups to come together and formulate agendas in safety and privacy provides for solidity for the movement. The role of social services in the place-claiming strategies of gay men and lesbians cannot be underestimated. With a few exceptions this very practical side of the gay and lesbian struggle in the United States has been overlooked in the rush to record and celebrate more public aspects of the struggle.

The growth of the gay and lesbian movement in Los Angeles has involved an unusually comprehensive approach to providing social services, often decades before comparably progressive cities. As a result, a vast and diverse array of social

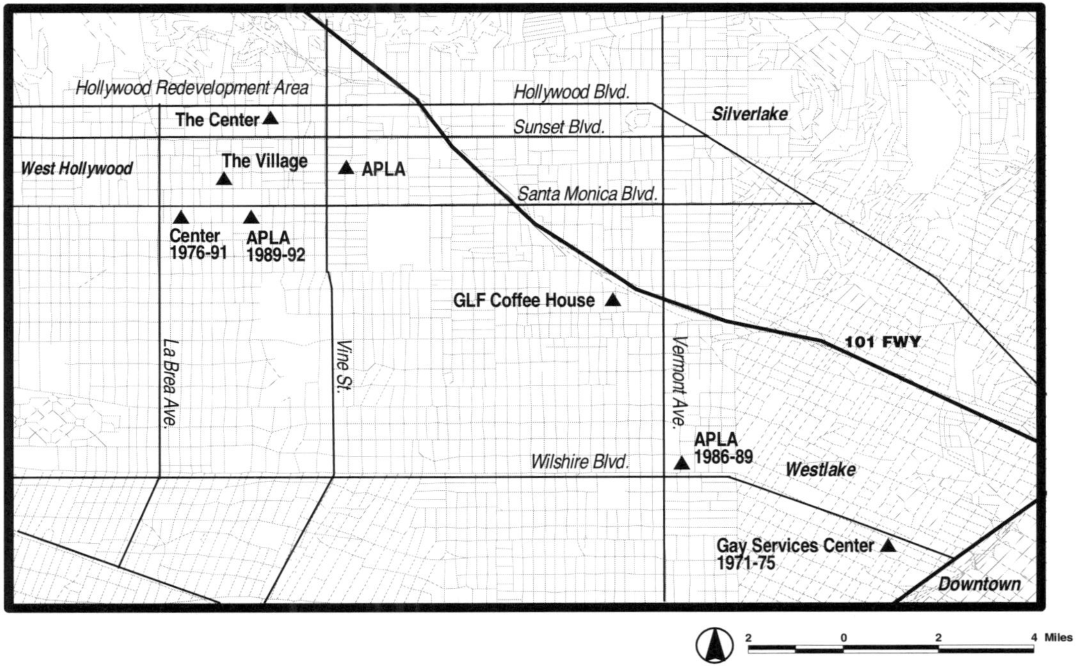

Map 3. Gay and Lesbian Center and AIDS Project Los Angeles Locations

organizations in Los Angeles fuels the ongoing transformation of the movement into a more powerful collective force through engagement with activist and mainstream politics at the local, state, and national levels. In many ways, these institutions symbolize the increasing clout and visibility of the community, with impressive buildings, staff, and operational budgets. As permanent and recognizable symbols of place-claiming strategies, the growth and expansion of these institutions reflect the increasingly mainstream status of gays and lesbians. The community's growing institutionalization and geographic expansion complicates standard definitions of marginalization for gays and lesbians during a time of relative acceptance and growing political power.

Mainstream histories and analyses of the institutional evolution of Los Angeles's gay and lesbian community tend to suggest that organizations have simply bought their way into their increasingly secure status. These analyses ignore the activist struggles and coalition building that made these institutions strong, and focus instead on the financial clout of a few major donors. Although an expanded client base and access to funding have both allowed and required these community institutions to aggressively pursue greater visibility and presence, it is the long history of grassroots gay and lesbian mobilization efforts that makes this current phase of relative ease and acceptance possible. This chapter looks at the decision of two major local gay and lesbian organizations—the Gay and Lesbian Center (the Center) and AIDS Project Los Angeles (APLA)—to move to Hollywood as part of one the most ambitious redevelopment projects undertaken by the City of Los Angeles. This unusual public-private partnership between the gay and lesbian and AIDS/HIV communities (not traditional participants in the city's redevelopment decisions) and the city's redevelopment authority raises a number of questions about institutional development and place claiming in Los Angeles. In particular, this coalition implicates the changing geography of the AIDS epidemic and its impact on the gay community and the history of activist struggles in the city. The various locations of these institutions since their founding track the spatial and political expansion of the gay and lesbian community over the past three decades.

Moving these agencies to central Hollywood after decades of community growth centered in West Hollywood continues the somewhat contentious shift begun in the mid-1980s away from the security of a more visible gay community. For a number of reasons, West Hollywood was no longer viewed as the only place to locate gay and lesbian organizations. Most immediately, high rents and low vacancy rates meant that some organizations, especially those with complicated space needs, had very few options when looking for a new building. At the same time, some organizations were beginning to feel that staying in the city would hamper outreach to those outside the mainstream of the community, including people of color and youth. Relocating to Hollywood marked a new level of independence of the gay and lesbian community. To understand this transition, let us investigate the locational conflicts and debates over the boundaries, dimensions, and meaning of place claiming by the gay and lesbian community.

Social Institutions and the Growth of Community Power

> In part, activists do not recognize the flaw inherent in the mass-based permanent organization model because they are attracted to the possibility of organizing the lower classes at extraordinary times . . . when a great deal seems possible. . . . But insurgency is short-lived. Once it subsides and the people leave the streets, most of the organizations which it temporarily threw up and which elites helped to nurture simply fade away. As for the few organizations that survive, it is because they become more useful to those who control the resources on which they depend than to the lower-class groups that the organizations claim to represent. Organizations endure, in short, by abandoning their oppositional politics.[1]

Classic arguments about the role of community institutions in movements born in activist and grassroots struggle exhibit a definite wariness about the role of community organizations in social change. Similarly, tension over institutionalization within the movement has been an important marker of dissent within the gay and lesbian community. The movement, both in Los Angeles and elsewhere, has always been self-generating and the schism between organizers/activists and participant is not easily defined. This conflict over strategy ultimately reflects disagreement over community identity and community location. Since the days of liberation, community institutions have served as both social service providers and as bases for oppositional activism. And because of the discrimination gay men and lesbians face, providing a safe space has been crucial to sustaining energy and focus of the movement.

Two of the most visible gay organizations in the city, the Center and the APLA, have expanded their sphere of influence beyond Los Angeles and are now considered nationally influential. Since its founding, the Center has been the largest gay and lesbian organization of its kind; while APLA, at its zenith, ranked as the second largest AIDS services institution. Many observers link the explosive growth of these two organizations to the new political power base of gay and lesbian Angelenos that has supported significant political advancements at the state and local level in recent years. In mainstream politics, two of the signposts of this success are the elections of two openly lesbian politicians—Councilwoman Jackie Goldberg in 1992 and California State Assemblywoman Sheila Kuehl. Both women have had significant impact on the way Los Angeles and its movements are viewed across the country and have made Los Angeles increasingly relevant in national organizing. As a 1993 *Los Angeles Times Magazine* article reported, the political and fund-raising support of gays and lesbians in Los Angeles is now seen as the national vanguard of the next wave of gay activism:

> Whether raising millions of dollars for AIDS in the grip of the worst national recession since the 1930s, nipping at Hollywood's heels, taking to the streets by the thousands for raucous protests or raising hundreds of thousands of dollars for the Clinton campaign, the gay men and women of Los Angeles are shaping the national agenda of the gay rights movements and forging a new sense of themselves.[2]

And Urvashi Vaid, former director of the National Gay and Lesbian Task Force, referred to the city as "the jewel in the gay and lesbian crown."[3] To a large extent, money from Los Angeles has provided the financial support to fuel many national gay and lesbian initiatives.

Southern California gays and lesbians contributed an estimated $3.4 million to Bill Clinton's 1992 presidential campaign in Southern California, which was considerably more attuned to gay and lesbian concerns than his reelection efforts four years later. In the years since, gay and lesbian donations to state and local campaigns provide critical support in most elections. During Barbara Boxer's 1992 campaign for the U.S. Senate, the gay vote truly became a deciding force. The Boxer campaign opened an office in West Hollywood (the first time a state Democratic Party candidate had done so), registered fourteen thousand new voters in three months, and fielded a two-thousand-person volunteer staff of whom approximately 40 percent were gay or lesbian. "I could not have won my election without the support of the gay and lesbian community," announced Boxer in Los Angeles a month after taking office.[4]

Whether this has translated into a more grassroots support of gay and lesbian issues within the broader political context remains to be seen. Certainly a powerful element in the gay and lesbian community has been the money certain sectors of the movement have been willing to raise for both local and national causes. Of those gay U.S. donors who gave more than $1,000 to major gay organizations, more that half were Southern Californians.[5]

Within the community, and to observers outside the community as well, it is not clear whether this new "clout" creates positive visibility and power for all gays and lesbians or simply further elevates a power elite that previously had wielded influence in mainstream politics. Certainly, many of the donors who emerged in the 1990s as central figures in this new publicly gay elite brought with them the credibility of their connections outside the movement. Predictably, many of the new leaders have been criticized for seeming to come so late to the cause of their own community. Thus, their contributions are both welcome and suspect, as activists acknowledge the necessity for their support and demand that they become more responsible to the community. Moreover, many also fear that the new influence of Hollywood on the Los Angeles gay and lesbian community pulls these organizations further into the realm of assimilated and wealthy Westside gays and lesbians.

In terms of place claiming within Los Angeles, this "new gay muscle," as the *Los Angeles Times* dubs it, has been most apparent in the Center's and APLA's building campaigns of the early 1990s. In the late 1980s both organizations were desperate for space following a decade of tremendous growth—APLA because of the continued increase in AIDS cases and the Center because its services were reaching more gays and lesbians, including populations outside West Hollywood. The histories of these organizations and the specific relationships between location and the expansion of the gay and lesbian organizing in Los Angeles indicate an important relationship between the geography of the city, the changing locations of gay and lesbian neighborhoods, and the expansion of the movement beyond West Hollywood.

The Los Angeles Gay and Lesbian Center

The Gay Services Center, as it was originally known, emerged out of the Gay Liberation Front (GLF) in mid-1971. The GLF—which had chapters in a number of major cities including San Francisco, New York, Boston, Chicago, and Los Angeles—formed almost immediately following the Stonewall Riots of June 1969. In Los Angeles, as in other cities, the GLF was responsible for initiating gay liberation as an alternative to the assimilationist homophile movements of the 1950s and early 1960s. Unlike these earlier organizations, which concentrated primarily on educating closeted gays and lesbian about their history and existence, the GLF focused on street protests, targeted actions against the police, and held the first gay pride parades.[6]

The GLF is best remembered as a direct-action, street-based group allied with other student movements of the later 1960s.[7] In Los Angeles, however, the GLF also provided the organizational and tactical base for the current gay and lesbian social services network. The institutionalization of the GLF into a social services movement differentiated the Los Angeles experience from other cities, where the move toward social service provision occurred much later. Although the GLF eventually gave way to these more institutional community-building activities in other cities, the intense street focus of the GLF remained active in other cities until the mid to late 1970s. As the group's influence dissipated, many GLF activists formed successor organizations (such as the Gay Activists' Alliance) that continued to emphasize direct action and public protest. Although the GLF did organize around a number of social issues for gays and lesbians, including homophobia in health care, psychiatry, and the media, the group generally worked to change mainstream institutions and attitudes, rather than set up parallel institutions.

In Los Angeles, the GLF's high visibility made the group's meetings and social activities into informal orientation sessions for those new to the movement or to the city. Not only were they the first (according to organizers) gay organization to list themselves in the phone book (so that young people arriving at the bus station downtown would know immediately where to go), they were also the first to establish a hot line. One early staffer of the hot line remembers:

> We just gave out whatever information or support we could to gay and lesbian callers. . . . We didn't have a lot of information to dispense, and our entire list of sympathetic doctors and lawyers as well as pertinent addresses was laid out in a loose-leaf notebook. . . . On a typical night we might get a dozen calls requesting information about gay liberation or the location of a bar, a half dozen calls about avoiding the draft, a few questions about treating venereal disease, and a couple requests for crash pads. Occasionally, someone called to report police activity in a certain toilet or park. There were a few calls from desperately unhappy teenagers on the verge of suicide because they thought they were gay. Sometimes frantic parents called, wondering whether their children's homosexuality was their fault in some way.[8]

Soon after establishing the hot line at their Vermont Avenue office, the GLF opened a coffeehouse on Melrose Avenue in the heart of Hollywood to serve as a casual drop-in and information center. It became popular not only for newly arriving gays and lesbians, but within a few months, also for people not involved in the movement (many of whom were not gay, according to local activists) who were sleeping in the coffeehouse and creating, as the Los Angeles Police Department (LAPD) insisted, a "menace."

At the time, major figures in the GLF in Los Angeles included Morris Kight, an activist with experience in both the nascent gay liberation movement and campaigns to stop the war in Vietnam, and Don Kilhefner, another gay liberation organizer and veteran of the Student Nonviolent Coordinating Committee.[9] Together, they abandoned the GLF's direct-action model and organized the Gay Survival Committee, a social services agency operating out of Kight's and Kilhefner's homes in downtown Los Angeles. Both Kight and Kilhefner believed that the movement needed to use the momentum generated at the height of the GLF's influence to create a network of services for the gays and lesbians who were daily arriving in Los Angeles in search of gay and lesbian community, often leaving behind jobs, family, and security. As Kight recalled, social services were an essential part of, rather than alternative to, a radical political agenda:

> Gay liberation doesn't just mean marching in the streets saying "Give me a 'G' . . . Give me an 'A' . . . Give me a 'Y' . . . Give me a 'P' " [and so on, spelling out GAY PRIDE]. . . . We felt that the movement needed a more organized response . . . a social services response to that with a very powerful role of advocacy. The Center was not only a major and the first ever social services agency, it was the headquarters of great advocacy, and we advocated with great regularity and brilliance.[10]

For Kight and Kilhefner, street activism alone could not fight the greatest threats to community stability: the hostility of mainstream organizations to the needs of gays and lesbians and the lack of social services. They and others in the burgeoning movement in Los Angeles saw that most social services in the city were not keeping pace with a growing openness about sexuality and recognized the very real potential for mistreatment at these traditional service centers. The movement, therefore, had a responsibility to provide these services independently. Not all members of the GLF, however, concurred with Kight and Kilhefner when they tried to convince others that street protest should give way to organizational institutionalization. Some felt that they were backing away too quickly from GLF's hallmark decentralized street-based structure, choosing instead a false sense of security and permanence incompatible with radical action. Kight was somewhat bitter about the conflict created by this decision, and recognized it as a major turning point in the movement. As a place-claiming strategy, the development of the Gay Services Center marks a key shift away from gatherings at temporal or private locations to public permanence.

John D'Emilio noted that this "mania for organization" was one of the clearest legacies of the Stonewall Riots and the gay liberation movement it engendered: "At the time of Stonewall, there were about fifty homophile organizations in the United States; by the end of 1973, more than a thousand lesbian and gay groups existed. This impulse to create organizations and institutions able to knit a community together and to deepen a sense of collectivity was a product of the Stonewall generation."[11]

By 1972, the Gay Services Center[12] moved into two decrepit Victorians at the corner of Wilshire Boulevard and Lexington Avenue, just west of downtown. Since the 1930s, there had been a small core gay neighborhood in the Silverlake and Echo Park areas of Los Angeles (as well as the more recent community in West Hollywood), and downtown had long supported a relatively stable gay community. This downtown presence centered on the turn-of-the-century Bunker Hill neighborhood, an area of flophouses and other "red-light" activities—all of which were demolished in the late 1960s as part of Los Angeles's first urban redevelopment project.

As Kight described it, gays were drawn to the decaying Bunker Hill and Westlake neighborhoods by cheap rents created by the evacuation of wealthier residents from the area, and by the relative anonymity of the new neighborhood, with its mix of immigrants and workers. Beginning in the 1940s, the first gay bars in Los Angeles were located around Bunker Hill—including Maxwell's Bar at the corner of 3rd and Hill Streets and The Crown Jewel at 9th and Hill Streets. Fred Frisbie, an early Mattachine Society member, recalled that Maxwell's was a seedier bar that attracted "hustlers, drunkards, vice cops, and nellie queens," whereas The Crown Jewel attracted more of a business crowd. To gain entry into this bar, a driver's license was required. For many, this proof of identification during a time when few Angelenos drove prevented many gay men from visiting this or other locations. Also, fear of reprisals made the idea of carrying any identification almost impossible for many.[13]

As the redevelopment of Bunker Hill loomed, the gay community began to migrate westward from Bunker Hill to Crown Hill and Union Hill, and, finally, in the mid-1960s, to Westlake Park. Located on the edge of downtown and now the hub of Central American immigration to Los Angeles, at the turn of the century the area was one of the first residential enclaves west of downtown. By the end of World War II, a number of the city's major cultural institutions had located on the boulevards surrounding the park (now renamed after General Douglas MacArthur), including the Chouinard Art Institute, the Los Angeles Philharmonic, the Otis Art Institute, and the Artists' Workshop. As the wealthy residents moved out to newer residential developments further west and in the hills, Westlake Park in the 1950s and 1960s transformed into a bohemian neighborhood. Into this slowly decaying but intellectually vibrant atmosphere the Center moved, drawn by, as Kight suggested, the much larger and more visible artists' community, the range of cultural institutions nearby, and by the low-cost Victorian houses.

By 1975 the Center had outgrown the campus of adjacent houses—always on the verge of condemnation by the city—and had begun the search for a new location. Kight described the decision to leave the Westlake area and move yet farther west as an inevitable response to increasing poverty and crime in the area:

> We caught Westlake at just the right time in its history. It had been the center of culture. . . . It was the headquarters of the artists, it was gentle and loving and there were great houses. . . . The great rich had fled . . . we felt that our presence there for one was helpful because we were populating the area and we were providing social services and entertainment and we stayed until it became a dance of death . . . so it had served us well and its use had passed.[14]

Kight uses the term "dance of death" to explain the dependent relationship between the gay community and its diverse neighborhood in these formative years. The community center did not so much contribute to neighborhood growth as it fed off the vitality of the surrounding area. As artists and other neighborhood residents moved on as part of the general process of white flight in Los Angeles, the neighborhood declined and the Center suffered. This receptive role differs from the Center's later role as an instigator of neighborhood development.

The Center's new space, on Santa Monica Boulevard at Highland Avenue just east of West Hollywood, served as the home of the Center for nearly twenty years. The factors that made the new site attractive to the Gay Services Center—renamed the Gay Community Services Center soon after the move to Hollywood—reflect the common concerns of not only the Center and APLA, but also a host of smaller social service agencies serving the lesbian and gay communities in Los Angeles. First, the building was large, flexible, and relatively inexpensive. Second, the site was convenient to major bus routes and had parking. Third and most importantly, it was adjacent to, if not directly in, an emerging cluster of gay and lesbian neighborhoods in Hollywood and West Hollywood. Even as early as 1975, a pattern of development was emerging that looked far different from that seen in San Francisco or New York. These more prototypical cities developed with clearly defined areas to which the vast majority of gays and lesbians flocked—areas that could then be the obvious choice for locating gay and lesbian services. In Los Angeles, by contrast, a number of neighborhoods—including Silverlake and Echo Park, greater Hollywood, West Hollywood, and Venice—all had known concentrations of gays and lesbians, but no single area was overwhelmingly the nucleus of the community. As Kight described the new location, it was "the epicenter, that was the word I used in the press because I wanted to fix the word in the press's head, it was the epicenter of the lesbian and gay barrio/ghetto."[15]

Kight strategically saw the Gay Community Services Center as a magnet for the geographically dispersed community. Rather than relocating to a residential area that already had a gay presence, it instead moved to a site surrounded by industrial and commercial buildings used largely by the movie studios. As a result, the location did not inscribe any one gay neighborhood on the city's map and did not mark out a gay or lesbian zone. Nor was this an attempt to realign the community toward one area or one neighborhood. Instead this site was seen as a way to reach out to a number of emerging neighborhoods simultaneously, from the more radical and political areas closer to downtown and the growing residential and commercial zone in West Hollywood. From the early 1970s, then, the Center oriented itself toward serving the whole city, rather than a single neighborhood.

For its first few years in Hollywood, the Center struggled to achieve the balance between its roles as a drop-in center, with meeting space and cultural events, and as a crisis center, with legal services and counseling. With a largely volunteer staff, the Center maintained an atmosphere of social and political consciousness, with sufficient opportunities for informal organizing and a strong connection between the political direction of the community and the needs of individual clients. However, as the Center professionalized and the volunteer staff grew, the Center became less important as a place for political organizing. Although some remained disenchanted with this drift away from its radical beginnings, most of the street activists who stayed involved with the Center had come to realize the importance of the social services. As much as the Center tried to retain some of its character as a hub or organizing activity, the new location worked against these efforts. Because the Center was removed from any gay or lesbian residential concentration, it never attracted casual or walk-in visitors. Increasingly, as the gay community in West Hollywood grew, the Center became less convenient for evening meetings or social gatherings.

However, the needs of a still-hidden community obscured the distinction between social and social service functions of the Center that is so noticeable today. By creating a community center emphasizing social services, the founders built a "space that they wanted people to come to affirm their gay and lesbian identities since people were sociologically wounded and needed help," according to Jodi Curlee, who worked at the Center during its early days and later became the director of social services for the City of West Hollywood.[16]

In a sense, then, the two missions overlapped. During these early days of the liberationist movement, the community was small enough and the needs were great enough that the Center could only provide the most basic services, such as rap groups or referrals. The information most needed could be provided almost as easily and often with better success at a social function, such as a dance, than at a more clinical setting. The Center staff, mostly volunteer, were just as likely to use these services as provide them, which prevented the staff from appearing professional or disconnected from the community.

As the movement grew throughout the 1970s, two major shifts in the role and client base emerged, which help explain the function of the Center today. First, it vastly expanded its services (creating substance abuse programs, extensive professional mental health services, and job placement services), many of which later spun off into independent organizations outside the Center. Second, the maturing of the movement and the increasing diversity of the lesbian and gay population in the city further diminished the Center's role as neighborhood "epicenter." Kight suggested that the transition of many of the GLF activists out of the movement and into "mainstream" jobs and lives nearly eliminated the need for a neighborhood-type drop-in center. The geography of the gay and lesbian community no doubt contributed to the lack of interest in a neighborhood-defined center where no residential agglomeration existed.

One of the roles the Center has played since its inception is as a headquarters for a variety of more specialized groups and services. One former staff member described the Center's pivotal role in expanding the types of services available within the community: "The Center created other opportunities in the community and created growth in the community either by being a place people could go or by the talent of the staff that worked there."[17] The spin-off groups created by the Center (for lesbians and people of color in particular) became independent institutions, expanding the community beyond the greater downtown area. At the same time the Center remained a focal point for social services and a growing image of the community's strength.

Because the Center emphasized social services for gays and lesbians in crisis (usually those at the beginning of a coming-out process or those less able to assimilate into the white middle-class core of the visible community) a crisis emerged between the Center staff, its client base, and the emerging openly gay middle class. The focus on intervention was imbedded in the mission of the Center and its staff and volunteers. And because funding was limited, it was rarely available for community organizing or community-building programs (such as social events), because interventionist social services (including health care, runaway youth programs, and counseling) were seen as more important. Over time, many of the more explicitly "social" community center programs disappeared (including the dances, reading groups, art programs, and other opportunities for mixing), and the involvement of middle-class gays and lesbians evolved as they created large donor programs. This split resulted in a class distinction within the Center and the community between the "donors" (who were seen as more directly building the Center) and the "users" (who consumed the Center's resources). Over time, as the emphasis on fundraising intensified, some of those who were not donors to the Center complained that they had fewer opportunities to participate socially or fulfill any advisorial role in the life of the Center.[18]

The connections between the diversification of the gay and lesbian community and the institutional development of the Center characterize the evolution of the Center's client base and programs throughout the 1970s. Although no actual data on the numbers of gays and lesbians living in the various residential enclaves in Los Angeles exist, the movement of gays and lesbians west out of the downtown area generally followed the movement west of the largely white, middle-class population in the city as a whole. Pockets of gay gentrification in Lafayette Park, the eastern end of the Wilshire district, east Hollywood, Echo Park, as well as the traditional centers in Silverlake and West Hollywood, constituted the map of an assimilated gay community.

Increasing mobility within the community and this emphasis on crisis services shifted the place-claiming role of social service institutions from that of creating a magnet to attract new gay businesses and residents to one of responding flexibly to the varied ways lesbians and gays were settling in Los Angeles. Westlake had been one of the focal points for GLF organizing (along with Silverlake, where the group often met), but by no means was the only neighborhood where gays and lesbians lived. Throughout the early 1970s and 1980s, the fervor of radical organizing dissipated and the movement consolidated its focus toward the narrower goal of social services provision. The area around the Center did see an increase in visible gay and lesbian presence, but not at a rate much faster than in many other neighborhoods across the city. By 1984 and the cityhood drive for West Hollywood, the majority of the neighborhoods west of the Center (including those in West Hollywood) had been transformed by the growing and increasingly visible gay population. However, the selectivity of the Center's clients (poor, in crisis, coming-out) made it a geographical draw regardless of its location. For those who did not use the services of the Center, its existence still served an important informational and symbolic role.

Throughout the 1980s, as the Center expanded beyond the limits of the building on Santa Monica, a number of services were relocated to other buildings, both nearby and farther west. The Center also worked to reach out to segments of the community who were unused to visiting the Center, by creating new kinds of social events aimed at bringing in those who were neither "in crisis" nor donors. Many of these events occurred at the Center but were also located farther west to attract the gays and lesbians living in West Hollywood who were seen as the most critical audience to retain. Increasingly, the Santa Monica location was hardly central to gay and lesbian life in the city. In many ways, the Center remained an island, attracting only a very few other gay and lesbian institutions as neighbors.

Far surpassing the effects of these geographic shifts, the onset of the AIDS epidemic marked the greatest change for the Center and the gay and lesbian community as a whole. The Center responded aggressively, first establishing an AIDS clinic in West Hollywood and an on-site testing program. As had happened earlier with the diversification and spin-off of programs from the Center, the vastness of the AIDS epidemic required a more comprehensive approach. With the expansion of the epidemic, the Center tried to respond to the many effects of HIV and AIDS on their clients' lives, including homelessness, job loss, poverty, mental health issues, and cultural barriers to treatment. Increasingly, the Center found itself inadequately prepared.

New social service agencies drew the burden as well as the funding away from the Center as more specialized programs emerged to cope with the epidemic. Eventually, the Center was no longer "the only game in town." On the plus side for the Center, the epidemic expanded not only the client base, but the volunteer and donor base as well, leading to a new level of cogender and cross-cultural organizing.[19]

Thus, throughout the 1980s and into the 1990s, as the planning for the move to Hollywood got underway, the practical significance of the Center for Los Angeles's gay and lesbian population leveled off, while its symbolic importance grew. Place claiming became a more complex process, not simply of gaining visibility by being on the streets, but of using this new visibility in ways that would change the city as a whole. Gays and lesbians, with new social acceptance, were poised to participate in city politics as major players.

AIDS Project Los Angeles

Since its founding in 1983, APLA has been the primary community-based organization serving persons with AIDS in Los Angeles County. Second only to the Gay Men's Health Crisis (GMHC) in New York in terms of budgets, the APLA has more than twenty programs for clients with AIDS, including a buddy program, phone hot line, referral to other agencies for specialized care, advocacy for clients using county health services, mental health and dental care, and home health care support. APLA also operates a residential program, with apartments for clients receiving Section 8 housing assistance. Beyond direct client care, APLA's programs also include a speakers' bureau, school-based education, public awareness campaign, and public policy development.

As a comprehensive AIDS service provider, APLA serves clients across Los Angeles County. As always, their clients reflect the demographics of the disease, with gay men no longer the predominant group. However, APLA is still based in the gay and lesbian community, especially for volunteers, paid staff, and donors. As a universally recognized symbol of gay presence in the city, APLA remains an important marker of place-claiming strategies. Next we look at how APLA evolved and relocated to accommodate the changing geography of AIDS in Los Angeles.

APLA began as a telephone hot line program in an industrial district of central Hollywood, as an offshoot of a program at the Gay Community Services Center. Almost immediately it moved to a building across from Plummer Park in West Hollywood and began taking clients and offering direct services. Throughout its history, the locational decisions at APLA have been driven by two factors: the facilities must be accessible for clients, and there must be enough space to provide services as the rate of HIV and AIDS infection has grown (and recently leveled off) in Los Angeles County.

Until the mid-1980s, APLA's client base centered in the gay community, leaving little reason to question its location in West Hollywood or its primary emphasis on the gay male population. As was the case around the country, particularly in the hard-hit cities of New York and San Francisco, the first responses to AIDS came from the gay community (with lesbians quickly becoming a major part of the community response). It became "friends helping friends."[20]

A study of the GMHC, which in many ways mirrors the development and services of APLA, points out that these organizations grew quickly to positions of importance within the wider mainstream community. First, the epidemiology of AIDS required the AIDS-specific focus of GMHC or APLA. In addition, the fact that they were grassroots efforts based in a marginalized community gave them a certain amount of freedom to experiment. Both organizations were able to provide services such as education and outreach to affected communities that neither state public health institutions nor other community-based institutions such as churches, schools, or social service networks could take on without fear of stigma.[21]

This independence from mainstream regulatory structures (both literal and symbolic), along with the overwhelming need to respond to the AIDS epidemic, allowed APLA the latitude it needed to create innovative programs. As the epidemic evolved, however, APLA was overwhelmed by trying to provide services to a growing number of clients in a limited amount of space. In 1986, they made two major location decisions, both of which exemplify the tension between its roots in the gay community and the need for AIDS-related services in communities outside the gay and lesbian base. First, APLA moved its administration functions to a building at Wilshire Boulevard and Vermont Avenue, while the front-line case managers stayed in West Hollywood. This location was chosen exclusively on the basis of affordability, because APLA would have preferred to stay in West Hollywood near the client base and the other services. One volunteer who later served as APLA's Director of Operations noted that this move was painstaking and foreshadowed the criticism the agency would later draw within the community. This "first real schism" within the organization was interpreted as an attempt to separate management from the day-to-day stress of dealing with clients; as a result APLA was labeled "bureaucratic" by clients, the community, and its staff and volunteers.[22] The APLA was the target of intense scrutiny, largely because it was seen as abandoning its grassroots base and volunteer support.

In contrast, the second move in 1986 was an effort to reach farther into the AIDS-affected communities of Los Angeles County, with the opening of a food bank program in Silverlake. Silverlake, often regarded as the second home of the gay and lesbian community in Los Angeles, is equally known as an immigrant neighborhood, its population dominated by people from Central American and Southeast Asia. Gay life in Silverlake has long existed alongside these other populations, giving the neighborhood a markedly different character than that of West Hollywood. Locating in Silverlake allowed APLA to create a physical presence in a nongay neighborhood as practical evidence of its commitment to all people living with AIDS in the county, without giving up either proximity to the "home base" in West Hollywood or ties to the gay community.

The food bank program, from its earliest days, saw a wholly

new group of clients from those seen at the case management services in West Hollywood. White gay men continued to be the primary users of the buddy program (which matches AIDS-affected clients with a volunteer who serves as a friend and supporter in the negotiation of services, including prescription pickup, grocery shopping, rides to doctor appointments, and so on), case management, and other client services. By contrast, the food bank clients tended to be poorer, women of color burdened with complex issues, often including housing, child care, and different health problems. Although Silverlake was a convenient location for clients, relations with local residents were not good. Partly, this was because the Latino community, like other nongay communities across the country, lacked information or were misinformed about AIDS. And even though the new location made outreach efforts easier, clients and staff were routinely harassed and on occasions attacked by young Latinos, prompting the Guardian Angels to institute patrols in the vicinity of the food bank.[23] Within a year, the NOLP program moved to the corner of Fountain Avenue and Vine Street in central Hollywood, where it remained until 1988.

In 1989, APLA consolidated its programs, leasing space on Romaine Street in Central Hollywood, a move that for the first time brought the diverse clients and volunteer base of the agency under one roof:

> When we all went to Romaine, it was obvious at APLA that AIDS wasn't gay and white and that the agency wasn't gay and white in terms of volunteers, staff, and clients. . . . From day one there were people of color, women, and children using our services.[24]

Within the agency and the larger gay community, the years APLA spent at Romaine were important for creating its image not only as the premiere service agency for people with AIDS in Los Angeles County but also as one with an uneasy relationship with the gay and lesbian community. Although its volunteer base continued to resemble the tradition from which

APLA merged, the donor core was increasingly comprised of the power brokers in the gay and entertainment communities (often where the two overlap), creating tension within the gay community. In addition, the explosive growth of the agency since its beginnings as a small phone bank in the Center into a multimillion dollar agency has invited criticism that the agency is too large, too bureaucratic, and out of touch with its roots. Within the agency, however, many staff reiterated that APLA has an enormous responsibility to grow and serve the entire city, precisely because of their relatively secure funding base and history as a grassroots gay organization. The agency's visibility, stature, and resources create an obligation, often voiced not only within the agency but by other AIDS service organizations as well. The APLA staff, in turn, recognize their responsibility as coalition builders for the HIV/AIDS community. As one APLA staff member explained,

> APLA has the most resources to do the work for all the folks living with HIV. . . . We don't have enough resources, but we have the most; we have more than most agencies. Thus, APLA has an obligation across the board to help fulfill the roles that other agencies cannot. APLA has to play an intricate role in negotiating with other agencies that are not as well funded, supported, or visible.[25]

Repeatedly, staff and volunteers at APLA insist that they never expected (or wanted) the organization to grow into a twenty million dollar organization with more than four thousand current clients (and more than twice that number of deceased clients); instead, it was forced into its role by the energy of its staff and volunteers and the inaction of other agencies, both public and private. The institutionalization of both APLA and the Gay and Lesbian Community Center has resulted in unique and groundbreaking relationships between the gay community and the City of Los Angeles, resulting in a shift of the locational base of the community outside both West Hollywood and Silverlake.

Hollywood Redevelopment and the Community Power

By the end of the 1980s, both APLA and the Center were searching for new space. Although they expected to stay within the dense core of clients residing in or near West Hollywood, they were prepared to look as far afield as necessary for affordable space. West Hollywood, although a desirable location for both organizations, was seen as "leased up" and prohibitively expensive. In addition, both agencies were concerned with the upper-middle-class white image of West Hollywood and wanted to find a location without such stereotypical associations.

What makes the relocation of these agencies particularly worth discussing in the context of community boundaries and the politics of place in Los Angeles is that both were attracted to the city's largest redevelopment project along Hollywood Boulevard—"the most famous street in the world." Wherever these two organizations chose to move, their decisions would necessarily alter both the community's boundaries and the politics of place within the gay and lesbian community. The fact that both agencies eventually joined forces with the city to create a definitive gay and lesbian presence in a relatively unmarked location makes their move even more influential. In the wake of this somewhat coordinated decision, the effects were much broader, restructuring the relationship of the community to the politics of the entire city.

These gay- and lesbian-identified institutions made the necessary connections with the city council, redevelopment authorities, and neighborhood residents and in the process effected unexpected realignments of the traditional political and urban redevelopment coalitions in the city. This chapter in the city's gay and lesbian movement illustrates the importance of fund-raising within the gay and lesbian communities and the strength of community organizing. Both made possible a new place-claiming strategy connected more to the city's politics of growth than the internal dynamics of the gay and lesbian movement.

The politics of urban redevelopment emerge from the ongoing struggle between the competing interests of a range of individuals and organizations, from business elites and city officials to arts organizations and the media. The creation of a mutually beneficial partnership between the public and private sectors—what John Logan and Harvey Molotch have called "growth coalitions"—determines the course of, and its relationship to, the local politics of place. Their analysis focuses on the role of the local growth machine in setting the course of expansion and, often, the real estate prices through which growth is either accelerated or curbed. Most importantly for this discussion, they emphasize the ways in which resources—human, technological, and material—are "exploited and moved around" in the pursuit of higher and better exchange and use values and the role of place as constitutive of these machinations. Places, in the growth coalition analysis, are the physical and substantive evidence of not only development in the city but also of the social relationships that are required to produce this expansion.[26]

For a study of place-claiming strategies, the investigation of the social relationships attached to specific places in the city illuminates the outside actors who, despite their isolation from the internal dynamics of the movement, play an important role in creating a context for locational decisions. Both APLA and the Gay and Lesbian Community Center participated in the formulation of a growth strategy for Hollywood, revealing the extent to which the movement had gained mainstream recognition and to which their place-claiming strategies were seen as having an effect on the city's development.

Like Los Angeles as a whole, Hollywood Boulevard developed in the early twentieth century in large part through the expansion and centralization of the movie industry and its resulting commercial and tourist activity. Soon after the end of World War II, however, suburban development drew both the movie audiences and the studios out of the city in search of cheaper land. Once the studios left, much of the tourist draw—

the chance of seeing stars on the street or in the clubs—disappeared as well, hastening the decline of the area. Although Hollywood Boulevard remains one of the top tourist destinations in the city, it also has become a notorious destination for teenage runaways attracted, in part, by the lingering myth that stars are made in Hollywood.[27]

Redevelopment in Hollywood began traditionally enough with a 1983 directive from the Los Angeles City Council, followed in 1986 with the approval of a redevelopment plan. Generally, the plan sought to create opportunities for large-scale commercial developments geared to the tourist market. These major developments would, if successful, help spur economic revitalization along the boulevard, encouraging smaller establishments (many of whom had stores in the area for decades) to improve their buildings and businesses. For the residential neighborhoods along the boulevard, the plan also offered urban design and streetscape improvements there and in the adjacent streets.

Substantive work on the boulevard was stalled until 1991 by litigation challenging the validity of the plan. Nonetheless, while the plan was held up in the courts, a number of strategies were developed and adopted to address the social needs of the neighborhood and to finalize a design and transportation scheme. Not surprisingly, none of the plan's elements mention gays and lesbians as a residential constituency, a business presence, or a provider or consumer of social services. Yet soon after these major redevelopment plans were approved, the gay and lesbian community, primarily the Center, became a recipient of redevelopment funds. Soon after, APLA also moved into the redevelopment area. With a combined employment of four hundred, these two agencies created a significant gay and lesbian presence on the boulevard.

The open invitation to gay and lesbian leaders to participate in Hollywood redevelopment discussions appears to have been brokered by the Community Redevelopment Agency (CRA) and Councilman Michael Woo—long recognized as an ally of the gay and lesbian community—in part because of the desperate situation on Hollywood Boulevard. A fundamental realignment of the traditional Los Angeles growth coalition and the redevelopment process was necessitated not simply by the growing influence of certain gay and lesbian leaders in the city but because the obvious and traditional solutions to Hollywood's decline (massive real estate investment by commercial developers) were not working. Local residents and traditional growth coalition members, such as the Chamber of Commerce, knew they needed more drastic and innovative measures than normally were used in Los Angeles. Ten years of residents' pressure and aggressive media reporting finally forced public officials to show concrete progress.

By the late 1980s, many of the grandiose deals for revitalizing the boulevard had not materialized and the situation in Hollywood was indeed desperate and ripe for innovative solutions. As John Kaliski, chief architect for the city's Hollywood project during the negotiations for the Center and APLA relocations explained, "Hollywood, by design and by default . . . is ending up with a ground-up rather than a top-down redevelopment process."[28]

The Center seized the opportunity to participate in the redevelopment process that was created by the emphasis on community participation and innovative solutions. According to both the Center and the Redevelopment Agency, redevelopment officials were the first to suggest to the Center's leadership that it look for space within the area designated for redevelopment, a choice that would make the Center eligible for financing through the redevelopment plan. After looking at a number of sites in the Hollywood area, the Center agreed to purchase, with a loan from the CRA and extensive private donations, a 44,000-square-foot building on Hudson Avenue, just south of Hollywood Boulevard, which had formerly been occupied by the Internal Revenue Service. The purchase and renovation costs on the building were $6.5 million.

According to the committee in charge of relocation, the search was driven by three factors: the desire to remain within a three or four mile radius of the current location, the need for public transportation access and secure parking, and the potential for funding support from the city.[29]

Torie Osborn, the executive director of the Center during the search, joined the Citizens Advisory Committee (CAC) and was later named chair of that body by Councilman Woo. As viewed by the CRA staff working on the move, her participation on the CAC almost guaranteed the success of the Center's search for funding within the redevelopment process. Osborn became involved in the neighborhood issues, served as a key negotiator between the competing interests represented by the CAC, and, most importantly, positioned the Center not as a gay and lesbian organization but as a social services organization whose clients happened to be gay or lesbian. The CAC's Social Needs Committee sponsored a report that identified six priorities for the area: day care for children and youth; low cost medical care; mental health services; job training, development, and placement; short-term shelters, transitional housing, and innovative homeless prevention programs; and services for non-English-speaking immigrants and refugees (primarily Hispanics, Soviet Armenians, and Asian Pacific Islanders). Deemphasizing the gay and lesbian community-building aspect of the Center's mission and focusing on its key services placed the Center squarely within the Hollywood Redevelopment Area Plan's mandate.

Although the focus at the Center was (and remains) the provision of services to gays and lesbians, the Center provides services in line with a number of the city's top priorities for Hollywood's redevelopment. As one CRA staffperson on the project explained:

> It was important that the Center did direct social services. There was a reason for it coming to Hollywood—it has the demographics, the poverty, the bus lines for accessibility. It wasn't really a gay community thing as it was a social services

> issue, which is an important goal of redevelopment [in Hollywood].[30]

Ultimately, the city council approved a $1.3 million loan to the Center, paid out of redevelopment revenues. The substantial financial assistance to the Center was made possible by the recasting of its role from one exclusively concerned with the lesbian and gay community to one of more generic social service provision. In 1994, the Center opened its new building.

However, the alignment of the Center's interests with the general aims of the redevelopment plan's social needs had its critics. A *Los Angeles Times* article that appeared immediately following the approval of the city loan included criticism from area residents who questioned the allocation of such a large percentage of the available funds (including the bulk of the annual budget of the Social Needs Plan) to one project. And, as could be expected, the decision-making process by the CRA also was under fire. The criticism did not directly challenge the use of city funds for gay and lesbian social services per se, but rather stemmed more from the highly political nature of the loan agreement and the extraordinary measures used to secure the funding, including transfers from economic development accounts and other sources.[31]

The CRA defended its assertion that the Center served a major part of the Hollywood Redevelopment Area neighborhood:

> The Gay and Lesbian Community Services Center is an extremely well known, vital, well-run organization that provides extremely critical services to the Hollywood community and I don't think anyone disputes that.[32]

In reality, however, the Center's ability to serve residents remains in flux. Although the council office in Hollywood claims that 30 percent of the council district's residents are gay or lesbian, this figure cannot be verified and comes from no specific analysis. The Center, in addition, serves only a small percentage of the area's gay and lesbian residents, particularly those in crisis, youth runaways, people with AIDS, or other specifically targeted groups. Youth outreach, HIV testing, and a state-of-the-art AIDS clinic currently occupy most of the Center's Hollywood Boulevard building. In 1998, the Center opened a second space in Hollywood—The Village at Ed Gould Plaza—to house community outreach and education programs, including meeting space, theater space, and offices for other community organizations. This new space has been extraordinarily successful in expanding the client base and bringing back to the Center many of the more assimilated gays and lesbians who in previous years would have been seen primarily as donors. In 1999, the Center returned to the Santa Monica site with a new youth services facility.

Center staff and clients also voiced reservations about moving to Hollywood. They were worried about the accessibility of the new site and afraid that the Hollywood Boulevard area was generally unsafe and specifically treacherous for its clients. The Center attempted to allay these concerns in a number of ways. A comparison of crime statistics for the area around the old site on Santa Monica and the new site on Hudson Avenue showed, surprisingly, that the crime rate on Hudson was lower than it had been previously. The city also announced plans to hire a private security firm to patrol the boulevard. And, finally, the parking within the building for staff and clients (which was not previously available) convinced the critics of the move that the new site would not increase client or staff vulnerability to gay bashing.

Staff at the Center did not believe that they would have greater access to clients at their new building, even though the CRA felt that there were substantial numbers of gays and lesbians living in the target area. But the city seems to have misunderstood the actual client base of the Center, which was and remains people in crisis, not the media image of the upwardly mobile gentrifiers. Some of the specifically targeted client groups, in particular the growing number of street youth, were particularly disrupted by the move to the boulevard. The Center provides transition shelter, counseling, HIV and AIDS services, and basic necessities for homeless working as prostitutes on Santa Monica Boulevard. According to staff, client numbers were "way down" after the move for two reasons. First, the runaways saw the Center as too far away from their hangouts on Santa Monica Boulevard, most of which were within blocks of the Center's former location. They also feared the gangs on the boulevard, which were seen as generally hostile to gays and lesbians. In addition, at first they did not think the new building was "youth-friendly." There was more security, it had an institutional or corporate interior design, and there was no place for them to hang out. As a result, the youth services division adapted its programs to compensate for the new site, finding ways to make the Center easier to use, so they did not have to come in as frequently or spend as much time there. To compensate for the Center's move, a mobile van unit began distributing food, clothing, and safe-sex kits to clients on the streets.[33]

The geographic importance for gay and lesbian activism of the Center's move to Hollywood was not just the potential for a lesbian and gay renaissance on Hollywood Boulevard; it also represented more than an expansion of the community beyond traditional boundaries. The place-claiming strategy employed by the Center was fueled by practical needs but sold to the community as a symbolic gesture—declaring a new, more permanent presence of the gay and lesbian community in Los Angeles at a citywide level, and demonstrating the community's ability to raise funds for its needs collectively. Torie Osborn, speaking at the Center's twentieth anniversary in 1991 about the then-upcoming move, connected the victory of the building campaign to the tragedy of AIDS and the vision of a post-AIDS gay and lesbian community:

> In the middle of the AIDS holocaust, and in the middle of the continuing battles we fight, this is a statement of permanence, a

> symbol of the legacy that we will leave for future generations of young lesbians and gay men coming up. . . . Ironically, it is being made possible by bequests by gay men who have fallen to AIDS.[34]

The new building made permanent this connection through the creation of a "donor wall" off the main lobby, built of bricks honoring significant donors to the building campaign. Many of the bricks are inscribed "in memory of" or "for" lovers and friends who have died of AIDS.

Ed Gould, chair of the search committee for the Gay and Lesbian Center's Board of Directors, further connected the achievement to a sense of justice finally coming due for gays and lesbians, rather than to the specific services or other practical advancements made possible by the move to larger quarters:

> We tapped into an acknowledgment that this community deserves something far better that it ever had in the past. . . . We tapped into the sense of permanence that was never there before, the Center feels very real and permanent, that never existed before. The sites the Center occupied before or the types of facilities we are used to . . . were never permanent. This move was viewed as a way of making our presence more permanent, more real, with more pride and involvement. The bottom line is that we deserve something like this.[35]

For APLA, the move to Hollywood made glaringly obvious the ever-increasing spread of HIV and AIDS in Los Angeles County and the changing geographic distribution of the disease. Although gay men continue to be at the epicenter of the epidemic, APLA's commitment to serving all affected communities has necessitated a shift (geographically and ideologically) away from the gay and lesbian community. One of the repeated criticisms of APLA is the perception that management has continually attempted to "degay" the agency, as evidenced by its marketing and fund-raising campaigns.

Discussions begun at the Center continue about how the relocation to Hollywood has raised issues of client access, the base in the gay community, and the reality of Los Angeles's gay geography. And, as at the Center, the meaning of permanence and the representation of history and struggle for place in the city became an integral part of the place-claiming strategy at APLA. However, unlike the positive claims Osborn made about the power of permanence and visibility, the agency and AIDS activists more generally were reminded that institutionalizing the AIDS organization was a negative reminder of the inability of the agency, the volunteers, the government, and ultimately the world community, to stop the spread of a deadly disease. Thus, the move to Hollywood remains for APLA a bittersweet accomplishment.

The discussion of HIV and AIDS services is in many ways a question of numbers: Where are the new cases? Who are the highest risk groups? What percentage of the population is infected? Planning at APLA, by necessity, has had to be flexible to allow for new programs that target specific at-risk groups. Although not always successful or well received outside the core gay male population, the agency has attempted to respond to new characteristics of the epidemic. However, since the early 1990s, the demographics of the disease have shifted in ways that first raised questions about the ability of APLA to lead a fight against AIDS in Los Angeles and then required successive shifts in the agency's resources and agenda. Beginning in the early 1990s, fewer than half of the clients lived within reasonable commuting distance of the agency's headquarters. Transportation to the agency, therefore, has been a major concern for the client base, particularly given the high incidence of poverty among people with HIV and AIDS. As with the Center, APLA considered public transportation access a major limitation in site selection, second only to the cost of real estate. Although the purpose of their most recent move was to allow for the consolidation of APLA services under one roof, the agency has continued to explore possibilities for decentralization, particularly through creative partnerships with AIDS service organizations in other areas. The food bank was the first to accept radical decentralization, opening a second site in South Central Los Angeles. Additional sites were subsequently opened across the city.

The move of APLA to Hollywood is therefore integral to the agency's response to this changing geography of AIDS and to its plans to accommodate the needs in other communities without ignoring the needs of gay men. For although the spread of AIDS outside the gay community has fundamentally altered the mandate of the agency, the history of the agency, the volunteers and staff, and the donor base contributes to a strong gay and lesbian identity. Planning and policy at APLA constantly balance these needs.

Thus, in 1992, APLA acquired and renovated a 127,000-square-foot former ABC studio space two blocks south of Hollywood Boulevard, on the edge of the redevelopment area. Much of the funding for this move to Vine Street and Santa Monica Boulevard was made possible by tax-free municipal bonds and massive private donations, including a one million dollar donation from music producer David Geffen, for whom the new building is named. Although the CRA did not directly or financially assist APLA in its search for space, as it had the Center, there was, apparently, some discussion about whether there was space for APLA on the boulevard itself and whether there were any compelling reasons to place a direct services agency there. The fear of creating a "social services ghetto," of "dumping people on the boulevard"—not exactly the most positive or supportive place for someone struggling with AIDS—convinced the CRA that other locations needed to be found near, but not on, the boulevard.

When the ABC studio space was acquired, city officials worried that studio space was irreplaceable and should not be converted into nonentertainment uses, but these concerns were not enough to stop the project. The willingness of the city to allow this conversion from an entertainment-related use to a social service-related use suggests both the dislocation of the entertainment industry in Hollywood as well as the clout of APLA.

The symbolism of this move to Hollywood, however, has been most resonant within the AIDS community. The move was emotionally painful for the staff and clients:

> The main psychological nightmare wasn't because of the distance, it wasn't because the building was murky, it wasn't because the building has no windows; it was the fact that we were institutionalizing AIDS and this was a goddamn city block that we needed. . . . What [the staff] now realizes is that it doesn't matter what I do, I can't stop it and in the beginning we thought that we could, that eventually we would shut the doors and go home and go on with our lives. The building said that we cannot stop this and this is what it is going to take to deal with this.[36]

This feeling that the move into this larger, more institutional space meant that the end to the AIDS epidemic could no longer easily be visualized or fantasized has been the most dramatic evidence of the meaning of place for APLA. Phill Wilson, Public Policy Director for APLA, described, at the dedication of the new facility, the earnest goal of the agency's building campaign:

> As we dedicate this building, let us be ever mindful of the most important dedication ever. Our dedication to hasten the day when we will lock the doors on this and every other AIDS institution on the planet in celebration of the end of this pandemic.[37]

Like the Center, APLA overcame significant practical issues to locate in Hollywood and take advantage of the affordable real estate—including parking, safety, and distance for clients to travel. Assurances from city officials were critical in the decision-making process. However, although the Center easily embraced the power of permanence offered by the new space in Hollywood, the politics of AIDS continually destabilized the agency's programs and budgets, making the establishment of such a major and seemingly inflexible facility inconsistent with the needs of the community. In the early 1990s, those on the front lines of the AIDS epidemic equated this new building with a resignation to the virulence of the epidemic and to the lack of any cure for the disease. By the end of the 1990s, of course, changes in the politics and treatment of AIDS dismantled this mindset and forced yet another realignment of the geography of AIDS treatment.

In 1997, APLA announced the layoff of more than two dozen workers and stopped filling available vacancies. Budget shortfalls, stemming in part from a drastic reduction in individual and institutional donations, led to service cutbacks and elimination of nonessential programs. The decrease in funding, however, had its roots in the new advances in HIV treatment and in the diversification of AIDS services, both in the community and commercial sectors. As Ferd Eggan, the city's AIDS coordinator understood already in 1996, "the AIDS industry is going to have to shrink."[38] Although APLA announced at one point plans to sell its Hollywood building and move to smaller quarters, the Geffen Center continues to provide services to more than eight thousand clients a year, with a volunteer staff of more than two thousand.

The New Boundaries of the Gay and Lesbian Community

Initially, the relocation of the Center and APLA brought nearly five hundred new employees to the Hollywood Boulevard area. The city had hoped that this influx would spur economic revitalization by drawing service industries to the area. Hoping to hasten this growth, some Center employees bought homes in the area, signaling reinvestment if not gentrification.[39] Despite some modest improvements in the area, however, the boulevard remains generally as it has been for the past two decades, a depressed area with very low end tourist attractions, still a must-see landmark for out-of-towners, but more for its decline than its activity.

The problems of Hollywood Boulevard spread far beyond the particular politics of the gay and lesbian community. Nearly every year the city announces another "major" commercial or entertainment project destined to turn the street around. In the meantime, however, both the Center and APLA continue to build a presence in the area. Each of these agencies is now a major local employer and physically a major presence on the boulevard. The Center's staff have been involved in the arts planning for the boulevard, helping two independent galleries to move to nearby space.

In comparison with APLA, the Center's new location is much more integrated into the life of the boulevard. There is also a sense at the Center that the boulevard is adjusting to its presence and that the gay and lesbian community will embrace the area. As one employee of the Center put it, "Hudson will eventually be a gay/lesbian street."[40] The city council, in fact, renamed Hudson Street to Schrader Boulevard, honoring Rand Schrader, the first openly gay judge who, as a board member, was instrumental in the fund-raising for the Center. In less than twenty years, the Center moved from condemned buildings in a marginal neighborhood to its new facility. Similarly, in less than ten years, APLA grew from a hot line in the Center itself to its own, similarly expansive home. To achieve this growth, the gay and lesbian community raised significant capital and generated serious public awareness. To a great extent, this funding ensured that these organizations could be seen as generators of new residential and commercial growth, rather than unwelcome neighbors.

4 Separate Space and Separatism

Lesbian Culture and Community

For the past thirty years, lesbians and other women activists in Los Angeles have created places that accommodate and advance their activist agendas. Although gay men also have used community centers for organizing purposes, separatism has most often been defined in relation to heterosexism, and therefore cogendered (at least in name). For lesbians, however, the construction of separate organizations or community spaces has been as much about establishing cultural and political identity independent from gay men as it is about creating places of refuge and celebrating autonomy in a heterosexist world. Their place-claiming strategies, then, have necessitated a break with the mainstream gay and lesbian movement, which requires a commitment to the commonality of gay men and lesbian concerns. Separatist efforts add an extra dimension to the meaning of identity and visibility as strategies for place claiming. Because of the competing agendas within the lesbian movement, the notion of separatism is distinctly more complex than contemporary literature and political discussions would suggest. The history of lesbian organizing in Los Angeles has been one of trying to define this separateness, and the character of these refuges reveals the politics and ideologies present in local lesbian communities. The politics of place within the lesbian community emerge in part from this search for an inclusive separatism.

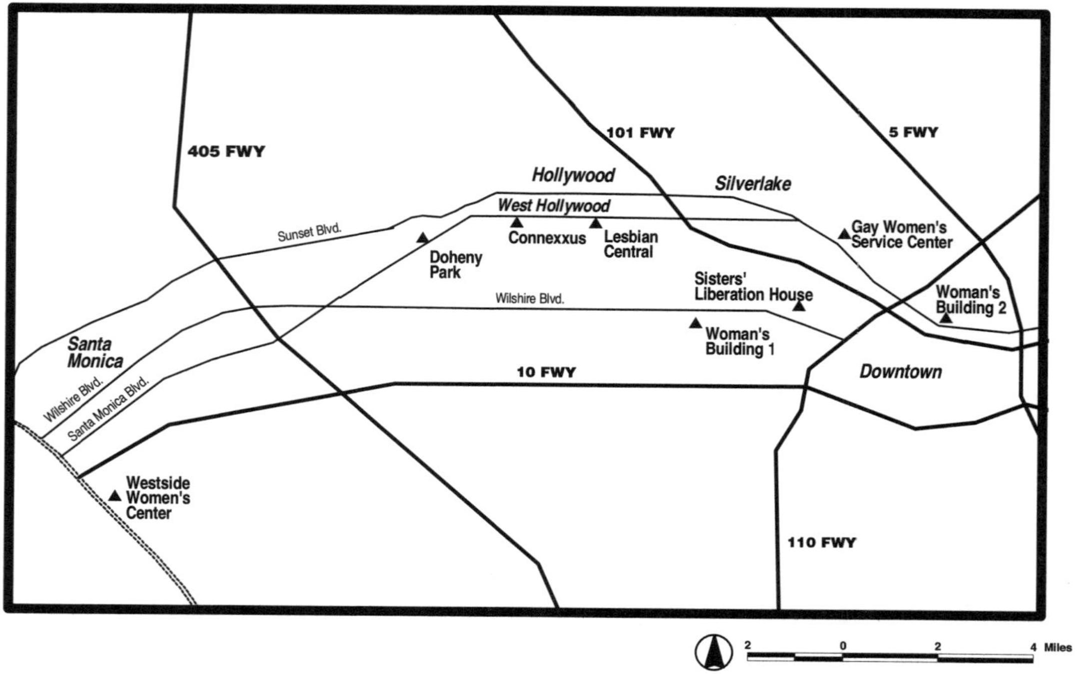

Map 4. Lesbian Community and Activist Sites

Attempts to claim safe space have been critical to the development of the lesbian movement. In Los Angeles, the struggle for autonomy has centered on a search for security, not simply in the physical sense (as in protection against assault), but also on a symbolic level as well, as abstract notions of home, community, and even utopia drive many activist efforts. Combining symbolic ideals with physical, political, and economic reality, lesbians have created places that define and reflect their collective experience. At the same time, lesbian politics have negotiated contentious debates about the boundaries of difference within this collective. Lesbians of color, working-class-identified women, and bisexuals have been more vocal in lesbian place claiming in Los Angeles than have their counterparts in the gay community. In part because of these insistences on inclusivity and specificity, the clear articulation of separatism as a symbolic practice has not generally led to organizational success.

Central to the search for lesbian space in Los Angeles has been the fight for autonomy—within both the feminist and gay rights movements. The community organizations and spaces built by lesbian and bisexual activists in Los Angeles make visible the shifting politics of their community, as lesbians move in and out of movements that have at times been either misogynist or heterosexist. The negotiation of these competing demands rarely has been simple. Although some gay activists work on multiple agendas, lesbian activists tend to note that they are more likely to continue to straddle multiple movements—civil rights, peace and social justice, domestic violence, or antinuclear, for example. Their lack of recognition as lesbians within these other movements has at times provided the impetus for separatist organizing. The recurrence of separatist ideals and practices results from the shifting terrain of lesbian activism and the crossover between activist agendas.[1]

In Los Angeles, two efforts to institutionalize women's need for separate space—the Woman's Building, a landmark women's art space, and Connexxus, a lesbian social services center—exemplify the multiple activist agendas of the lesbian community. To differing degrees, each straddled the often-competing contexts of the emerging visibility of lesbians and bisexuals within the gay liberation movement, the women's movement, the lesbian feminist movement, and the contemporary lesbian and gay movement. Three distinct phases, each with corresponding spatial manifestations, mark the development of lesbian culture and community in Los Angeles. Initially, lesbians claimed visibility in the context of the larger women's movement (as reflected in the history of the Woman's Building). As the gay liberation movement emerged, lesbians first participated in central roles and soon demanded the establishment of autonomous lesbian spaces. This phase ultimately focused on the call for a social service center distinct from the gay-dominated community services center and resulted in the founding of Connexxus, a quasi-separatist social services center based in West Hollywood, which struggled continually over the participation of both straight and bisexual women. In the still-continuing third phase, as the interest in separate facilities waned (and Connexxus and similar centers closed), lesbians largely have returned to cogender spaces, often in leadership roles.[2] Along the way, they have expanded social and economic outlets analogous to those available in the gay community and created a more marketable presence of lesbian entrepreneurs (primarily in West Hollywood) compared with the smaller, community-based, often-cooperative ventures of the late 1970s and early 1980s.

Lesbian Enclaves

Most work on lesbian concentration in the city emphasizes differences in the ways gays and lesbians use the city, rather than on the specifics of lesbian place claiming alone. The lack of a geographic concentration of lesbians in any major American city stands in stark contrast to the prevalence of gay male presence, creating a very different experience of the city for lesbians. Both lesbian and nonlesbian historians and geographers have searched for tangible evidence of these differences, importing a gay male model of community formation. Not surprisingly, many of these efforts to map lesbian community have been unsuccessful, because they rarely address the critical, and complicated, politics imbedded in the development of lesbian-identified places and neighborhoods. When recognizable enclaves, analogous to gay male constructions, are found, lesbian life flourishes. When such signs are not visible, lesbian life is often considered nascent, or nonexistent. Ignoring the significant presence of lesbians within feminist struggles more generally, scholars of lesbian history tend to overlook the construction of lesbian spaces as part of a feminist politics of place. This avoidance of such a significant aspect of the lesbian struggle perpetuates a monochromatic image, one that ignores both the important alliances between lesbian and feminist movements, as well as the more radical dimensions of lesbian community formation. This is often done at the expense of a similarly rigorous explanation of lesbian separateness, presenting, instead, separatist efforts as one dimensional and counterproductive.

At the heart of most representations of lesbian life in contemporary urban environments lie two assumptions: First, lesbians have a less urgent need for a geographically concentrated or physically manifested community than do gay men; and, second, lesbians, by virtue of their gender, rather than their sexuality, do not, or cannot, participate in an urban culture that is dangerous and inaccessible to women. Various explanations, from the greater need of gay men to escape societal homophobia to the innate male need to define and capture territory, have been used to suggest that lesbians simply do not require physical community. Continuing a tradition of urban analysis rooted in the nineteenth century, those searching for evidence of lesbian community see the city as innately hostile to women. The most intelligent formulations of this argument are resolutely feminist, revealing both the conscious attempts to restrict women to domestic and private spheres and the failures of planners to create hospitable urban spaces that would allow women to enter public life. According to Dolores Hayden, in *Redesigning the American Dream: The Future of Housing, Work and Family Life*,

> A political program to overcome the otherness of women and win all female and male citizens, and their children, access to safe, public urban space requires that the presence of women and their children in public space be established as a political right; and that gender stereotypes be eliminated from architecture, urban design, and graphic design in public space.[3]

The presence of women in the city (like the present lesbian community) necessitates, therefore, the active engagement of feminist activists in the redesign of cities and neighborhoods. History, through the experiences of feminist activists from the nineteenth-century Settlement House workers to the Take Back the Night marches of the 1970s, provides numerous models for the possibility of lesbian space. Geographical analyses of women's experiences more generally exist, and those begin with an understanding of the gendering of space in the city, a process that limits women's (including lesbians' and bisexuals') access to public and private space either directly (through economic restrictions) or indirectly (through the threat of crime). Few of these sources incorporate any in-depth discussion of the specific concerns of lesbians in the city (except as the archetype of the independent woman). Instead, existing works focus on the presumed parallels between heterosexual and homosexual or bisexual women. The idea that women are excluded from public space even after they have achieved parity with men in terms of income, work opportunities, or freedom from family responsibilities establishes an alternative map of lesbian space that works from the objective reality of women's lives in the United States.

Included in this analysis of the "unsafe" city lies the peculiarly lesbian belief in the Lesbian Nation—community as an emotional, or even spiritual, construction that defies physical barriers. Bonnie Zimmerman traces four roots of this strand of lesbian communal life: the legacy of preliberation culture centered in the unpredictable and illegal life of the lesbian bar, the "communal ideals of the 1960s counterculture," radical feminism, "which emphasized the virtues of universal sisterhood and women working together to create new institutions," and the symbolism of Lesbos passed down through generations and across cultures as the ideal of female life. Out of these origins comes the myth of the Lesbian Nation, one that "exists more happily in literature and myth than . . . in real life."[4]

Together, the myth of a lesbian nation and the understanding of urban life as generally inaccessible to women constitute the core of specifically lesbian studies of urban geography. Beginning with Deborah Wolf's work on the lesbian community in San Francisco, the absence of physically defined lesbian urban life followed the feminist argument that economic constraints epitomize the differences between gay men and lesbians. This argument is echoed in Manuel Castells's analysis of the Castro district. His analysis inferred an absence of any lesbian community in San Francisco (at least as measurable by urban planners) when set against the gentrification of the Castro, presumably by gay men. Both of these analyses emphasize lesbian communities rather than lesbians themselves. Although it is most likely true that lesbians are evenly distributed among the population, the question remains: Which lesbians have nothing to lose in becoming a visible (or perhaps closeted) member of a lesbian community, and which lesbians remain apart from these communities, in relationships with men? Sy Adler and Johanna Brenner—also geographers—attempt to contextualize this research:

> Wolf pointed out that since lesbians tend to be poor they live in older, ethnically mixed working- class areas, in low-rent apartment buildings or small, low-rent houses. "Since much of the socializing in the [lesbian] community consists of visiting friends, women without cars try to live near each other, so that gradually, within a small radius, many lesbian households may exist." Indeed, Castells himself noted that lower incomes mean less choice regarding the location of home and work and that lesbian concentrations were emerging in the kinds of areas described by Wolf, particularly low-rent neighborhoods with counter-cultural communities.[5]

Adler and Brenner begin their analysis of lesbian space in an anonymous city by acknowledging the role economic disparities between gay men and lesbians play in their differential use of urban space. They then explore a more complicated notion—namely the "differences in [lesbians'] capacity to dominate space"—a difference related to the gendering of space in the city. Using mailing lists of lesbian organizations, institutions, and businesses to locate census tracts with a significant proportion of lesbian residences, Adler and Brenner assert that, in fact, lesbians have developed distinct enclaves along the lines of those inhabited by gay men. However, their research does not look at the dimensions of these businesses or, more importantly, the importance of these organizations for the neighborhoods in which they exist and for the lesbians who use them. In fact, the absence of scholarship that explores aspects of lesbian spaces outside the home would seem to perpetuate the stereotype of the chosen invisibility of lesbians.

In the wake of critical studies' emergence as an alternative to a rigid and simplistic understanding of identity, a few case studies have begun to look at the growth of more visible lesbian enclaves in urban areas. Tamara Rothenberg's study of Park Slope, a well-known lesbian neighborhood in Brooklyn, New York, begins with the assumption that the neighborhood is lesbian coded and proceeds to define this community through a series of interviews with residents and business owners. Rothenberg describes community-building in Park Slope as the result of "social networking"—the casual agglomeration of lesbian residences reinforced by the location of a number of lesbian social and community organizations. Park Slope, as described by Rothenberg, comes across as a place where life is simply easier for lesbians. Another study of lesbian neighborhood development, this one in Vancouver, Canada, recalls earlier work on gay male neighborhood development with its identification of cheap housing stock as the most important indicator of gay community development. This study contrasts the process of neighborhood development by men and women in Vancouver in two neighborhoods, cataloguing the following features of gay or lesbian neighborhood development: differences in housing stock (apartments for men versus houses for women), community spaces (more permanent for men, less so for women), and perception of the neighborhood as sexualized space (again, more so in the gay neighborhood and less so in the lesbian one).[6]

Absent in the broader history of lesbian community building, however, is any explicit analysis of the role of lesbian activists in the development of gay enclaves (like West Hollywood). When activism is referenced, these authors emphasize its role as a social activity, obscuring the ways such activism led to specific decisions about the location, visibility, and viability of gay and lesbian neighborhoods and institutions. These geographically focused explorations of lesbian community development focus on the material evidence of lesbian lives in the city, overlooking the particular politics of the communities they investigate. As a result, individual activists disappear in these accounts, with lesbian community building an economic, rather than political, process.

At the other end of the spectrum, however, Lillian Faderman's historical projects have connected names and faces with the development of lesbian communities. In *Odd Girls and*

Twilight Lovers Faderman traces the transformation of the lesbian experience from the 1930s to the 1990s, building a lesbian history that responds to the economic realities of each successive era in the broader history of the United States. The expansion of the national economy in the 1920s and later during World War II created jobs for lesbians within the mainstream economy, as a low unemployment rate and need for workers facilitated women's economic freedom. Alternatively, the Depression in the 1930s marked a restriction of women's (and therefore lesbians') freedom as the scarcity of work led to a rhetoric that targeted working women as contrary to the national interest. Lesbian community, prior to the liberation movements of the 1970s, was, according to Faderman, reactive—dependent on the vicissitudes of economic prosperity. With the rise of the women's and gay movements, however, lesbian politics and economics collided. The "blueprint for a lesbian-feminist community" included a vision of lesbians' economic independence so that women "would not have to fear that they would lose their livelihood because they 'came out.' . . . As one writer phrased it, 'Hopefully, we will soon be able to integrate the pieces of our lives and stop this schizophrenic existence of a straight job by day and lesbian political work at night. It keeps us in a permanent culture shock and drains our energies.' "[7] Lesbian community formed around this economic vision with the establishment of food co-ops, medical clinics and other social services, and independent businesses of all types (including the emblematic auto repair shop). For Faderman, this era seems to represent the high water mark of lesbian community, the moment when lesbian politics are most clearly articulated and connected to lesbian urban reality.

Faderman sees the current era, beginning in the mid-1980s, as representing a downturn in lesbian consciousness. She notes that the explicit lesbian politics developed through the 1970s have given way to a more market- and media-driven community. Class aspirations replace class consciousness as lesbian entrepreneurs (or "luppies," to use a disparaging phrase Faderman borrowed from 1950s activist Phyllis Lyon) search for respectability and "a politics of accommodation." Faderman views this as a lifestyle, rather than a shift in politics. Her sources (none of them activists) emphasize a search for happiness, job security, and professionalism in tones that contrast sharply with the unveiled defiance of 1970s lesbian feminism. In fact, her sources (all apparently over the age of forty and therefore part of the lesbian-feminist generation) emphasize their journey from the radicalism of the 1970s to the complacency of the 1980s:

> I think the whole picture has changed. The women in our group have it all together. They're happy with what they are doing. They all have good jobs. They're career women who chose to be career women. They have nice homes. They have the money to take the kinds of vacations they want to. They don't wish for anything to be different. Our group is happy.[8]

As Faderman's categorization of these women as "luppies" suggests, the seemingly apolitical approach to community building of the later 1980s and early 1990s frustrates many with a longer view of the lesbian struggle in the United States. In their book *Homo Economics*, Amy Glickman and Betsy Reed describe the "lesbian chic" of the 1990s as evidence of lesbians' seamless inclusion in the new respectability of gay community. Gays and lesbians become consumers, rather than activists, with community defined more by the interests of advertisers and corporations than by a community-based politics.

A complete understanding of lesbian place claiming must take into account more than residential pattern alone, or the simple effects of economic parity. As has been the case in Los Angeles, for lesbians as well as gay men, the specificity of the city's geography and the diversity of its population negate the usefulness of or perhaps even the desire for a single, tightly knit lesbian or gay neighborhood. Minor lesbian enclaves have waxed and waned over the past thirty years, a number specifically tied to the location of defense industry plants in southern, central, and northern Los Angeles County. At most, two stable centers of lesbian concentration emerged in Los Angeles (one in West Hollywood and another in Long Beach). In neither case has the location of social service organizations had any noticeable effect on the location of these enclaves. The struggle to create places and attachment to place independent of residential concentration characterized more fully the place-making practices of lesbians in Los Angeles.

To look at residential evidence alone ignores the centrality of lesbian activist strategies and ideologies to the claims on place. Although lesbian culture has been well theorized, the strategies of lesbian politics have not been as broadly discussed, particularly as lesbian politics interact with the city.[9] This failure to connect the actions of lesbians with their effects on the city is reflected in the belief that the physical dimensions of lesbian culture are less important than the mental dimensions. As Julia Penelope wrote, "The spaces we create for ourselves may have physical boundaries, but, more importantly, they're an idea we nourish in our minds."[10] Although lesbians have had fewer opportunities than gay men to engage in residentially focused place claiming, the life of the mind parallels, rather than surpasses, the life of the streets.

Lesbian Feminism and Autonomous Activism

During the 1950s and 1960s, before the arrival of the modern women's movement and gay liberation, lesbian culture in Los Angeles was largely confined to the few lesbian bars located in the San Fernando Valley and Hollywood. Little more than anecdotal evidence exists to explain the specific geographic concentrations of lesbians in these areas. However, the proximity of these bars to major aircraft and other war-related manufacturing plants—as well as the film studios—supports a connection between the availability of employment for women and the rise of a public lesbian culture. Joanie Presents and Club Laurel, two popular San Fernando Valley clubs of the postwar years, were pioneering not only because they offered a social space for lesbians, but also because they were both owned by women.

Other accounts of pre-1970s bar culture in American cities describe a pattern of locating lesbian bars in inhospitable parts of town. Joan Nestle's classic essay, "The Bathroom Line," describes the world of a working-class bar in New York City that circumscribed the extent of lesbian visibility and experience for its patrons:

> Because we lived in the underworld of the Sea Colony, we were surrounded by the nets of the society that hated us and yet wanted our money. Mafia nets, clean-up New York nets, vice squad nets. We needed the Lesbian air of the Sea Colony to breathe the life we could not anywhere else, those of us who wanted to see women dance, make love, wear shirts and pants. Here, and in other bars like this one, we found each other and the space to be a sexually powerful butch-femme community.[11]

Similarly, in Los Angeles, the bars were "rough" places, located in "seedy" parts of the city (North Hollywood, Baldwin Park, Pico Rivera, and Hollywood). Drugs were definitely part of the bar scene. To protect patrons from hostile outsiders, and from each other, aggressive bouncers carefully controlled the comings and goings. Bar culture was not solely about drinking. Most of the bars sponsored softball teams that attracted other lesbians as well. "These women were tough," recalls one bar patron, "they drank beer and played ball, that's all they did."[12]

At the same time, however, in Los Angeles, the particular landscape of the city and opportunities for home ownership after the war meant that these bars were also part of an emerging suburban lesbian community. These women generally sought the same middle-class dream offered to veterans by the postwar subdivisioning of the San Fernando Valley where houses could be bought for ten or fifteen thousand dollars. Independent women forced out of the better-paying wartime jobs in the military or production plants turned to secretarial jobs in the Hollywood studios. In this way, the prefeminism lesbian culture of Los Angeles could be maintained even after it declined in other cities.

From the beginning, lesbian feminists searched for political strategies to organize lesbians and lesbian communities with visions of new consensus-driven societies. Early lesbian feminist texts and manifestos talked about creating "separate spaces," and a "Lesbian Nation."[13] Lesbian feminism, as Arlene Stein explains, arose out of the search, by lesbian activists, to create an autonomous movement that did not require concessions (in terms of strategies or goals) to either gay men or straight women in the lesbian community:

> Lesbian feminism emerged out of the most radical sectors of the women's movement in the early 1970s. Young women who "came out through feminism," as the saying went, attempted to broaden the definition of lesbianism, to transform it from a medical condition, or, at best, a sexual "preference," into a collective affinity which transcended rampant individualism and its excesses as well as compulsory gender and sex roles. It was a movement that spawned a vibrant and visible lesbian culture considerably more multidimensional than in previous decades.[14]

Lesbian feminism aimed to move lesbian culture out of the bars and into the new politics of the feminist and gay liberation movements. Paralleling developments across the country, the development of lesbian-feminism created a division, with the working-class bar culture generally ignored by the younger activists. This was both a political and a spatial segregation, as very few women made the transition from the bar culture to the new political and social organizations. Jeanne Cordova, who came out in the Los Angeles bar culture in the mid-1960s and did make the transition, becoming a leader of the lesbian-feminist movement, described the schism:

> During my lesbian feminist years I didn't go to the bars very much; a whole generation never really went to the bars at all. [With lesbian feminism] there were alternative places to be, [the feminists] all went to a bar once or twice but compared to the openness of a sisterhood environment they thought it was a real comedown and they didn't understand like I did that [bar culture] had its own scene.[15]

To reinforce the distinction between themselves and the gay liberation movement, lesbian feminists located their Los Angeles institutions away from the Gay Services Center (then located in Westlake). The Gay Women's Service Center on Glendale Boulevard in Echo Park (arguably the first social service space for lesbians in the United States),[16] the Sisters' Liberation House on South Oxford Street near downtown, and the Westside Women's Center at Second and Hill Streets in Santa Monica all opened in 1971 or 1972 and facilitated the growth of the lesbian feminist movement in Los Angeles. As was typical of each of these spaces (and similar ventures in other cities), the Westside Women's Center was a community-run space that offered both services (such as group counseling) and organized social events, housing smaller community organizations, among them the *Lesbian Tide*, a lesbian magazine with national circulation. The lines between the lesbian movement and the women's movements were never clearly drawn, with each of these organizations attempting to redefine itself in response to a rapidly growing and evolving community presence. Conflicts over the use of the space and the desire to balance separatism with outreach to women just entering the movement or community (feminist or lesbian or both) often led to rapidly shifting organizational agendas and structures. The history of the corner at Second and Hill Streets in Santa Monica, where the Westside Women's Center was opened, reveals this shifting terrain. Over the course of just five years, that corner supported at least a half-dozen lesbian or feminist organizations, many of which were reformulated or splinter groups. The difficulty activists had in defining separatism or separatist space was often at the heart of these transformations.

Art and Politics at the Woman's Building

In Los Angeles, one of the most compelling and innovative examples of this attempt to create lesbian space within the context of the women's movement emerged at the Woman's Building, a public center for women's culture in downtown Los Angeles. Founded by three women active in the feminist art movement and on the faculty at the California Institute of the Arts—Sheila de Bretteville, Arlene Raven, and Judy Chicago—the Woman's Building energized women's cultural expression in Los Angeles and set the standard for women's art collectives across the country. The Woman's Building, which opened in 1973 and closed in 1991, evolved out of the Feminist Studio Workshop (FSW), which had been established by de Bretteville, Raven, and Chicago as the first independent school for women artists. The Woman's Building provided a larger context for the FSW, by providing space and support for other political and social ventures. The building also housed at various times galleries for exhibitions and other women's organizations and businesses, including a women's bookstore, travel agency, theater companies, coffeehouse, thrift store, and the local office of the National Organization for Women (NOW). Originally housed on Grandview Street near MacArthur Park, the Woman's Building moved to a three-story warehouse on North Spring Street just north of downtown Los Angeles, on the edge of Chinatown. Then and now this end of downtown Los Angeles is very much a transitional industrial space attracting artists to the available warehouse space but never generating a significant residential or commercial concentration.[17] Most of the organizations that had shared space in the Grandview Building did not move to the Spring Street site, allowing the Woman's Building to expand

and concentrate its arts programs.

Artists at the Woman's Building aimed to create a space where "the arts and feminist education [are not] separated from the other activities of the burgeoning women's community."[18] Understanding the Woman's Building and its role in creating lesbian space in Los Angeles requires a careful unraveling of the many objectives of the Woman's Building founders—to exist in Los Angeles, to govern itself as a feminist organization, and to encourage difference and individuality through artistic expression and personal growth. In the book commemorating the fifteenth anniversary celebrations, Sheila de Bretteville described the vision of the space and the project of the Woman's Building:

> I have always seen you as a place of gathering, a place for learning about each other with each other. Asking not only "who I am and how I have come to understand myself as a women?" but also "who is that other woman who appears to be different?" Community and diversity would be valued and those women relegated to the margins of mass culture would be brought to the center. Differences would not be effaced, all would be included. For me, to be in Los Angeles is to be on an active city street, claiming our place, making the patriarchal world include us as we are not as it images us to be.[19]

Although the Woman's Building served all women, not solely lesbians, it was seen as a place where, as artist Cheri Gaulke explained, "women could relate to each other as women and a lot of women who came to the Woman's Building as heterosexuals became lesbians (myself included) there."[20] Without the obvious tensions within other feminist organizations in the 1970s, the Woman's Building exposed women to lesbian relationships and politics, often for the first time. Rather than ostracizing or marginalizing lesbians, artists at the Woman's Building generally accepted lesbianism as a politically important stance.

Lesbians involved with the Woman's Building spoke of the

lesbian presence as an essential and formative part of the building, given its historical and political context. Just as the Woman's Building struggled to be a place for women of color, from various class backgrounds, and at all levels of artistic education and ability, the attitudes toward sexuality and lesbianism were open and accepting. In contrast to the often-wrenching struggles that characterized other women's as well as lesbian organizations—the unending search for consensus, agonizing attempts at diversity and inclusion, debates over tactics and strategy—the Woman's Building avoided many of these conflicts. Terry Wolverton, who came to the building as a student in the FSW and later became executive director, explained this relative calm as the result of the building's emphasis on art and art making, a focus that "created a kind of permission and a kind of terrain where it was understood that women weren't all the same and [that women] needed the space for self-expression."[21] The lack of a "censorious atmosphere," then, allowed lesbians to participate in the Woman's Building and express their lesbianism in many ways and to varying degrees.

This seemingly permissive and exploratory environment inevitably led to some disagreements over the appropriate use of the building's space. The artists continually exploded the limits between public and personal space, and these shifting boundaries manifested in the work and organization of the Woman's Building. Because the building created both a private space for women making art and a place "that welcomed the public to come in and experience women's culture,"[22] users and observers occasionally clashed. Cheri Gaulke recalled a point at which the two purposes—public and private—attempted to merge and often clashed, where the "private blobbed out into the public space."[23] Without a paid staff at the building, participants in the educational programs had to be available to coordinate events, take care of administrative duties, and, inevitably, take time away from their artistic work to interact with the curious public. Occasionally, women found it difficult to maintain the public persona of the building after a full day of art making. When the artists' projects dealt with feminist issues—separatism, rape, violence toward women, and other manifestations of discrimination and harassment—the need to put on a public face and welcome strangers into these private spaces and experiences meant suppressing the emotions raised by the examination of these sensitive topics. The women at the building maintained an uneasy balance between the public and private dimensions of the building. As a public gallery, it required some deference to traditional decorum and social mores; as a private space for women, it was a place where these traditions were being challenged and subverted.

Much of the work produced by women at the building directly challenged notions of public and private space, often in ways that can also be read in later gay and lesbian activist projects. Suzanne Lacy's project, "Three Weeks in May," documented rapes in Los Angeles on a large map hung in the city hall underground mall. Lacy recorded each rape on the map with a large stamp, along with nine smaller stamps representing the 90 percent of rapes that go unreported. She also staged guerrilla actions every day of the three-week installation, including self-defense classes for city hall employees, street theater events at lunchtime, and the spray painting of body silhouettes at sites where rapes were reported. Many of the performance art techniques developed at the Woman's Building dealt with issues of image, the media, and the use of public space, techniques that later appeared in the direct-action campaigns of groups like ACT UP and Queer Nation and has influenced the work of later feminist artists.[24] While the violence of rape literally shrinks the map of the city for women, as different areas of the city are marked as dangerous, the reclaiming of these spaces through a woman's own graffiti made the violence visible and challenged the silent process of erasing women from the city streets.[25]

These projects expanded the scope of the Woman's Building as artists reclaimed parts of the cityscape previously marked as out of bounds for women. In one "reclamation" project, artists examined public transportation, publicizing its role as the primary mode of transportation for immigrant women commuting to jobs in sweatshops downtown or as maids in houses on the westside of Los Angeles.

The project that most defined the role of the Woman's Building as lesbian space for artists was the Lesbian Art Project, a collective effort led by Arlene Raven, an art historian and Woman's Building cofounder, and Terry Wolverton, a writer at the building. The Lesbian Art Project included classes at the building, work-sharing seminars and exhibitions, collective theater pieces led by Wolverton, and social events. Wolverton recalled the Lesbian Art Project as one that aimed to broaden the scope of the Woman's Building and to respond directly to the need of lesbians across the city for community space. Wolverton recalled: "I think the biggest rationale was that we wanted to create a positive, celebratory, and interesting culture for lesbians; we wanted to broaden and expand the culture that existed for lesbians."[26]

In the fall of 1979, a collective was formed at the Woman's Building to curate the Great American Lesbian Art Show, sponsored in collaboration with the Gay Community Services Center. In 1980, the Woman's Building presented a national review of the state of lesbian art while lesbians around the country held concurrent shows with support from Los Angeles. Photographs from these other shows, which ranged from full-scale exhibitions at galleries and museums to more underground shows in studios, garages, and private spaces, were collected in Los Angeles. Slides from the various exhibits were later compiled as an archive with copies sent to four gay and lesbian archives across the country. Maps of the United States and Los Angeles illustrated the scope of the show beyond the space of the Woman's Building.

As Wolverton explained, the impetus behind the show was

to use multiple locations to increase the visibility of lesbians and lesbian art and overcome the obstacles to staging a national show. At that time, the organizers in Los Angeles had little contact with the mostly closeted lesbian artists they believed were doing work across the country, women who could not be brought to Los Angeles for the show. At the same time, the curators wanted to illustrate lesbian culture and art at a scale beyond a single neighborhood, community, or collective:

> Because we couldn't make possible everything we wanted to do with physical space we chose this alternative way of trying to do that. . . . We put out a whole booklet about how to organize an exhibit and then we had our show. . . . So it was kind of creating a conceptual space, expanding the space, bringing women into the space when we couldn't do that physically. We knew that there were lesbian artists out there doing all kinds of things and we wanted to make that manifest, make that visible.[27]

The Woman's Building, at its best, functioned as a permissive and uncontested arena where lesbians and straight women worked together without the political conflicts seemingly inherent in the women's movement more broadly and in many other feminist and lesbian organizations in Los Angeles and elsewhere. Importantly, the search for new forms of artistic expression did not eclipse the political conflicts, but, rather, provided an alternative space that encouraged dialogue. At the same time, many of the projects undertaken at the Woman's Building and the Lesbian Art Project in particular created connections between the artist community and the larger community of Los Angeles. The Woman's Building, the Lesbian Art Project, and the Great American Lesbian Art Show attempted to transcend the gallery space, move art into the public sphere, and create tangible evidence of the diversity of lesbian views and politics. As Gaulke said, "Raising consciousness wasn't enough; it wasn't enough to stir up a bunch of feelings."[28]

The Woman's Building closed in 1991, in part because fund-raising efforts were less than successful and more importantly because many of the artists believed that a separate women's space was no longer necessary. Other galleries in the city had begun to organize shows of women's work, and many artists chose not to show their work at the Woman's Building, for fear of "ghettoizing" it.[29]

Leaving the Men Behind: Creating Connexxus

Whereas the Woman's Building represents the strategy of creating lesbian space within the context of a broader women's movement (this time committed to women's artistic expression), the more constant struggle of lesbians in Los Angeles has been for a community center solely devoted to their needs. Although the Gay Services Center did provide services for women, lesbians were not specifically recognized by this nascent organization until 1984, when the Center finally added the word lesbian to its title and mission (becoming the Gay and Lesbian Community Services Center). At the same time, the Center instituted a program, Lesbian Central, devoted solely to the needs of lesbians. Throughout its history, tensions plagued the Center and these conflicts between cosexual services and a safe space for lesbians were never resolved. Out of these organizing struggles at the Center, however, emerged Connexxus, which operated for five years.

Place-claiming issues at Connexxus illuminate the struggle over the lesbian participation in the liberation movement, the challenge to create institutions reflecting lesbian diversity, and the difficulties in choosing a single site for social service organizations intended to serve the entire area. Overarching all these tensions was the struggle to create autonomous, women-only space in the increasingly cosexual movement.

The level of discord at the Community Services Center over the participation and representation of women on the board, staff, and among its clients is difficult to gauge from a distance. Women who ran Lesbian Central, including the director and others who eventually left the Center to start Connexxus, described the situation this way: Battles were constantly waged and truces were uneasily reached. The fact that, as Lauren Jardine, director of Lesbian Central explained, "there wasn't anything else in town," meant that lesbians struggled to make a place for themselves within the boundaries of a community center they felt was antithetical to their needs.[30]

Lesbian Central occupied a small area on the first floor of the center, near the main entrance, which allowed women to enter Lesbian Central without having to go into the rest of the building. This was not viewed as separatism, but as the claiming of separate space, a distinction that seems rather fine but reflects the particular politics of the time. And when the lesbians at the Center raised money independently to renovate the space, many of the gay men became angry, which further divided the two groups. Lauren Jardine, director of Lesbian Central during the years immediately prior to the opening of Connexxus explained the separatist ethos:

> At that point we were still very much into an autonomous separatist women's movement so that rather than ghettoization we saw it as an affirmative stance that there was a separate space called Lesbian Central. . . . It was off grounds to men unless there was a special event to which men were invited, there was a constant fight at the center about men not being able to come in that facility. That seems primitive now but at the time made perfect sense.[31]

The "turf wars" at the Center continued simmering with disagreements about the degree of ghettoization versus empowerment even after the creation of Lesbian Central. The conflict intensified when Del Martinez, a vice president and board member of the Center and highly respected social worker trained in the Settlement House movement in Chicago, was denied the executive director position despite strong support from staff and the community. The lesbian community generally believed that the Center overlooked her application because, as an older, Latina lesbian, she did not look "right for the part." The Center, many presumed, wanted a white man for a more corporate and professional image to front its expansion. Charges of racism, sexism, and ageism and a threatened walkout by the women at the Center did nothing to dissuade the board of directors. The event triggered an en masse departure of women from Lesbian Central and the beginnings of Connexxus.[32]

Connexxus existed as an autonomous, largely volunteer organization in the City of West Hollywood from 1985 to 1989, when it closed because of financial instability and failure to attract new women to the board and the volunteer staff. As originally envisioned, Connexxus ambitiously aimed to create what the Center could not—a community-operated space that provided social services unavailable to lesbians elsewhere. Harking back to the first years of the Center, the emphasis at Connexxus was on building community and creating safe space. Beginning with the human services provided at Lesbian Central (counseling, rap groups, classes, social events), Connexxus hoped to develop a business/services/entertainment complex for women-owned businesses, arts organizations, professional offices, health club, and similar community-oriented activities.

Its location in West Hollywood remained a contested and divisive issue through the years. Del Martinez and Lauren Jardine, the founders of Connexxus, both insisted that West Hollywood was the only logical choice at the time, despite the controversy this decision caused.

Just as Connexxus was nearing the final planning stages, the local voters approved cityhood for West Hollywood. As both Martinez and Jardine recalled, the sense of possibility that cityhood offered was an overwhelming factor in the decision: "There was the feeling that lesbians would move to West Hollywood," recalls Martinez, adding,

> We both said there is only one place we have to locate, because [West Hollywood] was going to be a mecca and we wanted to be

> there. Particularly in the early years of the city we wanted to be there, that was what was exciting, can you imagine being in your own town?[33]

In addition, the founders felt that the city would be more user-friendly, particularly because, at the time of incorporation, three of the first city council members were gay or lesbian. Finally, although they considered Culver City, Santa Monica (prohibitively expensive), and Silverlake (too much of a gay, rather than lesbian, enclave), West Hollywood was seen as being equally inaccessible to everyone. Since there was no one place where enough lesbians lived, Connexxus wanted to locate in a place that might in the future attract lesbians. Connexxus first opened offices on Santa Monica Boulevard, in the center of the gay nightlife. After a year, it moved to a larger space on La Cienega Boulevard (also in the heart of West Hollywood), where it was able to offer space to other organizations for meetings.

When Connexxus began to offer programs, organizers discovered that lesbians—particularly those in need of social services (especially those who were still closeted)—simply did not live in West Hollywood. But to receive funding from the city, Connexxus needed to prove that a certain number of its clients resided or worked in West Hollywood. Although they managed to meet their West Hollywood quota, the majority of their clients came from outside the city boundaries.[34]

Connexxus staff tried with particular intensity to address the diverse ethnic, racial, and class demographics of the lesbian community. The organization's isolation from other community institutions, however, meant that there were few opportunities to release the tensions created by their desire to accommodate every perspective. Where other organizations (such as the Community Services Center) were used to groups leaving over personal and political disagreements, Connexxus, as a consensus-driven organization, committed itself to working out every major and minor disagreement.

Despite continued outreach to, and needs assessment of, lesbians living in the city, few West Hollywood residents attended anything other than the dances and other social gatherings. Both Jardine and Martinez emphasized these attempts to create programs for West Hollywood residents, noting their futility because, in their opinion, West Hollywood lesbians were less likely to need the crisis-oriented social services—including coming-out groups and therapy—that Connexxus offered.

Part of this lack of outreach resulted from the class and race divisions within the center that were, as stated earlier, at the core of Connexxus's difficulties. Lesbians from the east side of the city, including many lesbians of color and working-class women, saw Connexxus as too white and too middle class, whereas women from West Hollywood and other parts of the Westside (primarily white women) saw the center as downwardly mobile. Eventually, however, it became evident to the women at the Center that sufficient numbers of women simply did not live in West Hollywood and those that did had no need for social services.

For lesbians of color, West Hollywood existed off their maps of lesbian Los Angeles. Those women who did participate reported that many lesbians believed that "Connexxus was in Beverly Hills . . . and they felt intimidated or simply not interested in going to the facility to find out what it was all about."[35] Although Connexxus was considered a substantial improvement over the programs offered at Lesbian Central, particularly because Del Martinez's leadership suggested greater diversity and sensitivity to the needs of lesbians of color, the location in West Hollywood continued to be a serious obstacle. According to Carla Barboza, one of the board members responsible for outreach to communities of color at Connexxus, lesbians are more likely to live in their own ethnic communities than in a distinct lesbian neighborhood: "Their world is centered around their culture and their class and their neighborhoods and West Hollywood is simply a fantasy."[36]

Leaders within Connexxus, however, maintained that, despite the seeming homogeneity of the city, West Hollywood offered lesbians the best hope of uniting the community on common ground. More practically, organizers recognized that the program needed the city's financial support and could not easily leave the city, regardless of the limitations the location placed on client outreach. Nevertheless, some committed volunteers proposed that Connexxus develop satellite services around the city to serve populations less likely to travel to West Hollywood. Eventually, a site was found in East Los Angeles and Connexxus East/Centro des Mujeres was opened. Interestingly, Barboza recalled that this center similarly remained disconnected from its neighborhood population, although it did attract women who had not been to the West Hollywood site. She described the Centro as providing an impetus for "solidifying" a number of independent programs and efforts:

> I don't think it created a community, I think it simply offered a space where Latina lesbians could come and find each other and themselves, whereas prior to the creation of Connexxus East I don't know of any other location where Latina lesbians could come and have rap groups and start a social network and find a place they could call their own . . . it created a location for people to congregate and sort out their identities.[37]

Lesbians involved with both initiatives described Connexxus and Connexxus East as separate, not separatist, space, which created an important and unusual distinction between the ideology of separatism and the practice of separate space. Although Connexxus evolved from a dispute with the cosexual policies of the Gay and Lesbian Community Services Center and the perceived inequities of that arrangement, the founders made a delicate distinction between the need for separate space as a practical need rather than separatist ideology. Connexxus aimed to provide for lesbians what the Woman's Building sought for women generally—a space for generating greater community visibility and strength. Very clearly, organizers contrasted this with the more familiar notion of separate space—a place where women could live and work independently, without regard for an integrated gay and lesbian movement. While this evolution was occurring elsewhere, not solely in Los Angeles, it reflects the tentatively political nature of the Los Angeles lesbian community and its somewhat reluctant acknowledgment of the need for inclusiveness in a city with few spaces for gathering. Although some separatists used Connexxus's services (and raised objections over the use of the building by some straight women's groups, such as NOW), separatism was generally considered a fringe element in the community.

Ultimately, Connexxus was forced to close the West Hollywood facility, citing a lack of commitment from new volunteers and absence of secure and long-term funding. As lesbians began to develop political affinities with gay men, both within the context of AIDS and in the broadening fight for civil rights legislation, the pool of potential volunteers and clients dwindled. Connexxus East stayed open as an independent facility, and the June Mazer Archives, which had been a program within Connexxus, also became independent.[38]

Many organizers interpreted the closure of Connexxus as signaling an important transition in the history of lesbian organizing. For some, this transition was a positive one, leading to a new, more equal sharing of community space between gay men and lesbians. For others, this transition was a step back, with lesbians accepting once again a backseat status to the needs of gay men. The impetus for this transition, however it was read, was seen by all as the inevitable result of the growing AIDS epidemic. Given the slow response of the federal government, it became clear by the mid-1980s that an answer to the AIDS epidemic would require massive commitments of money and time from the gay community. Lesbians who had been involved with Connexxus as funders, rather than clients, turned away from the women-only atmosphere of Connexxus to support the newly created AIDS organizations.

The immediacy and urgency of the AIDS crisis caused many women to reconsider the efficacy of separate space for lesbians. In 1986, Connexxus became directly involved with gay and lesbian community politics for the first time as an agency, working on the statewide campaign against Proposition 6, a libertarian initiative to prohibit gays and lesbians from teaching in California's public schools. This fight was viewed by many at Connexxus as a call to move beyond the boundaries of the lesbian community to create the coalitions necessary to stop the rising backlash against gay and lesbian visibility in California:

> It felt like a threat to our identity. It was also a call to wake up and work with our gay brothers. . . . It was the first time that we had been able to coalesce and come into action together . . . we really believed we could lose . . . you could feel the community rise up with the coalition.[39]

Because of the ties made during the "No on 6" Campaign and the severity of the AIDS epidemic, many organizers within the community determined that the need for Connexxus had dissipated. The younger women in line to take over Connexxus from the founders moved instead into positions of leadership within the new coalitions of gay men and lesbians created by the AIDS crisis. With this new urgency for collective action, the desire for the separate space that Connexxus represented became irrelevant.

Independent of the struggles over lesbian diversity and lesbian separatism, AIDS created a situation where lesbian space was no longer justifiable on its own terms. AIDS represented an unfathomable increase in the stakes for gay and lesbian visibility; the response to this new attack on gay and lesbian rights galvanized a generation of lesbians who had not been involved with community organizing before but responded to the needs created by AIDS. In light of the new wave of energy for cogender organizing, the priority for a place like Connexxus seemed less and less urgent. "It was like most of us had been awakened and we developed friendships and alliances with these men and we couldn't ignore AIDS anymore."[40]

Lesbians in Los Angeles, like those in San Francisco, New York, and other cities, joined the new direct-action groups—ACT UP and Queer Nation—despite their overwhelmingly male membership. One of the bases for the new cogender identity was the commonality of concerns between lesbians and gay men and the power of cogender organizing. New theorizing about the movement began to assume the participation of both lesbians and gay men, and agendas no longer focused on the specific needs and concerns of lesbians alone.

However, not all women were comfortable with this shift away from lesbian-focused organizing, and the disenchantment that many women had felt with the community at Lesbian Central became an issue once again. Carla Barboza, who admitted that she has not been directly involved with lesbian community organizing since the closing of Connexxus, voiced a common complaint: "We don't get support for anything but are expected to support wholeheartedly with our resources and energies and our emotions whatever happens to the men."[41]

The importance of Connexxus as a separate space remains, despite the tensions its closing created. Many of the lesbian activists today, including those involved in cogender organizations, entered the community through the rap groups at Connexxus. In a city where lesbians had long been invisible, Connexxus created a presence at a crucial moment in the community's development. For women who had worked in the background of the gay liberation movement, the women's movement, and other political struggles, Connexxus offered tangible evidence of their own strength as a lesbian collective and allowed them to work on their own issues, uninterrupted. Del Martinez, the woman most credited with the Connexxus vision, recalled the unimaginable power this institution represented for lesbians of her generation:

> I came from Chicago. We are talking about the city where we used to get raided all the time, and we used to jump out of the bar windows and run down the streets in fear for our lives. I remember the first dinner that Connexxus had, it was at the Biltmore Hotel—our first founders' dinner—and my friend Karen was a founder all the way from Chicago . . . so she came and we sat in this ballroom and I looked at her and she looked at me and I said, "Did you ever in your life growing up in Chicago believe that you were going to be hanging out with six hundred lesbians in a major hotel in a major city in this country?" And I am sixty years old and I have known I was gay since I was fourteen, so you know that I never dreamed in my whole life that this was going to happen.[42]

In response to the void created by Connexxus's closing and increasingly in the years since, the Gay and Lesbian Center has developed additional programs and aggressively targeted lesbians as clients and funders. Shortly after Connexxus's closing, the Center opened its Community Outreach and Education Project, developed with the help of the Connexxus board, the City of West Hollywood, and Torie Osborn, the first lesbian executive director at the Center. Although the Center rejected Connexxus's arguments for an autonomous women-only space and separate programming at the Center, the new education program ensured that lesbian programs were developed and nurtured. Julie Anderson, one of the early directors of the Center's program, expressed what has become the operating principle at the Center, for lesbians as well as other groups outside the mainstream of the gay movement:

> I believe in separate space for any group that has been oppressed. . . . The Center is cogender but when you go into a rap group that is lesbian only, it is very clear that it is a lesbian-only space.[43]

Depending on one's point of view, this shift away from an autonomous lesbian-identified space to lesbian space within a more integrated lesbian and gay movement is either the inevitable result of the community's efforts to integrate in the face of AIDS and the decimation of the movement's male leaders or yet another example of the internalized homophobia and misogyny in the movement more broadly. In any case, the new map of lesbian space includes highly fractured and transitory spaces. In 1994, responding to a health survey that revealed that the majority of lesbians never visited a health care provider, the Center opened the Audre Lorde Health Clinic, which provides basic gynecological services, HIV testing, and referrals to other lesbian service providers. However, despite this innovative program, and the fact that more than half of the Center staff and management are female, the perception remains strong in some sectors of the lesbian community that the Center is less dedicated to lesbian concerns.

Lesbian Activism in the 1990s

A few weeks before gay pride weekend in 1994, flyers began appearing in the usual places—telephone poles, in front of A Different Light Bookstore in West Hollywood, at the Center in Hollywood, and outside clubs and bars—calling for "Single and looking dykes, married dykes, riot girls, lipstick lesbians" to rally for the Lesbian Love March, scheduled for the Friday night before the weekend-long gay pride celebration. As scheduled, more than two hundred women marched from Doheny Park on the border of Beverly Hills and West Hollywood, down Santa Monica, through the throngs of gay partygoers cruising Boystown, to West Hollywood City Hall. This event, which has now become a yearly ritual and now renamed generically the dyke march, stands out in a city where gay politics has largely stepped back from the streets and into the semipublic spaces of bars and clubs, churches and temples, and gentrifying neighborhoods. Since the landmark protests against Governor Pete Wilson's veto of state job discrimination protection for gays and lesbians in 1994 (see Chapter 5), gays and lesbians have taken to the streets fewer than a dozen times, and, except for the 1997 protests after the killing of gay Wyoming college student Mathew Shepard, never with any real focus or depth.

A deeper look at the dynamics and spatial politics of this event reveals much about the constraints on public activism in a city where gay power and gay economics have been institutionalized. The roots of the dyke march lie only partly in Los Angeles. Organized by women already involved in Los Angeles's gay and lesbian activist politics, including organizations like ACT UP, Women's Action Coalition, and Queer Nation, the march was inspired by an intervention on the eve of the 1993 March on Washington. That protest, organized by a newly formed group, the Lesbian Avengers from New York City, with help from women's caucuses from ACT UP chapters around the country, aimed to find a place for women at an event dominated by mainstream gay activists. "Ignite the riot," the rallying cry for the Washington march, recalled an alternative history of the Stonewall Riots that held that lesbians, not drag queens, sparked the chain of events leading to the riots and the gay liberation movement. Sarah Schulman, one of its organizers, described the Washington march:

> That night we all gathered at DuPont Circle and the women kept coming and coming. We started marching (in true Avenger style—without a permit), and soon realized that the numbers were absolutely huge. Around 20,000 lesbians marched through Washington, D.C. that night—the largest lesbian event in the history of the world. By the time we turned down Pennsylvania Avenue, we completely ruled the street. The Avengers stopped in front of the White House to eat fire and then we moved on to the Washington monument. You could see the ecstasy in the eyes of the marchers, many of whom had come from small towns and oppressed communities all over the country. . . . It was one of the proudest moments of my life.[44]

After the march, back in Los Angeles, reverberations from the success of the renegade dyke march and the official march, which had permits from the city and the National Park Service, quickly faded away, with little shift in the tone of local gay politics. A dyke march in San Francisco that June (on the eve of their gay pride weekend) finally inspired a group of Angelenos to attempt a similarly confrontational and unsanctioned gathering.

From the beginning, however, organizers in Los Angeles recognized their geographic limitations and settled for a community-building event, rather than a confrontational issue-driven protest. As Mary Pickert, an Angeleno veteran of the Women's Action Coalition and other activist organizations, had not attended the Washington, DC, march but had heard about the "fire-eating, bare-breasted women" in Washington and San Francisco, she rationalized that "in San Francisco, you can get a thousand women out on the streets for anything."[45] Thus, the organizers in Los Angeles concentrated their efforts on celebration as a first stage in long-term organizing; the issues, they felt, would come later. To deflect attention from what might be seen as confrontational (or excessive) politics, organizers abandoned publicizing the event as a dyke march (which they felt would scare away many lesbians in Los Angeles), and called it the Lesbian Love March. As the flyer suggested—with its invitation to lesbians of all types—the march intended to celebrate the diversity of the Los Angeles lesbian community.

Despite attempts to reach out to the nonactivist sectors of the lesbian community, organizers found it difficult to overcome the preference for pleasure, rather than politics. Handing out flyers at the entrance to Girl Bar, a widely popular lesbian dance club in West Hollywood, Judy Sisneros and Mary Pickert encountered women resistant to, or generally disinterested in, the notion of a lesbian-only march. Most women, they felt, simply did not understand how marching in public could affect their already privileged lives. Rather than antagonism, the prevailing response seemed to be one of confusion and misapprehension. The owners of the Girl Bar, however, ordered the activists off club space for creating a disturbance (in part because the flyers women did take were then tossed on the dance floor). Organizers figured that because the march was scheduled for a Friday night—the biggest night of the week for the Girl Bar—the bar owners objected to the march because it would draw women away from spending money at the club.

Within the small lesbian activist community, organizers encountered resistance of another kind. These opponents felt that pandering to the "socialite" lesbians would compromise the spirit of the march. As the date approached, organizers reworked the program to reflect these conflicting interests and expectations. At one extreme, organizers hoped for "a huge street march of dyke activists . . . exposing lesbians as part of the gay community."[46] More moderate organizers hoped to use the march "to build community" for all lesbians including the "bi, queer friendly, sitting on the fence, queer for thirty years."[47] At the other end of the spectrum, some aimed only for a celebration—"like a party in your garage,"[48] or "a street party."[49] Organizers represented different stages of political involvement and experience, and, like the lesbians they were trying to attract, had vastly different reasons to walk down Santa Monica Boulevard on a Friday night. Mary Pickert, however, summed up the overarching desire of the group—to create and build a community from its roots in multiple attitudes and niches:

> Planning the march and being part of the march affirmed the idea that being a lesbian or a dyke is being part of a diverse community that we as members of the community do not always appreciate. In Los Angeles, in particular, it is not often that we, the gay and lesbian, or lesbian community come together unless it is for a political action. I think the dyke march works to alert us all to community and, hopefully, work to build appreciation for the community that is not always there.[50]

By creating this event collaboratively, with celebration as the common goal, the organizers of the Lesbian Love March simply followed the Los Angeles tradition of adapting national activism to a Los Angeles audience, by making an action a spectacle. The march aimed to publicize a community that did not view itself as one, not to show the power of a community that was already there. If the less-activist lesbians were temporarily politicized by the event, no one expected that they would become part of the movement. Instead, the march was seen as a way of using festivity (outside the commercialized space of the official parade) to energize women as a collective force.

For women who were new to activism, it is clear that the dyke march created a space for lesbians to push their idea of community a little further. Bunnie Meyer, a male-to-female transgender, walked her first dyke march in Los Angeles just six months before her reassignment surgery and became an organizer the next year. For her, the dyke march created an entry for outsiders into the lesbian community in Los Angeles:

> Working on the dyke march did push my feeling of self-empowerment. When you are taking the streets with all these other people proud enough and sometimes brave enough to be there, you catch a feeling of community and with that, power. Once you gain that feeling of being okay and being empowered, it cannot help but influence your daily life. [51]

Another first-time activist who had attended but not participated in street protests in the past felt that the sheer number of women (like herself) who used the march as part of their own coming-out process outweighed the arguments that the event was never radical enough: "I personally supported the vision of a politically oriented march, but it seemed obvious to me that simply getting the dykes out there as an alternative to the Christopher Street West 'parade' mentality was political enough. Although I have to admit I took such pleasure in making fake Los Angeles Police Department no-parking signs and wheat pasting huge dyke posters. I guess I was more radical than I thought."[52] Overall, even though more women were marching, there was not a corresponding growth in activism.

As a community-building spectacle, the Lesbian Love March attempted to provide something for everyone. After a two-mile march, women gathered in the parking lot behind West Hollywood City Hall for a rally that was much more like a party. Speeches were hampered by poor acoustics and lack of attention, although a band did keep women in the streets for a while longer—before most women drifted off to the Palms, West Hollywood's venerable lesbian bar across the street. Mary Pickert described the first march:

> Leaving the Lesbo Love Park after we assembled, and with the drummers and the banners, we took to the streets, while the police, bewildered, tried to figure out what this mass of women was going to do. . . . We actually created this march—and after all the work, the midnight wheat pastings, the talking and talking about the march to friends, the handing out of flyers all around town, the endless meetings—and now, it was all happening. And women did come, did participate, and were happy to be there.[53]

Although attendance at the dyke march increases every year and continues to operate as a freeform precursor to the highly regulated Christopher Street West parades, this display of an antiestablishment faction (critical of both gay and mainstream politics) is not representative of contemporary politics in Los Angeles. And even though the march has stayed in West Hollywood, organizers struggle each time with the inevitable debate over the appropriateness of this highly structured space for such a radical event. As with Connexxus, these discussions have always been resolved in favor of West Hollywood, although each year the organizers battle over moving it out of the city. As has always been the case with gay and lesbian organizing in Los Angeles, leaving West Hollywood rarely is easy. Some women advocated using the march to take over ostensibly straight spaces, such as a local mall, the Sunset Strip, or the trendy Melrose Avenue shopping street. Here, they felt the presence of five hundred lesbians would confront stereotypes. Others have pushed to move the march into Silverlake—a neighborhood long viewed as a cheaper, more radical, and ethnically diverse gay space. As with past street protest activities in Los Angeles, these discussions ultimately return to the same two limitations—the need to reach a very fragmented gay and lesbian population, and the struggle to be visible on the deserted, often-inhospitable streets of Los Angeles.

The greatest tension over the years, however, has been over the tendency toward institutionalizing the march, leading to fears that the event was being co-opted by less radical activists and traditional gay and lesbian organizations. Part of this is because the role of the event has never been resolved, nor has it been an occasion to clearly articulate an activist agenda for the lesbian community. In fact, admit the organizers, no one really listens to the speakers. Instead, like the Christopher Street West festival it was intended to counteract, the dyke march is itself becoming institutionalized as a festival without political content. The event and after-party are still free (in contrast to the fifteen dollar entry fee for the gay pride festival) and still unattached to any organization (although the Center and a number of local clubs have offered to sponsor the event). Organizers continue to assert that independence from other events and organizations is critical. Their resistance is unusual in a city where Absolut vodka, Coors, and other major corporations sponsor most events. Dyke march organizers raise funds for the march by asking for donations, asking clubs to sponsor fundraising parties, and (one year) holding bake sales around the city, and they have never aimed for nonprofit status.

Most importantly, perhaps, the dyke marchers have maintained a resolutely antiregulation stance and have refused each year to apply for a city permit. Although they march in West Hollywood to create a crowd, challenge stereotypes about who occupies space in West Hollywood, and to be part of the community, they maintain an uneasy standoff relationship with the city government. This stems more from a commitment to independence rather than recklessness. Like other activists—from ACT UP to the AB101 demonstrators—they march in West Hollywood because they must, but in a way that continues to challenge the city's sense of itself:

> From my point of view, the most significant thing is the fact that each year the city and/or some group wants to control the dyke march and each year the answer is the same: We are lesbians here to take the streets and we neither ask for nor want your permission. The city of West Hollywood has dangled cash and other enticements. Should West Hollywood want to provide, with no strings attached, an after-march party site for the convenience of the marchers and reap the benefits of noise control, the committee has no problems with that. Should West Hollywood want to provide port-a-potties or other amenities that a city could provide, the committee has no problems with that. As soon as there is a string attached, there is no deal and no interest in dealing.[54]

Perhaps because of the tenuous relationship with the City of West Hollywood, the growing power and continuing anti-establishment stance of the dyke march is the clearest descendent of the early Gay Liberation Front (GLF) activism, with the sophistication of the ACT UP organization. Dyke marchers have found a way to use the space of West Hollywood as transitional and temporary. Like the map of gay and lesbian Los Angeles more generally, the dyke march adapts to the needs of the changing community. Without established or universally recognized public spaces for gathering and protest, each successive wave of gay and lesbian activists has remapped the city for itself, adjusting and often initiating changes in the geography of the gay and lesbian city. At the same time, many of the limitations of both West Hollywood and the rest of Los Angeles continue to suppress the power of the movement—that across the barriers of space, it is still difficult to create a truly diverse movement. The dyke marchers continually questioned their ability to attract a diverse population. Outreach to universities, clubs, and other gay and lesbian organizations have through the years failed to build a multiethnic coalition of activist lesbians, despite the committee leadership of a number of lesbians of color.

The persistence of the dyke march does not, however, mark a new era in street activism. Although this event challenges the commercialized and corporatized nature of the Christopher Street West pride events, its more enduring lesson is the possibility of activism that invites participation in the public space of Los Angeles without a clearly articulated activist agenda. When community leaders (such as the director of the Gay and Lesbian Center) speak at a small rally before the march, they emphasize pride and success, rather than problems or conflicts within the community. The dyke marches, in both theory and practice, celebrate the experience of being out in public when the city's geography confines any public presence. These displays of community strength and sexual identity underscore the radical nature of occupying public space in Los Angeles. And it is this kind of radicalism, resulting more in personal transformation than collective power, that continues to underlie the nature of gay and lesbian interventions in this city. As Mary Pickert eloquently explained, the process of place claiming for gays and lesbians in Los Angeles starts with the simple (yet often-unattainable) premise that personal growth and empowerment, rather than societal change, matter most:

> Having done different kinds of actions over the years, I have always wanted to get people involved, and I hoped that the dyke march would empower other people. Los Angeles is an apolitical town, but I sense that if people could just get out there and look around, and move from you and I to we; maybe, despite our differences as queers we could find that we share certain things.[55]

5 Out of the Bars and into the Streets

Direct Action from Liberation to Transformation

During the 1980s, street protest became a defining feature of the gay and lesbian movement in Los Angeles and across the country. Beginning with the dramatic emergence of the AIDS Coalition to Unleash Power (ACT UP) in New York City and continuing with the formation of Queer Nation, Women's Health Action Mobilization, Women's Action Coalition, and the Lesbian Avengers, direct-action groups organized and inspired a new generation of gay and lesbian activists. Energized by massive protests criticizing government inaction on AIDS issues, activists developed new street-based tactics, culminating, in the mid-1990s, in a series of connected efforts demanding "radical visibility." Images from these aggressive public protests flooded mainstream media newscasts and became the subject of videos shown on—or banned from—public television. As part of the increasing public debate about gay rights these portrayals revealed a bold new public personae of the gay and lesbian rights movement. In response, the far right merged footage from these demonstrations with that from gay pride parades in highly sophisticated campaigns designed to carry its message of intolerance and public persecution. In short, the direct-action movement, as the newest incarnation of the gay and lesbian movement in America, changed the popular images of gay power and gay community

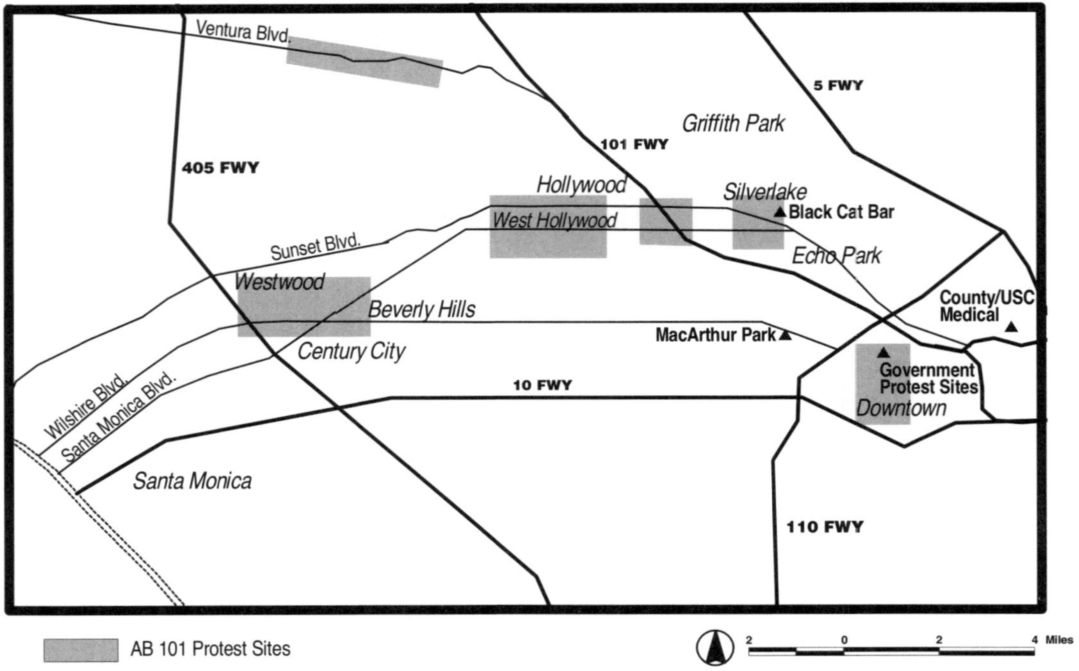

Map 5. Direct Action Sites

in profound ways. These actions have, in turn, altered the geography of gay and lesbian activism—especially as these protests extended out into spaces from which they had been or felt excluded.

Street protest has been a feature of the movement since the gay liberation era of the early 1970s. Then, as now, public interventions are seen as the most expedient and strategic way to gain visibility for a movement that aimed to change public perception about who gays and lesbians are, where they live, and what they want and need.

Using the streets transforms the notion of public space from one of uncritical openness and freedom, moving beyond what Iris Young has called the "ideal of impartiality," to "a zone of critical pedagogy."[1] The streets become a place for education, confrontation, and celebration of sexual difference. As Lauren Berlant and Elizabeth Freeman argue in their analysis of Queer Nation tactics in Chicago, street protest—particularly as it has evolved in the late 1980s—takes visibility to a new, more purposeful level and reworks our understandings of public space and its uses:

> Queer Nation takes from the AIDS Coalition to Unleash Power this complex understanding of political space as fundamental to its insistence on making all public spheres truly safe for all of the persons who occupy them, not just in psychic loyalty but also in everyday and embodied existence. To be safe in the national sense means not just safe from bashing, not just safe from discrimination, but safe for demonstration, in the mode of patriotic ritual, which always involves a deployment of affect, knowledge, ritual, and crucially, a kind of banality, ordinariness, popularity.[2]

As important as these new modes of protest and organizing have been in other major cities, the movement in Los Angeles has been less visibly a part of this transformation. Fewer major protests have been staged in Los Angeles, and fewer still have received the media attention given to protest in these other cities.

The reasons for these differences cannot be explained simply by either social or political conditions. The motivations for street protest elsewhere are the same: AIDS care and treatment, discrimination and harassment, or violence, for example. But the gay and lesbian community in Los Angeles has excelled in other forms of community organizing and groundbreaking political achievements. The limited use of street tactics in Los Angeles stems less from social or political inaction or apathy (as has been argued more commonly) than from other, site-specific obstacles.

Activists who have attempted place claiming through street protest are at the mercy of Los Angeles's sprawling and car-dependent geography, including the scattered gay and lesbian neighborhoods, and the obstacles created by demographic and economic stratification. Occasionally, protesters have defied these hurdles and literally taken back the streets, but the perception that the geography of Los Angeles cannot be negotiated has contributed to a reticence toward street protest and mass demonstration.

Los Angeles is not a Chicago or a Selma, cities forever associated with a single momentous event that shaped a social or political movement's tactics for subsequent activists. In 1991, however, as AIDS protests began to wane in Los Angeles, the gay and lesbian community erupted in a series of spontaneous protests sustained largely by nonactivists. This manifestation of gay and lesbian anger surpassed even the most vocal years of ACT UP protests. For two weeks, thousands of gays and lesbians took to the streets night after night to voice their opposition to a veto by the Republican governor of California, Pete Wilson, of Assembly Bill 101 (AB101), which would have extended job discrimination protection to gays and lesbians.

To understand the local reactions to AB101 veto is to glimpse the complexity of gay and lesbian politics, particularly the constant struggles to accommodate the diversity of the movement and the recurrent and unresolved debate pitting assimilationist strategies against more radical critiques. The

AB101 protests also can help us understand the geographies of such protests, especially when we examine them in the historical context of the two most sustained periods of activism in gay and lesbian Los Angeles: the Gay Liberation Front (GLF) of the early 1970s and ACT UP two decades later.

In late September 1991, Governor Wilson vetoed a civil rights bill that among other things would have protected gays and lesbians from employment discrimination at private workplaces. By legal standards, the law merely restricted only the most blatant forms of antigay job discrimination, and Governor Wilson and others argued that state Labor Code already protected gays, albeit not explicitly. AB101 exempted small businesses and churches, while state and local ordinances already covered most gay and lesbian employees in the public sector. The importance of the veto, however, was read largely symbolically and struck chords with thousands of gays and lesbians who, within hours of the announcement, took to the streets in West Hollywood:

> As the marching went into a week, then two, you could feel the world stretching, making room for this new thing we were bringing into being in Los Angeles, the city that trade unionists call "the scab hole" of the West; the city that San Francisco lesbian and gay activists used to dismiss as being "good for fund-raising, but not much else"; the city where nobody looks at anybody else outside their own clearly demarcated social turf. No one walks in Los Angeles. And no social movement could hold Los Angeles' streets for two solid weeks.[3]

The AB101 marches went almost entirely uncovered by local media despite the certainly newsworthy significance of as many as twenty thousand people taking to the streets on a nightly basis in traffic-stopping protest. Within the gay community, however, these marches have taken on a defining role, signifying for many the moment that Los Angeles's gay and lesbian community took ownership of the national movement and, as one article put it, moved "the center west."[4]

Nearly the entire city's established gay and lesbian leadership (including a major contingent from ACT UP) were in Washington, DC, attending a conference (and getting arrested for their own street protests) when Governor Wilson announced his veto. California activists in Washington immediately turned to San Francisco to gauge the state's reaction, fully expecting an immediate and public response. Activists assumed, perhaps naturally, that Los Angeles would remain silent. Contrary to these predictions and past experience, however, thousands of women and men who had not previously attended an ACT UP meeting, marched for anything, or even written letters to their assembly representatives supporting AB101 took to the streets. This continued presence created street visibility that could not be ignored by the national movement, even as the local media looked the other way:

> Images painted a picture of a city transformed. The California flag was torched; so was Wilson's effigy. Someone smashed a door at the Ronald Reagan State Office Building; John Heilman, a gay West Hollywood city councilman, alerted the sheriff that he was marching and not to disturb him; 15,000 gays and lesbians stopped traffic and business on city streets for weeks. . . . In short, a new community—more militant and diverse than anyone could have envisioned just two months ago—had emerged overnight.[5]

For the first time in recent Los Angeles history, and for the first time in gay and lesbian movement history, the streets of Los Angeles were the sites of sustained, often-anarchic protests, overwhelming neighborhoods from the Westside into downtown. In keeping with their spontaneous nature, untrained activists led the marches without set routes, coherent slogans, or media soundbites. In direct contrast to the previous five years of ACT UP organizing in Los Angeles, New York, San Francisco, and dozens of smaller cities, the two weeks of AB101 protests were marked by an absence of the kind of militantly democratic process that had created the highly successful actions in other cities. In addition, the focus of the protests was not a specific site or organization. Whereas ACT UP became famous for its theatrical protests at the Food and Drug Administration in Washington, DC, on the trading floors of Wall Street, or St. Patrick's Cathedral, the AB101 protests were diffuse, decentralized, and somewhat rambling. With only a loose coalition of organizations coordinating street efforts, the protests continued without advance planning or strategy sessions. Instead, people simply gathered on Santa Monica Boulevard in West Hollywood, for example, assembled at an intersection on the main strip after work, and headed off to destinations all over the city.

More than anything else, the AB101 protests defined new possibilities for gay and lesbian activism in Los Angeles. For the first time in decades, gays and lesbians took to the streets for common purposes, moving outside the boundary of the West Hollywood Boystown to defy the spatial logic of a city that had proved remarkably resistant to direct action visibility. Most nights, marches followed Santa Monica Boulevard out of West Hollywood to Beverly Hills and Century City, or east to Silverlake and Echo Park, often covering from five to ten miles. On other nights, groups of marchers met at locations outside West Hollywood: Ventura Boulevard in the Valley, Wilshire Boulevard in Westwood, or at government office buildings downtown. Marchers were motivated by the call to secure the governor's attention and show politicians across the state that gays and lesbians would not tolerate discrimination. Since these motives were not local, the targets were eclectic, as marchers assembled anywhere they felt a crowd might be gathered: the Hollywood Bowl, a Hollywood hotel where Jerry Falwell was staying, and the Los Angeles County Museum of Art. Many times, most of the participants had little or no idea where they were heading, and simply marched for the solidarity of being with so many other gays and lesbians in public. The marchers challenged each other and the city to think about the injustice that would drive thousands of people to march through streets, disrupting traffic, when most of them had never even tried strolling down the sidewalks. The ubiquitous chant—"Whose Streets, Our Fucking Streets"—like the marches themselves, suggests the utterly place-claiming nature of the actions:

> Like all good chants, it goes to the heart of the issues: it's not AB101, but basic civil rights and the fact that many middle-class gays and lesbians now realize that they have none. Before they can express their love in public, they must claim the streets as their own.[6]

For lesbians, people of color, the HIV-affected, and other disabled marchers, the geography of the protests often took on additional significance. People of color in Los Angeles spoke of being acutely aware of the dangers associated with walking through unfamiliar territory, especially when that trespass could be read as an aggressive confrontation (which, for some, a gay march may well be). Similarly, women warily walked through unfamiliar neighborhoods, and lesbians suffered a double vulnerability. For many HIV-positive marchers, the benefits of even a two-mile march had to be weighed against potential health costs. AB101 route leaders tried at times to acknowledge these different senses of geographic comfort. Often, however, the lack of centralized planning meant that these concerns were overlooked.

One of the most contentious marches (in this regard) targeted Silverlake, a historically Latino barrio that is also known as the second major concentration of gay men in Los Angeles. In the late 1980s, Silverlake had been the site of a spate of violent gay bashings and clashes between local youth and older gay residents. When the AB101 marchers gravitated toward Silverlake (in part to demonstrate the diversity of the protesting crowds), Joel Barraquiel Tan, a Filipino AIDS activist and writer, recalled that many people of color were dismayed by the confused motives that brought the protests to this area of the city:

> The Silverlake march made me nervous: We approached it with some fear. It was like, why did they decide to come to Silverlake, because I know the people who are going to be marching there and they do not live in Silverlake? . . . They are not going to understand; they are going to get shot at. . . . I was ambivalent about it, but I also wanted to be there to watch what went on so that there wasn't any blatant disrespect. I felt really protective of it; I felt ownership of that particular community.[7]

The mixed emotions Tan recalled are emblematic of the debates within the community as a whole as the marches stretched into their second week. Long-time activists had believed that the West Hollywood "boys" would never leave the gyms and get involved, but some did. Activists in the ethnic committees had long argued that the movement was geographically isolated from communities of color, but the marches went to Hollywood, Silverlake, and downtown. Republican professionals who had been closeted at work and voted for Pete Wilson came out publicly for the first time, denouncing the governor and their own party as a traitor. Although these transformations were welcome, activists soon realized that this new energy was not easily harnessed.

In the wake of the AB101 veto and as a response to the sudden emergence of new constituencies on the streets, many activists formed new organizations and coalitions. One of the most prominent of these, League America, attracted professional, often-closeted, lesbians and gays who wanted to respond to the rising backlash against the movement in their own way—through negotiation and behind-the-scenes pressure. As one founding member explained:

> There are many lesbian and gays who don't see themselves as militant but are angry at their second-class treatment. . . . The majority of lesbians and gays are dealing with the closet in some form in their lives, and League America is safe for them.[8]

At the other end of the political spectrum, Colors United Action Coalition was founded by African Americans, Latinos/as, and Asian Pacific Islanders who felt ignored by the movement leaders during the AB101 protests. Demanding participation and representation at event after event in the wake of the veto, Colors United demanded immediate access and respect for all people of color within the gay and lesbian movement. Tan, the organizer who quickly became the spokesperson for the group, described Colors United as a way of building strength within and between ethnic communities so that people of color could contribute effectively and on their own terms:

> The one thing I could see that we were really trying to do was to create safe space. I always saw us as a great experiment by using what we saw made sense for folks who were in the group. . . . We were all so homeless, because people who have latitude are extremely privileged in that they can speak different dialects and they can recognize different customs, but most of the time they are very alienated.[9]

Within a movement that used visibility to counter discrimination, the concern for respecting privacy and personal space underscored the protests for all activists, but especially for gays and lesbians of color. According to Tan, for many gays and lesbians of color in Los Angeles the over-arching emphasis in the AB101 discussions on sexuality regardless of race, gender, and class recalled pre-AIDS activism in which people of color were virtually invisible. In a community forum soon after the first wave of the AB101 marches, Colors United presented an alternative to the constant search for visibility within the largely white spaces of the city that focused on organizing on more local and personal "turf":

> With our reclaimed power, we are empowering our own home communities and organizations to join in the efforts to enlighten, expand and educate the gay and lesbian community, society, and the world collective at large. With our community organizing and bar outreach we seek to and have embraced communities that have been marginalized and neglected. Communities such as

> Monterey Park, East Los Angeles, and South Central Los Angeles. . . . Each outreach is an opportunity to learn, enjoy and grow, not a "colonial expedition" or a "mission." Because we have been colonized and ghettoized in the past, these are neither our motives nor our methods. We seek to find our place in the ecology rather than disturb it.[10]

Colors United Action Coalition called on mainstream gay organizations to move beyond street marches that potentially suppressed dialogue in favor of spontaneity. Focusing instead on the divisions within the movement as acted out on the streets, Colors United sought to engage the debate about civil rights on a broader basis. For them, activism on the streets was a tactic for privileged gays and lesbians who generally already had access to the streets. For gays and lesbians in Los Angeles without such easy access, other strategies became more important. One of the lasting legacies of Colors United, for participants, was simply the creation of "a family of people who do for each other, and if we ever need to come together again, I will guarantee you, we will."[11]

Very quickly, the target moved past the specifics of job discrimination protection to the problems made visible by the marches themselves: police harassment and entrapment, the invisibility of what turned out to be a very large and powerful community, and the diversity of agendas and strategies. AIDS activists worked at harnessing the energy created by the veto for their own struggles, while other activists, like Colors United, concentrated on the larger structural issues dividing the community. Because the legislation was extremely weak and of dubious importance to a broader struggle for gay and lesbian civil rights and because the implications of the AB101 veto were largely symbolic, it was particularly difficult for the new organizations to agree on an activist agenda. For Colors United, better civil rights legislation was never on their agenda. As for League America, employment discrimination was of some concern, although their demands were broader. In fact, the groups tended to agree that the legislation was not the issue. Instead, dialogue between the groups focused on the meaning and failure of assimilationist strategies by gays and lesbians from all communities. The very common act of being in the streets together created a basis for the dialogue Colors United desired:

> Such cooperation within the gay community suggests that the "Queer vs. Assimilationist" cold war may be dissipating. "The people who most wanted to assimilate were told they couldn't by the veto," says Queer Nation's Jenna White. "And now they may no longer care to."[12]

Leaders felt that the coalitions forged between those on the streets and those in corporate boardrooms and electoral politics elevated both gay and lesbian politics to a more establishment role and the Los Angeles movement to one of national importance. Community institutions like the Gay and Lesbian Community Services Center (the Center) and neighborhoods like West Hollywood gained a new significance as people who rarely, if ever, ventured into these public spaces began to recognize their significance. Local stores created community bulletin boards, and the Center's hot line was flooded with calls. Gay and lesbian street culture did emerge and flourish briefly, in part because the situation was changing so rapidly that the streets of West Hollywood were the only place you could get accurate, up-to-the-minute information.

Los Angeles since AB101

Los Angeles activists capitalized on the momentum generated by the governor's veto of AB101 for a short time after the marches, but by the time a revised workplace discrimination bill was signed a year later, the landscape had simmered down again, and the belated victory attracted little attention. This burst of energy followed by a long stretch of relative quietude mirrors the experience of the last twenty-five years. Political maturation and national coordination has diminished the power and presence of take-to-the-streets-style activism across the country, and in Los Angeles, geography as well as politics and ideology has driven direct-action strategies underground. The most lasting effect of the revitalization of this movement has been the continued presence of Los Angeles activists on the national scene as organizers, politicians, and donors to the large public policy organizations, including National Gay and Lesbian Task Force and Human Rights Campaign.

Understanding the significance of the AB101 protests, not as an isolated incident but part of a longer tradition, requires looking back to ACT UP and the earliest days of gay liberation. The GLF and ACT UP, both transplants from New York (GLF in the 1970s and ACT UP in the 1980s), were certainly overshadowed by their counterparts in New York and San Francisco, but they were also, inevitably, following a course altered by context.

Los Angeles's importance as a generator of gay and lesbian street protest began in the mid-1950s with the founding of the Mattachine Society. As mentioned in Chapter 1, at the end of November in 1950, Harry Hay, along with friends Bob Hull, Chuck Rowland, Dale Jennings, and a man known only as R, met at Hay's house in Silverlake to discuss creating a gathering of gay men with similar interests and the possibility of a homosexual rights organization. This group of acquaintances became the core of the Mattachine Society, the first national organization of gay men or lesbians.

The goals of the Mattachine were deceptively simple:

> To develop in its members a strong group consciousness free of the negative attitudes that gay men and women typically internalized. As the first homophile organization, the goal was not liberation, or even assimilation, but acceptance by mainstream society. They believed in a fundamental difference between homosexuals and the heterosexual majority, and affirmed the uniqueness of gay identity, projected a vision of a homosexual

> culture with its own positive values, and attempted to transform the shame of being gay into a pride in belonging to a minority with its own contribution to the human community.[13]

The relationship between the Mattachine and the geography of Los Angeles is subtle. The Mattachine held no protest marches or demonstrations, and with the exception of one highly publicized trial against the entrapment of a Mattachine member, did not register in the public eye. Meetings took place in members' homes, usually in Silverlake, and their locations were a closely guarded secret. The place-claiming strategies of the Mattachine, if they existed at all, were primarily personal—as the group supported each member to recognize, accept, and carefully act on sexual desires. As a tangent, Silverlake, and the adjacent neighborhood of Echo Park, long known as the Red Hills (because of the large numbers of Communist Party members and other leftists living there), began attracting other gay men. These mainly white and middle-class men became the pioneers in the gradual transformation of the area into a gay enclave.

The Mattachine's first public action in Los Angeles was a legal challenge to police entrapment. Dale Jennings was arrested in February 1952 and charged with "lewd and dissolute behavior." Jennings claimed that he had been accosted by police, a standard practice of the Los Angeles Police Department (LAPD). After a meeting of the Mattachine, the members decided to fight the charges and formed the Citizens Committee to Outlaw Police Entrapment and quickly initiated a media campaign. When this elicited no response, they organized an underground network to publicize the trial among the gay community by distributing leaflets in bars and among gay shop owners in West Hollywood. The charges eventually were dropped after the jury deliberating Jennings's case deadlocked.[14]

Following the momentum of the Mattachine's steady attack against police harassment, a nonassimilationist gay community emerged to bridge the tactics and goals of the waning homophile (the term widely used in the 1950s and 1960s by both gay and lesbian activists) movement and the energy of the impending liberation movement. Although later considered conformist and assimilationist by liberation activists, the homophile organizations were the first to argue for the rights of homosexuals as an oppressed minority.

The most interesting omission in the national consciousness about Los Angeles's role in gay and lesbian history is the protest at the Black Cat in 1967, eighteen months before the liberation movement was "born" at the Stonewall Riots. The Black Cat, located at 1909 Sunset Boulevard in Silverlake, has been the site of a gay bar periodically since the 1940s. On New Year's Eve 1967, the LAPD raided the bar, arrested most of the patrons, and injured a number of those arrested. The usual response of homophile activists had simply been to ensure that arrests were done properly and that those arrested received a fair trial without settling for lesser and still damaging charges. However, after the Black Cat arrests, younger gays energized by the student protest movements chose to use the incident for change, rather than accommodation. In concert with the *Los Angeles Free Press,* which had been organizing against police harassment across the city, more than two hundred gay activists picketed the Black Cat on 11 February 1986. In hopes of appeasing the police, none of the picket signs carried the word "gay" or "homosexual." The protest was considered largely successful (because it was not broken up by police), even though the other protests the *Free Press* hoped to stage in Venice, the largely African American neighborhood of Watts, and the predominantly Latino section neighborhood of Pacoima never materialized. An article in the homophile magazine *Tangents* declared that this was the beginning of a new era in gay culture in the city: "All over the city, homosexuals are determined that they will no longer 'cop out' to the lesser charge if they are arrested. And when someone else is arrested, they will come forward as witnesses, even though police may bring pressure on their employers."[15]

Changes, however, did not come quickly, and the homophile movement's leaders continued to dominate the community's institutions. The Stonewall Riots in June 1969, of course, changed this rather stagnant movement in a matter of days. What began as a routine police raid at the Stonewall Inn, a gay bar on Christopher Street in New York's Greenwich Village became the turning point for gay and lesbian civil rights. Like so many other gay and lesbian bars around the country, it operated without a liquor license and had reputed connections to organized crime. When the police raided the bar, patrons, including Black and Puerto Rican drag queens, gathered on the street and jeered the police. Movement historian John D'Emilio described the scene on the streets the following night:

> By the following night, graffiti calling for "Gay Power" had appeared along Christopher Street. Knots of young gays—effeminate, according to most reports—gathered on street corners, angry and restless. Someone heaved a sack of wet garbage through the window of a patrol car. On nearby Waverly Place, a concrete block landed on the hood of another police car that was quickly surrounded by dozens of men, pounding on its doors and dancing on its hood. Helmeted officers from the tactical patrol force arrived on the scene and dispersed with swinging clubs an impromptu chorus line of gay men in the middle of a full kick. . . . For the next few hours, trash fires blazed, bottles and stones flew through the air, and cries of "Gay Power!" rang in the streets as the police, numbering over 400, did battle with a crowd estimated at more than 2,000.[16]

Within days, the GLF emerged from this battle. The GLF, who saw itself as part of the New Left, added its demand for gay rights to the political agenda being pursued by the student and youth movements across America. To affirm their connection and affinity with these other causes (in which most GLF activists had been involved), the GLF participated in the landmark events of the early 1970s. Activists went to Washington as part of the November 1969 moratorium, participated in the Congress to Unite Women in the same month, ran workshops at the National Student Association, and spoke at rallies for the imprisoned Black Panther leaders. In short, they were present at nearly every other major student event in 1969 and 1970. The philosophy of the liberation movement, as reprinted in the New Left newspaper *The Rat,* reflected a new sense of urgency, which, for the first time, tied the oppression of homosexuals to that of others involved in struggles for human and civil rights:

> We are a revolutionary group of men and women formed with the realization that complete sexual liberation for all people cannot come about unless existing social institutions are abolished. We reject society's attempt to impose sexual roles and simplistic myths. We are going to be who we are. At the same time, we are creating new forms and relations, that is, relations based upon brotherhood, cooperation, human love, and uninhibited sexuality. [B]abylon has forced us to commit ourselves to one thing—revolution![17]

The GLF quickly spread to Los Angeles. Led by a new generation of gay political activists, most GLF members had not joined the Mattachine but were either affiliated with the broader homophile movement or had not yet been involved in the gay movement. Morris Kight, a Los Angeles transplant long involved in antiwar politics in the city, came to the GLF with political capital and skills earned in other social justice movements. In keeping with the liberation movement's commitment to involvement in issues other than those of the gay community alone, the Los Angeles GLF "declared 'its unity with and support for all oppressed minorities to fight for their freedom' and expressed its intention 'to build a new, free and loving Gay counter-culture.' "[18]

In June 1970, the GLF burst onto the city's consciousness with a march down Hollywood Boulevard to commemorate the first anniversary of the Stonewall Riots. Morris Kight recalled that the march was originally conceived as twenty-five simultaneous actions located at strategic "symbols of oppression, repression, and exploitation," including churches, schools, synagogues, police stations, recruiting stations, and employment agencies. After these separate actions activists would then meet up to form a massive march through the city's central neighborhoods. Although this multipronged strategy was intended as a way of redrawing the boundaries of the gay and lesbian community, in effect making gays and lesbians visible across the city, Kight and other GLF organizers eventually decided on a single march down Hollywood Boulevard for, as he said, obvious reasons:

> It's a world-famous street and we wanted to be where the people were, where the media were, where the action was. Moreover, in those days, it was a little bit of a gay community—it isn't so much now . . . but at that time it was—and so that's how we used Hollywood Boulevard.[19]

Los Angeles Free Press, who published the only estimate of the crowd, set the number of marchers at twelve hundred with approximately thirty thousand onlookers.[20] This Christopher Street West parade (named in honor of the Stonewall riots) was similar to the AB101 marches because it was entirely free form, with no more than half a dozen organizations represented and the vast majority of participants marching unaffiliated. Described in the *Free Press* as "a political Mardi Gras,"[21] the spectacle itself created the political message, independent of any banners, leaflets, or chants. As the *Free Press* reported,

> In a burst of inspired magnificence, Hollywood's gay community proved once and for all that they are free. . . . At its zenith, "Christopher Street West" was one of the highest points of achievement of freedom-loving people in the history of the world. Participants and observers alike shed tears of joy. . . . Carried along in a sea of love and emotion, the 1,200 gays sang, danced, marched, rode in floats and encouraged their brothers and sisters to stop observing from the sidelines and to join in the celebration.[22]

In an eerie foretelling of the struggles later gay and lesbian activists in Los Angeles would wage against charges of political apathy, Kight recalled that within hours of the parade, as the next year's events were being imagined, activists argued that the event had not been "radical enough," and that commercialism had already begun to taint the movement. In a statement published in the *Los Angeles Free Press*'s 1970 "Gay Liberation Supplement," Kight responded:

> And as might be expected, we are hearing the first loud squawks that it will not be radical enough. As for its idea content, all will depend on the sponsors and participants. Already the policy has been set down that it will be non-exclusionary, all ideas will be welcome, and all who wish to march can do so. As for radical content, the sky's the limit, but that Gays proudly announced their Gayness and proudly paraded it in the streets was considered by many as the most radical goddamned idea they'd ever had.[23]

Unlike the larger and better-organized GLF factions in Berkeley and New York, the Los Angeles chapter never truly connected to the network of student-led protest movements across the country. Although the Berkeley GLF was founded by activists who had been part of the Free Speech Movement, the Los Angeles GLF had few allies in the city. For the most part, the student protest movements in Los Angeles were sporadic and overshadowed by the more sustained activities in the Bay Area.[24] Instead, the Los Angeles liberation movement concentrated on social events and outreach efforts. At its zenith, the GLF sponsored a series of "gay-ins," three of which were held in Griffith Park (Los Angeles's largest park, nestled in the Hollywood Hills) in 1970 and 1971. As a site for a public coming out of the gay community, Griffith Park was seen as a necessary pilgrimage site for the movement's integration into the Los Angeles landscape. According to Kight,

> We chose the merry-go-round (in Griffith Park) because that was a prominent section and easy to find—the road leading up from Los Feliz Boulevard led straight to it and there were places to

> park up near there. You could see up through the whole area—the merry-go-round here and the mountains there. It seemed like a perfect place and it was stunningly liberationist.[25]

The GLF intended these festivals as challenges to the police policy that effectively banned any public gathering of gays and lesbians. Like the hippie love-ins and similar gatherings of the early 1970s, these free festivals were intended to change the public perception of gays, lesbians, and (moving beyond the Mattachine) bisexuals, and to encourage tolerance and acceptance of alternative sexualities and difference in general. The usual speeches and rallies were accompanied by music and dancing. In addition, professionals and activists offered free legal advice and other services designed to help gays and lesbians come out at work and home and fight against common forms of discrimination such as firing, eviction, or improper treatment by doctors and psychiatrists. As precursors to the festival atmosphere of the later gay pride parades, the gay-ins opened up the boundaries of the few limited gay commercial areas in West Hollywood, Silverlake, and near downtown and encouraged gays, lesbians, and bisexuals to gather in public places considered hostile. Although Griffith Park had long been a cruising area after dark for gay men, the idea of celebrating in the middle of the day with one's gay and lesbian friends exploded misconceptions (both internal and external to the community) about gay culture.

As with all GLF events, the LAPD targeted and harassed the Griffith Park gay-ins. Morris Kight, a primary organizer of these events, described an encounter with the police during the third and final gay-in. Emphasizing that police harassment inevitably accompanied gay and lesbian gatherings, in both public and private places, Kight told the story with an undissipated contempt for the police and a fair amount of glee over the gay community's response and the police's ignominious defeat:

> The [third gay-in was] at the merry-go-round and the police really came to that one, really seriously—black and white

> uniforms and riot masks and their batons held at riot gear. They lined up on the hill near the ranger station to march down. I went up to see them and said, "If you want to cause a riot and hurt a lot of people including yourselves, that's exactly what you are going to get because the crowd is angry. The crowd is having fun, nobody is violent, nobody is armed, nobody wishes to do any physical harm, they want to have fun, and your presence is offensive. Why don't we agree that you will leave, I will go away and go back down and associate with the people, and you will quietly withdraw. Because if you don't you will have a violent riot here today." They withdrew within twenty minutes.[26]

Kight's response to the police and his characterization of the gay-in as a harmless gathering of friends epitomizes the place-claiming strategies of the liberation movement in Los Angeles. Drawing equally (if unconsciously) from both situationist politics and hippie celebration, their actions temporarily appropriated areas of the city. Coordinated groups of gays and lesbians demonstrated to police and the city that they posed no threat to the safety or morality of the larger community. Ultimately, this strategy aimed at normalizing the presence of gays and lesbians—individually as well as collectively—in places where gays and lesbians previously had been invisible.

In addition to the gay-ins and the Christopher Street West parades, the GLF also engaged in a number of targeted actions, or "zaps," which called attention to police abuse, employment discrimination, and other issues of legality. Reflecting the international focus of the GLF—born, in part, out of the desire of the GLF activists to tie the gay rights struggle to other revolutionary race-, class-, and gender-based struggles around the world—many of their actions targeted international discrimination against gays and lesbians, including protests at the French and Spanish consulates. Like the gay-ins, these actions attempted to create visibility in a political context, demanding the inclusion of gays and lesbians in making decisions that affected the conduct of their lives and the boundaries of their legal and illegal presence.

Women's involvement in the liberation movement was, like their involvement with the development of the Gay Services Center, fraught with debate and tension. The Lesbian Feminists (who organized under that name) did participate in some of the early GLF actions (including the parade and the gay-ins) but left the organization as lesbians slowly emerged as a more autonomous group. Separate from the GLF or the wider gay community, the Lesbian Feminists coordinated a dozen or so GLF-style zaps, including a memorable First National Lesbian Kiss-In at the Los Angeles County Museum of Art, on Los Angeles's centrally located Miracle Mile.[27]

One of the most surprising aspects of this era of activism was the extent to which the targets were defined by the mundane rather than the symbolic. Activists considered accessibility, safety, and convenience as much if not more than discussions of politics, ideology, and visibility. Morris Kight, considered by many the "architect" of the liberation movement in Los Angeles, recalled the importance of balancing the practical with the political. Many of the concerns on his list seem, if not exclusive to Los Angeles, certainly more pressing and relevant to the local activists:

> I tried to select [targets] from a variety of things. The indicia I used were: Would it be a recognizable place? Would people know where it was? Would it be near bus transportation (because a number of gay folk are below the poverty level)? Was parking easy enough? Was it a well-known address? What would be the atmosphere there? We used, for example, De Longpre Park for an enormous number of demonstrations and for perfectly rational reasons. So I tried to select easily recognizable addresses with ease of public access—one where parking was easy and where there would be some affinity.[28]

Finally, the GLF began minimally and with limited success to confront the racism that haunted this and all future street protests, including both ACT UP and the AB101 movements. With the notable example of Greg Byrd, Los Angeles's first

GLF chairman, whites dominated the GLF membership. And although the GLF organized out of homes across Hollywood, Westlake, and Silverlake and maintained an unofficial headquarters at Satan's, a straight bar in Silverlake popular with the hippie crowd, the protests were conducted only in majority white areas. Morris Kight qualified this spatial segregation, citing respect for the more pressing concerns facing ethnic neighborhoods and communities:

> I felt that it would be improper for radical lesbian/gay liberation to go into East Los Angeles or to Watts or to South Central because I felt that it would not be the affinity and they had problems enough of their own. While they had activities that we went to and supported, we went to and supported those because it was politically correct to do so.[29]

A network of more specialized, single-issue gay and lesbian groups quickly superseded the more comprehensive and amorphous GLF strategy, as splinter groups organized around such issues as civil rights and police reform. At the same time, distinct constituencies emerged within the gay and lesbian communities, including separatist movements. Many of the tactics of the GLF, however, became important parts of the gay and lesbian organizing. Among the most important was the tactic of "coming out," not as a personal acknowledgment but as a political act with communal benefits for the entire society, gay and straight. In addition, the GLF transformed traditional direct-action practices that spatially manifested political desire. Later movements such as Queer Nation adopted (without attribution) many of these tactics, including "kiss-ins" at malls and straight bars. In one of their more successful campaigns, the GLF plastered gay and lesbian bars with stickers announcing the establishment's liberation from the unwritten laws that disallowed same-sex touching.

The hallmark of GLF organizing was its revolutionary dedication to gay and lesbian visibility and recognition. The model for this visibility came not only from within the movement, as gays and lesbians theorized about what the "sexual revolution" would mean for American society, but also from other movements of the late 1960s and 1970s who engendered the atmosphere of radical political and social change. Because gays and lesbians from a variety of backgrounds came to the GLF from other political arenas (student organizing, Black Power, the women's movement), the liberationist gay and lesbian movement, unlike the Mattachine, remained open to a broad spectrum of political or social claims. Unlike the pre-Stonewall movement, endless negotiation and a centralized structure did not hamper the GLF. Their freestyle approach to organizing and protesting had ramifications across the city and for the geography of gay and lesbian lives. Although gay liberation created an atmosphere conducive to gay-owned businesses and was responsible for an explosion in gay and lesbian social services, liberation was not consciously directed toward building communities, except in the occasional case of communes and other small-scale living experiments unofficially organized by GLF members. In fact, the geography of liberation organizing in Los Angeles reflected the geographic decentralization of the city as a whole. As a result, although gay neighborhoods were strengthened in the early 1970s, the GLF street protests did not contribute to any direct spatial growth of the gay and lesbian communities. Place claiming in the liberation context had a broader societal and citywide focus.

AIDS Activism in Los Angeles

The contemporary gay, lesbian, bisexual, and transgender movement—if it can be collectivized—distinguishes itself from earlier incarnations in terms of legitimacy, political clout, diversity, tactics, and goals. This period began with the first meeting of New York ACT UP in 1987. Founded by Larry Kramer, an activist who had four years earlier started Gay Men's Health Crisis as a social service organization by and for gay men with HIV and AIDS, ACT UP created guerrilla-style protests to ensure funding, treatment, and research for people with AIDS. Seen as a model for strategic street-based activism, ACT UP's influence has extended far beyond the gay and lesbian or AIDS communities alone. Surpassing its original goals of bringing attention and action to the AIDS epidemic, ACT UP (and the direct-action movement it spawned) changed the connection between politics and community for most gays and lesbians in the United States, making one synonymous with the other. As the AIDS crisis evolved, ACT UP's commitment to nonhierarchical structure paired with the necessity of reaching its goals brought into focus a number of concerns unresolved by other movements. Central to ACT UP's sense of identity were the meaning and wielding of power within long-term organizing efforts, community strength and pride, and the integration of the community into the mainstream. Throughout its history, issues of race, class, and gender (as they mark and are marked by the epidemic) have dominated ACT UP's efforts as well.

Like chapters around the country, ACT UP/LA grew exponentially, from the first organizational meeting, quickly becoming a leading force in the local AIDS debate. Gay men and lesbians uninvolved in community politics joined longtime leftist activists (including a local group, the Lavender Left, which emerged out of the GLF). Lesbians who had previously seen few connections between gay and lesbian issues were joined by younger lesbians, whose issues more easily tied with gay men's concerns, as a visible part of ACT UP. Throughout 1989 and 1990, ACT UP/LA carried out publicly disruptive actions all over the city. By the end of 1990, however, mirroring changes in ACT UP chapters across the country, the Los Angeles organization entered a period of continual reorganization, as radical and mainstream agendas clashed. Charges of racism and gender bias—and the desire to channel ACT UP's energy into non-AIDS issues—led to the emergence of Queer Nation, a group dedicated to visibility and a more integrated gay, lesbian, bisexual, and transgender community.

In Los Angeles, Queer Nation organized sporadic visibility actions in 1991 and 1992 across the city. Targeting shopping malls, public high schools, churches, and other institutions with a history of hostility to gays and lesbians, Queer Nation's actions combined many of the tactics first used by liberation activists in the 1970s with the assumption of political power gained through ACT UP's success. Although, like ACT UP/LA, Queer Nation never reached the heights of popularity in Los Angeles that it had in New York or San Francisco, it did survive until 1993 and played an important part in the AB101 protests.

The tactics of these direct-action movements profoundly changed the geography of the gay and lesbian community in a number of ways. First, these strategies made visible those in the gay community who were, in the early days of the epidemic, shockingly invisible—namely, those infected with HIV. The central role played by HIV-positive people in ACT UP, the graphics and videos produced by ACT UP, and the media attention ACT UP drew from those outside the community revealed a more diverse and complicated demographics—both of gays and lesbians and of the epidemic. As the virus spread through communities of color, the tentative nature of the linkages between a mainstream, largely white and affluent gay and lesbian activist community and gays and lesbians of color graphically appeared. Whereas liberation had been, like many of the social movements of the late 1960s, predominantly white and middle class, the distribution of AIDS cases unflinchingly exposed the diversity of those affected and forced a shifting of the barriers that had been drawn around the more affluent enclaves of the gay and lesbian community.

Second, ACT UP and the activist politics that emerged in the wake of the AIDS epidemic reflected and supported new kinds of gay and lesbian neighborhoods and revealed the presence of same-sex desires and relationships in neighborhoods less connected to the gay and lesbian economic growth in the late 1970s and early 1980s. In Los Angeles and elsewhere, neighborhoods that had presented few visible signs of gay or lesbian culture began to show the possibilities of creating community in places less gentrified and more ethnically and racially diverse. The new direct-action movement, through its attention to diversity of race, class, and sexual desires, critiqued the simple promise of gay or lesbian enclaves and the implications of gay and lesbian economic mainstreaming. Eventually, these more affluent and established neighborhoods (such as West Hollywood) became themselves targets of more radical activists.

Direct-action protesters within ACT UP and later organizations publicly questioned the prominence and definition of West Hollywood and other, smaller, gay and lesbian enclaves in Los Angeles. Their disruption of the codification of gay culture paralleled academic debates around postmodernism and identity politics, particularly as activists explored alternative spaces and venues for protest and stretched boundaries of the gay and lesbian cultural space in new ways. Video, performance art, and innovative graphics expressed the ambiguity many felt toward the growing institutionalization of community spaces and their acceptance by the mainstream culture.

The range of actions ACT UP staged from late 1987 to early 1993 (its most productive and visible period in Los Angeles) reveals much about the nature of the direct-action movement, and the targets of its actions tell a lot about the spaces the community occupied. Paul Daniels, a member of ACT UP's Agitate Committee (responsible for plotting major demonstrations), echoes the frustration the group felt as the geography of Los Angeles stunted various street-based strategies:

> I think in Los Angeles when we are dealing with place as it deals with either geography or community and as it has to do with political movements, it also has to do with boundaries. In Los Angeles, we have such a huge environment—geographic and physical environment—that we have to cover and nooks and

crannies of communities everywhere. You have to take into account a lot of considerations.[30]

These considerations included the difficulty in creating a sense of urgency about AIDS, fear of police harassment, lack of visibility in the local media, difficulties in transporting activists to the various sites of protest, and the absence of a singular gay community from which to draw a core group of participants. ACT UP discovered few targets for effective protest in Los Angeles, despite (and because of) the city's geographic and demographic expanse. In the roughly five years that ACT UP visibly demonstrated in Los Angeles, fewer than a half dozen locations were notable as targets, rather than as convenient meeting places.

ACT UP/LA most frequently protested at downtown government offices. The relatively dense geography of Los Angeles's downtown and the concentration of public services and buildings resembled most closely the geography of New York, Washington, DC, or San Francisco. Fifteen times ACT UP staged sit-ins and die-ins at the County Hall of Administration during Los Angeles County Board of Supervisors meetings. The five-member Board of Supervisors (with a reputation for being dominated by white conservative interests) oversees the public health budget for the eighty-seven municipalities in Los Angeles County, which has a population of nearly nine million.[31] Other governmental targets included the downtown and Westwood federal buildings (fourteen times), the Sheriff's Headquarters (five times), Immigration and Naturalization Services Headquarters (twice), and the Nixon Library (once). ACT UP also targeted conservative politicians at their homes and protested health care policy and AIDS patient care at University of Southern California (USC) and University of California Los Angeles medical centers.

ACT UP/LA's fight for a government response to the AIDS epidemic centered on the need for a dedicated AIDS ward at the Los Angeles County–USC Medical Center. Over the course of the three-year struggle for an AIDS ward, ACT UP protested repeatedly at the Board of Supervisors and at the County-USC Medical Center, including a week-long round-the-clock vigil at the medical center in 1989. At one crucial sit-in at a Board of Supervisors meeting in 1989, ACT UP activists protested "to call attention to the Board's criminal inaction nine years into the AIDS epidemic which has already claimed the lives of 4,337 County residents."[32] Police arrested fifteen demonstrators and charged them with disrupting a public meeting. Protests at the Board of Supervisors continued throughout 1990 and 1991, with ACT UP carefully and loudly monitoring budget deliberations and the length of time patients had to wait for treatment (or a simple appointment) at the county AIDS clinic. At one typical action at the Board of Supervisors, activists risked arrest and were ultimately removed from the chambers:

> For the fifth time in just over a year, gloved sheriff's deputies who had hovered ominously over the proceedings with pistols and batons in full glare of television cameras, were ordered to handcuff and remove to the County jail anyone who refused to sit silently. Activists brandishing an American flag and tombstones scrawled with the phrase "Early Intervention / Health Care is a Right / 4-Months Wait = Death" were dragged from the room under the alternately imperious and distressed gazes of [Supervisors] Antonovich, Dana, Edelman, and Hahn.[33]

These protests were among the most visible actions led by ACT UP/LA and exemplified their insistence on garnering public support through media attention. Using outreach methods that had become the hallmark of ACT UP protesters around the country, the Los Angeles group attempted to circumvent the peculiarities of protesting in the city: the lack of pedestrian crowds and the difficulty of getting large turnouts of activists to the events. According to Daniels,

> We were particularly creative when it came to our use of the media. . . . We made big loud splashy things [because our]

> primary purpose was to get our message out to a broad public. We couldn't get our message out to a small specific public because it didn't exist—small specific little publics don't exist in HIV because HIV attacks everybody. So we made the biggest, loudest, noisiest demonstrations and the most visible actions we possibly could to capture media attention and that is how we got around having to be geographically specific.[34]

ACT UP resorted to geographic specificity only after contentious and often-dividing debate. ACT UP leadership presumed entire areas of the city to be out of bounds, despite the geography of the disease. Believing in increased homophobia in the African American and Latino communities and fearing the racism within their own ranks, ACT UP rarely ventured into neighborhoods in the southern or eastern areas of the city. ACT UP, like the GLF, struggled against the charge that they ignored communities of color and countered that their absence in these communities reasonably followed a general sense that their presence in these neighborhoods would be viewed as an intrusion, not just by the mainstream, but by gays and lesbians as well. In fact, as Daniels recalls, the Latino community leaders (including representatives from the Catholic Church and other neighborhood organizations) asked ACT UP not to undertake actions in certain parts of the city. Because these requests came also from organizations perceived to be less overtly hostile to the gay activists, they were respected.

Soon after the civil unrest in April of 1992 (following the beating of Rodney King and the exoneration of the police officers involved), the People of Color Caucus within ACT UP/LA tried to get the organization's meeting place moved from West Hollywood to a site more accessible to members living on the Eastside. As one ACT UP participant remembered, "We wanted to diversify the group and have more people of color in the group, but the majority of the people were still white and didn't live anywhere near South Central. Those people were rather frightened about going down to South Central at night to meet. It was very difficult even discussing it."[35] As a result of this controversy, some meetings were switched to Echo Park, but with the convenience of the site at Plummer Park, West Hollywood continued to be the preferred location. Many people of color dropped out of the group shortly after the 1992 civil unrest.

ACT UP attempted to reach out to the African American and Latino communities primarily by hosting information and outreach tables at community fairs and other events around the city. Unlike the governmental or medical targets, these places have less symbolic value for gays and lesbians, but were selected as places in critical need of AIDS and HIV information. ACT UP also regularly conducted outreach campaigns in West Hollywood bars to distribute safer-sex kits and information. However, ACT UP's sphere of influence was never as successful at infiltrating minority communities as it was in the gay enclaves west of downtown.

At times, however, the diversity of Los Angeles was successfully negotiated and even used to ACT UP's advantage. To mark the murders of AIDS activists in Mexico City, ACT UP marched from Echo Park to the Mexican Consulate on 6th Street near McArthur Park. In a blending of traditional Mexican Dia de los Muertos rituals and ACT UP guerrilla theater, a number of Latino activists from Los Angeles marched naked and covered in mud to the consulate, where they enacted a die-in while other marchers poured fake blood on them. As Daniels said, "It was very powerful and it was a very different kind of demonstration than we would have had in West Hollywood or West Los Angeles."[36] This attention to cultural boundaries and cultural expression has been a constant concern not just in ACT UP/LA but in AIDS activism across the United States. As Ty Geltmaker has commented in his comprehensive analysis of the struggle for the AIDS ward at the LA County/USC Medical Center, AIDS activists respected culturally based homophobia, understanding the struggles within communities of color against barriers of racism, accessibility, and cultural codes that cannot be crossed:

> White self-identified gay men were able to organize around AIDS because their publicly worn sexual marginalization was accompanied by ferocious assumptions of social entitlement and relative access to power and wealth. The new "communities" of AIDS cannot be expected to respond to their diagnoses with such a preexisting sense of common purpose and nascent power.[37]

This white self-identified power base that spearheaded ACT UP organizing in Los Angeles reflected not only the sense of social entitlement that middle-class gay men took for granted, but also the way West Hollywood operated as a stage upon which this sense of entitlement could be expressed. West Hollywood became a city in the midst of the first wave of AIDS cases, and the city was just two years old when ACT UP held its first meeting in the Plummer Park community room.[38] As Daniels recalled, the incorporation of West Hollywood paved the way for ACT UP, and support from the city council, while not always explicit, ensured that many actions that the LAPD would not have allowed were tolerated by the Los Angeles County Sheriff's Department in West Hollywood:

> West Hollywood does not want to alienate the gay and lesbian community [which is] effectively a third of the population. You get voted out of office very easily if you alienate the community too heavily. . . . West Hollywood has been very supportive of ACT UP.[39]

The most critical support was the city policy that allowed ACT UP to march without the parade permit required for all other protests. Some of the most powerful events ACT UP held were the spontaneous funeral marches for ACT UP members, during which the group would close down Santa Monica Boulevard, march through the streets past the gyms and clubs and restaurants, and light a bonfire at one of the major intersections. Although few onlookers actually joined the funeral marches, the fact that a permit was not necessary and that West Hollywood represented a large portion of the affected community facilitated these hastily arranged processions.

The disparity between the relaxed atmosphere of the West Hollywood strip and the intensity of ACT UP's message and tactics often brought underlying tension to the surface, according to Daniels:

> West Hollywood as a city is a funny milieu when it comes to the gay community. . . . [It is] one of the most homophobic and assimilationist gay communities in the world. . . . Because people were there for social reasons they resented us frequently for coming into the community and scaring them out of their social mood. I've had flyers ripped up and thrown in my face [and people] saying, "I'm not here to deal with this. I'm here to get laid, to have a drink. I'm here to relax." That was a common occurrence.[40]

Many activists saw the reluctance to appreciate the depth of the AIDS epidemic by communities across the city as the biggest obstacle to successful street protest:

> Of all the major North American urban centers caught up in the crisis of AIDS and the challenge of the new queer activism, Los Angeles is historically and morphologically most resistant to the public discussion and representation of death and degeneracy, except perhaps as lurid entertainment in Hollywood films.[41]

The combination of the apathy in West Hollywood toward protest and the centralization of the AIDS epidemic within its city boundaries in the earliest years of the crisis certainly complicated ACT UP's strategizing. Despite the constant threat of police violence and the absence of onlookers to provide moral support, most protests occurred not in West Hollywood but in Los Angeles proper. As long as the group targeted politicians and policies not supportive of the needs of the gay community (and other communities affected by AIDS and HIV), the group had to assemble elsewhere. ACT UP frequently targeted

Century City, Los Angeles's "second downtown" built—according to some observers—after the 1965 Watts Rebellion to counter the downtown city-builders' fears that violence could threaten the center of power. The Century Plaza Hotel has long been the location for visiting dignitaries (with a presidential suite) and for large political fund-raisers, thus making it a natural target for marches and demonstrations. Perhaps as a result of Century City's legacy as a political and corporate refuge, police crackdowns on demonstrations have been particularly violent there, but not just for ACT UP. Why the police retaliated so harshly in Century City was never clear to the ACT UP organizers; they did sense that although the area appeared to the demonstrators to be neutral territory, the police viewed it as a special place where disturbances could not be tolerated. Demonstrators were known to have been chased off the streets and through a nearby open-air shopping mall with billy clubs. Throughout the years that ACT UP dominated gay politics, activists were constantly aware that the police monitored their meetings and phone hot lines and that plainclothes detectives participated in their marches and videotaped them from the sidewalks.[42]

Other protests more directly seemed to fit Los Angeles apathy and prurient Hollywood-style interest. ACT UP staged several protests at the Oscar awards ceremonies, held either in downtown Los Angeles at the Dorothy Chandler pavilion, the county-owned arts center, or at the Shrine Auditorium south of downtown. At the 1991 Oscars at the Shrine Auditorium, approximately one hundred ACT UP and Queer Nation activists protested "AIDSphobia" in Hollywood. The activists denounced the studios for ignoring the AIDS crisis and the County of Los Angeles for an AIDS budget equal to just one-fifth the budget for a blockbuster film. Protesters carried signs declaring that thirty people would die in America of AIDS during the Oscar broadcast. The ACT UP newsletter issue published after that protest suggested the very personal connection

ACT UP members in Los Angeles made between AIDS indifference and Hollywood's responsibility:

> When celebrities fail to speak out about the lack of AIDS funds in the county in which most of them live, in the county which benefits most by the enormous sums of money generated by Hollywood, and in the county in which the number of AIDS cases is increasing faster than the national average, is it any wonder why we must agitate against this atmosphere which fails to show its social responsibility during this crisis?[43]

Not surprisingly, this protest was one of the more successful actions planned and carried out by ACT UP/LA, receiving more press coverage than any other demonstration. Although the continual protests at the Los Angeles County/USC Medical Center achieved more tangible benefits, stories about the Oscar protests appeared in four local newspapers, the major newspapers from New York and San Francisco, numerous local and national television newscasts, the gay and lesbian press, and the major Hollywood industry media. Where New York ACT UP actions often made the *New York Times,* the Los Angeles media only covered AIDS protests when they disrupted an event already being televised nationwide.

Geography, diverse demographics, ethnic segregation, and police brutality combine in Los Angeles in a way that requires a significantly greater degree of commitment from those taking to the streets; activists must cross more boundaries than in other cities and counter a perception of inherent apathy in Southern California. Ty Geltmaker gave the particulars of Los Angeles, providing a more sympathetic analysis than the usual charge of a generalized Angeleno:

> The battle for individual sovereignty over what Foucault called the "care of the self" is fought by gay men and lesbians each time they simply make themselves visible on the streets. This is true in all of America, but even more so in Los Angeles, the least pedestrian and most sprawled of metropolitan regions. Lacking the anonymous bustle and protective gaze of meandering urban

crowds, the privatized organization of space and transportation in Los Angeles places anyone who dares to walk rather than drive at heightened risk of being singled out as "different."[44]

As Geltmaker suggests, local activists created alternative styles of protest not always readable in the context of national ACT UP defiance. More practically, the low density and lack of public transportation posed real problems for ACT UP, because direct action relies on sheer numbers of bodies to emphasize the point that thousands of people in the county were being affected by HIV and AIDS. The contrast between New York City, where hundreds of people might stop on a street corner in the normal course of events, and Los Angeles, where the lone pedestrian on the street is rare enough to be noticeable, undermined the efforts of ACT UP to make the physical presence of AIDS palpable:

> In New York City they had a demonstration not long ago where they had 5,000 people show up because they can all just hop on the A train and go where they wanted to go—they closed down the Brooklyn Bridge for God's sake, and you know it's easy for them to do it on their lunch hour. In Los Angeles we simply cannot get people to travel the huge distances that we covered. We had members coming from Ventura, Orange County, over by Magic Mountain, and as far away as Riverside and San Bernardino. So we had people converging from all areas and they had to commit quite a bit of time in their days to do this and that was a problem and to this day that was one of the problems we have in maintaining a consistent and viable population core group of people who are able to show up at demonstrations.[45]

Activists involved in the GLF, ACT UP, and AB101 protests all reiterated the influence of the geographic and political obstacles Angelenos have had to confront since the founding of the Mattachine. Their solutions to these impediments demonstrate a necessary flexibility in the face of an almost geographically hostile terrain for street activism. In the case of the GLF, the organizers instead turned to social service long before their counterparts in other cities did. In ACT UP, after winning the fight for an AIDS ward (the most urgent local issue), the core of the membership focused on the national front, participating in coordinated actions in Chicago, Washington, New York, and San Francisco with increasing frequency. Alternative styles of protest, including phone zaps (coordinated phone calling of political officials), postering, and the merchandising of T-shirts also replaced the traditional street protest. Los Angeles, however, did not necessarily succeed with these approaches any better than other cities.

Although fleeting, the ACT UP and AB101 protests signaled the possibility of regenerating street protest in Los Angeles, and their unique circumstances suggested strategies for the future. These street activists created spectacles that regularly received media attention and energized a new generation of community leaders less entrenched in established organizations. Their efforts emanated organically from the cafes, gyms, and bars in West Hollywood. These protests astonished the less politicized because they differed in tone, style, and content from earlier efforts. Like the gay liberation actions, ACT UP and AB101 protests followed a local script, rather than one suggested by activists in other cities. Although the ACT UP efforts were ultimately overshadowed by their counterparts elsewhere, AB101 followed no script. Their success suggests that place claiming is organic and that visibility is place specific.

6 The Remapped City

The preceding chapters present Los Angeles as mapped by gay and lesbian activists. I have used the experiences of these activists to trace the shift from an underground movement, disconnected from the neighborhoods and public places of an expanding city, to a major social and political force, with connections across the country. The growing access of the gay and lesbian community to the mainstream political process can be read spatially, through the changing strategies employed by activists in Los Angeles. Together, the politics and practices of the movement constitute a strategic, if rarely acknowledged, claiming of public and private places. Since the emergence of the Mattachine in the 1950s, gay and lesbian activists have transformed themselves from an often-isolated group of assimilationists—mostly men—to a liberationist complex of both cogender and separatist organizations. The multiplicity of activist and community-building strategies now reflects a movement without boundaries. Each stage has intersected the geography of Los Angeles in ways that reflect both the power of the collective and the personal truth at the heart of this movement based in sexuality.

The immediate effect of these changing strategies and opportunities is a new geography of sexuality in Los Angeles and an expansion of the city map used by gays, lesbians, and bisexuals. Liberationist strategies sought to make the city safe for gays and lesbians, and their efforts addressed police harassment in both private and public spaces. Areas that had supported a clandestine gay presence became places for public celebration. The map of the city farther expanded for gays and lesbians as West Hollywood became a focal point of the movement's cultural and political organizing. Although West Hollywood remained a space primarily for white gay men (in appearance if not in practice), lesbians expanded their presence as well. More recently, as the community has acknowledged and begun to express a diversity of racial, ethnic, cultural, sexual, and political differences, it becomes more difficult to draw one map of the community or movement. What must be mapped now, beyond the locations of the community, is the interplay between the city's geography and its cultural identity and practices.

I began this project asserting that the stereotypical images of the movement and the city—complacent, suburban, assimilated—obscure the most interesting dimensions of activism in Los Angeles. The history and practice of activism presented here dispels, I hope, these characterizations. Angeleno activists have marched in the city's streets for more than three decades in celebration and in anger. Organizers have built institutions that have grown to reflect the complexities of the movement and the city. The point of this more realistic telling of the city's activist history is not, however, to create an image of Los Angeles that mirrors San Francisco or New York. Los Angeles's sense of the political is different; and the particularities of the gay and lesbian movement reflect this difference. Although the streets have been sites of activism in Los Angeles, the movement as a whole has not been street focused. Activists and others have created public spaces recognized as gay or lesbian, but West Hollywood is not the primary focus of daily life for the movement or the greater community. Place claiming in Los Angeles has included not only those strategies that support the continued growth of enclaves like West Hollywood, but processes as well that allow for a more decentralized and less publicly identifiable community. In this final chapter, then, I examine the competing desires in the Angeleno movement for visibility and community integration. Looking at these together creates a picture of the movement that acknowledges the collective drive of the gay and lesbian movement without denying the ways in which certain Southern Californian stereotypes of individuality (and isolation) affect the map of community building.

In analyses of Los Angeles, references to Hollywood operate both as trope and necessity. Los Angeles urban historians and critics use the cinematic representation of the city to highlight not simply the way it represents itself and is represented by the rest of the world, but as a way to get at the fragmented locations of culture and politics in the city. In this way, for lesbians in Los Angeles, the coming-out of Ellen DeGeneres—mediated by her character on the eponymous show in 1997—served this function.

For many, Ellen's coming out was the most important event in the gay and lesbian community in recent years, and in Los Angeles, this was even more the case. Twenty-nine percent of homes in Los Angeles watched the show; the percentage of gay and lesbian households is of course impossible to measure. Across the city, and across the country, viewing parties were held in homes, bars, and clubs.

The show, *Ellen,* and the politics of Ellen DeGeneres's coming out within the context of a television situation comedy reflected back the complicated meanings of public visibility, sexualized identity, and political strength that intertwine the contemporary lesbian experience. For the eight months that the show aired on a national network after the title character came out, the show, even more than Ellen DeGeneres the actor, was the most visible representation of a lesbian culture in late-twentieth-century America. Significantly, and recognizably, Ellen Morgan—the hesitant and personable neighbor—represented a lesbian culture (and by extension a gay and bisexual culture as well) reflective of the specificities of Los Angeles.

Ellen took place on two sets, an apartment and the bookstore where she worked. Both spaces balanced intimacy with communalism, centering on Ellen's daily encounters with a revolving cast of close friends and random acquaintances. Neither of these spaces changed after Ellen discovered her lesbianism. The lesbian content was entirely situational, centered on Ellen's attempts to negotiate her old life and new desires. Tied as the show was to the existing locations, however, the lack of any lesbian geographic markers was inevitable, but also more authentically Angeleno. In the famous coming-out episode and the one that followed, Ellen visited two lesbian locations, the Gay and Lesbian Center off Hollywood Boulevard and Little Frida's, the lesbian coffeehouse in West Hollywood. Afterward, however, the show relied on infusing the old stage sets with Ellen's new identity.

What then is the gay and lesbian Los Angeles of *Ellen*? On one level, it is all of Los Angeles. By acting out her lesbian sexuality in a straight space, Ellen typifies the experience of most gays and lesbians in Los Angeles, and elsewhere, comfortably living in a straight world as that world is in turn transformed by her presence. This new sense of assimilation brings with it a new strategic place claiming—transforming an otherwise heterosexually coded place into one that has particular meaning for gays and lesbians on a collective level. Through her use of certain places in the studio's version of Los Angeles to test and refine her new lesbian identity, Ellen is accomplishing in a moment the radical task of renaming the geography of this city. It is appropriate that the first gay series takes place not in New York or San Francisco but Los Angeles. For gays and lesbians in Los Angeles, this simulation of lesbian life in their city reflected their own experience of a place without obvious markers of sexuality. Throughout the show's short run with a lesbian title character, *Ellen* mirrored the struggle many gays and lesbians must undergo in their own coming-out processes.

As a political act, *Ellen* claims two kinds of space, both of which are about living rooms. Gays and lesbians and fundamentalists alike would probably agree that the show sexualized Wednesday nights at nine o'clock, its scheduled spot in prime time. Because overt lesbian content (whatever that might have been) was off limits, the show kept repeating the verbal cues used before the secret of the character's sexuality was revealed. Nonetheless, the fictionalized Ellen's presence on national television altered both the airwaves and the living rooms in which the show was viewed.

To many, particularly those committed to a more progressive politics of sexuality, the show symbolizes a national trend that is particularly entrenched in, but not exclusive to, Los Angeles. One Angeleno activist/observer described the city as "an Ellen-ized home to gay gentrification."[1] This sentiment epitomizes the difficulty with which the movement has understood Los Angeles. Is Los Angeles reflective of a trend, or leading one? Does the show encourage or simply mimic contemporary gay and lesbian culture? Whatever the answers to these questions of causality, the significance of *Ellen* is its reflection of the ordinary lives of gays, lesbians, and bisexuals who rarely, if ever, participate in a public culture of sexuality. There is an arrogance and prejudice, however, in assuming that the radicality of the private life—or one's home place—cannot also be an instigator of change.

Gay and lesbian activism has always confronted this fissure—between the inescapable fact that sexuality requires both personal and private acts and the recognition that societal change requires public engagement. In this latest incarnation, however, the assertion of multiple layers of identity politics—foregrounding questions of race, gender, ethnicity, and bisexuality—raises critical questions about the insistence on always being public. Instead, to critically map the alternative strategies of place claiming should necessitate a more nuanced reading of the turn away from street politics, or emphasis on creating a reassuring and comforting place of refuge. *Ellen*, of course, is still a television show, and hardly a manifesto for change. A transformative politics of the meaning of home for gays and lesbians has emerged on the margins of the community, as gays and lesbians of color consciously transform the city.

From the divide within the lesbian community—both between the lesbian feminists and the bar culture and between the gay integrationists and the lesbian separatists—to the growing strength of the African American, Asian, and Latino gay activist communities, the lack of a monolithic gay and lesbian community has kept multiple agendas alive, not all of which are in accord. These differences in politics have been physically actualized in different ways, resulting in distinct, if not competing, claims on place. The place-claiming strategies of the more politically powerful white male segment of the community—the establishment of physically imposing and permanent structures (the Los Angeles Gay and Lesbian Center [the Center], AIDS Project Los Angeles [APLA] headquarters, and the West Hollywood strip)—are not necessarily the same as those that emerge organically from communities of color or from the lesbian community in general.

In recent years gays and lesbians from Los Angeles's ethnic and racial minority communities have turned to organizing within their ethnic communities as well as the larger gay movement, in part to undo an often-entrenched homophobia. They, like lesbian activists in the 1970s, are uneasy about their role in a larger movement, and their place-claiming efforts reflect this. That there has been a rapid growth in the number of ethnically defined gay and lesbian organizations reflects a more general shift as these activists recognize that their sexuality cannot be divorced from their identities as people of color. As a result, the location of their activism and place claiming shifts back to these home communities. In his essay, "Does Your Mama Know About Me?" Essex Hemphill, a gay African American poet, challenges the allegiances of Black gay men in choosing their community:

> The best gay minds of my generation believe that we speak as one voice and dream one dream, but we are not monolithic. We are not even respectful of one another's difference. . . . Look around brothers. There is rampant killing in our communities. . . . We are

> a wandering tribe that needs to go home before home is gone. We should not continue standing in line to be admitted into spaces that don't want us there. We cannot continue to exist without clinics, political organizations, human services, and cultural institutions that *we* create to support, sustain, and affirm us.[2]

There has been an important shift in place-claiming strategies that answers Hemphill's call. The Center remains a site where activists of color gather for services—rap groups, social gatherings, counseling services. More frequently, however, organizing takes place in ethnic neighborhoods of the city rather than the gay-coded spaces, including West Hollywood. As a result, communities of color have been the vanguard of an effort to redefine the boundaries of place claiming for all gays and lesbians as they show, through example, the possibilities for reconciling a gay map of the city with other maps.

When communities of color identify home as their organizing place, it transforms the meaning of visibility, often into terms that are more respectful and tolerant of traditional cultural values than the larger gay and lesbian movement has been in the years since Stonewall. One of the founders of Los Angeles Asian Pacific Islander Sisters (LAAPIS), explained that lesbians of color remain, in many ways, rooted in the cultural norms of their ethnic communities, despite the compromises such dual identities require: "A lot of us don't want to make our parents feel embarrassed, so we don't like to be in a gay surrounding in our own neighborhoods, neighborhoods being your own ethnic community."[3] LAAPIS provided a "safe space for lesbian and bisexual Asians," concentrating more on creating opportunities for outreach to the Asian community than increasing Asian lesbian awareness within largely white gay and lesbian organizations. Like Connexxus East/Centro des Mujeres—the effort of the previous generation of lesbian activists—LAAPIS allowed Asian lesbians a place to develop social networks not predicated on access to West Hollywood and the more visible organizational sites of the movement. Accordingly, this activist explained, "At this point our first focus is toward visibility within the Asian community . . . when you want to make a statement you want to go home first."[4] In 1999, citing "a difficult obstacle with no immediate resolution"—namely a decline in "participation and commitment from our membership"—LAAPIS disbanded, indicating, perhaps, both the difficulty of organizing and the eventual redundancy of all such efforts.[5]

In Los Angeles, then, two metaphors for gay and lesbian place claiming coexist: coming out and coming home. Across the city, activism is most successful when both are accomplished. As even the most radically street-based activists admit, there is an untapped source of movement support to be found within the supposedly "apolitical" gays and lesbians.

Although many organizations for gays, lesbians, and bisexuals of color have challenged the boundaries of the movement, few have had a neighborhood presence. Like the earliest incarnations of the Gay and Lesbian Center, these organizations, if they have a physical location, do not build on or attract a gay and lesbian nexus. However, the notion of home as a place for organizing exists in Los Angeles not only in the form of these organizations, but also in the neighborhood that has always offered an alternative to West Hollywood—Silverlake. Like West Hollywood, Silverlake is represented by gay politicians; and it has a street life, a large residential community, and an annual street (pride) festival that celebrates gay culture. But unlike West Hollywood, it is demographically diverse; unlike West Hollywood it is a place where gay culture is not privileged.

Silverlake, by all accounts the second-largest (or densest) center of gay and lesbian culture in Los Angeles, reveals few traces of the community, apart from a half dozen bars and clubs as dimly lit and poorly signed as they were a decade ago. Far more evident are the businesses established by successive waves of Central American and Southeast Asian immigrants, from *pupuserias* to *clinicas*. If West Hollywood reflects the simultaneously celebratory and commercial face of the movement today, Silverlake reveals the more common pattern of gay and lesbian presence. This is a more conflicted community, one still struggling to find a public face in an environment that must be shared across culture and class. A 1998 controversy over the location of a gay sex club near a residential area on the outskirts of Silverlake (in violation of city zoning codes) appeared at first glance to be evidence of continuing distrust of gay establishments as places where drugs and crime are predictable and inevitable. The club's location far away from the sanitized bars of West Hollywood and in a largely poor, ethnic area led, however, to a necessarily more nuanced debate over the meaning of public, the political status of the community, and the terms of coexistence. Although the club had won a preliminary victory and zoning exemption from the city, largely through the efforts of openly gay councilwoman Jackie Goldberg, it chose to close down after the mayor's veto of the zoning exemption jeopardized once again the club's status. On the part of the largest gay and lesbian community, there was scarcely a response, evidence, perhaps, of a desire to avoid tainting the civic-minded image of the gay and lesbian community.

The public nature of this debate (and continuing references to the fight in subsequent political campaigns and elsewhere) obscured the reality of gay life in Silverlake. The residential life of Silverlake (expensive houses north of Sunset Boulevard and cheap apartments to the south) is more emblematic of the larger map of gay and lesbians in Los Angeles—one altered street by street and house by house. In a neighborhood as ethnically integrated as any in Los Angeles, residents have elected a lesbian city councilor and supported a lesbian assemblywoman. In any other city, these achievements would be clearly activist, but in Los Angeles they are becoming standard and part of the background of urban life.

Silverlake would not be the neighborhood it is today without the decades of public activism both in the neighborhood and across the city. The Mattachine Society was founded here, early gay activists "liberated the bars" and kicked out the police, and some of the first nonbar gay businesses opened on Sunset Boulevard in the heart of the neighborhood. The annual Sunset Junction Street Fair, begun in part as an alternative to the commercialism of the Christopher Street West Festival (the official gay pride event), now attracts both the gay and lesbian population (which considers itself more bohemian than their neighbors in West Hollywood) and the growing immigrant community. The largely residential character of Silverlake, as much as the decades of street activism, however, supports this easy accommodation of distinct cultures. For Silverlake, the private dimensions of gay and lesbian life are as important to the community's survival as the network of a gay and lesbian movement.

To see Silverlake as successful means, in part, rejecting an analysis that considers domesticity simply an indication of a less political community. Instead, as described earlier, the social and political environment of the city influences this pattern of visibility. Both the politics of the movement as it has sought to contain multiple ideologies and conflicts over race and gender and the politics of the city at large have required certain strategies of place claiming and limited the usefulness of others. The competing interests and strategies emerging at different moments over the last twenty-five years, then, complicate the map of gay and lesbian Los Angeles. Opposing strands of activism—simultaneously public and private, gay, lesbian, bisexual, transgender, and queer, and racially and ethnically coded—create overlapping maps.

Over the past three decades, changing notions of community and sexual identity have intersected with the movement's evolving politics in ways that both adapt to and alter the geography of the city. As the movement became more visible, and societal attitudes shifted toward tolerance, gays (more than lesbians) moved out from isolated enclaves. The targets of the Gay Liberation Front (GLF) actions—police stations, recruiting stations, individual psychologists, schools, and churches—were those places and institutions that continued to exclude or negatively classify gays and lesbians. Their actions in Los Angeles demanded immediate amelioration of the harassment lesbians and gays experienced every day. Activists worked to open up social institutions to gays and lesbians and to reduce the daily risk of entrapment, arrest, and social isolation. Because there were few pockets of gay residential concentration and almost no gay or lesbian businesses, protest had to move out of the few enclaves and into less safe areas of the city. With the exception of a few protests, like that mentioned in Chapter 5 at the Black Cat in Silverlake—a target of excessive police harassment and enforced-biased entrance requirements—gay protest did not take place on gay turf.

Within a few years, this agenda shifted toward the development of gay communities as a social, economic, and political presence. Accordingly the movement focused on creating and supporting places for these communities. Central to this development was the emergence of an independent lesbian movement that necessitated the creation of places for women, both within and alongside the often-inclusive, occasionally homophobic women's movement The most significant early shifts in the movement for gays and lesbians were social service centers, a more diverse array of gay- and lesbian-owned businesses, greater control of a gay consumer market, and greater visibility at offices and in their homes, which created an urban fabric that fostered and protected the movement. As this happened, and places for gays and lesbians developed in greater specificity (as the Gay Services Center spawned lesbian-only institutions and, later, institutions that were both racially and ethnically defined), the social makeup of the movement changed, as did the map of a gay and lesbian Los Angeles. The place-claiming strategies of the late 1970s and early 1980s reflect this urge to create solid, permanent institutions separate from the institutions that had been protested by the liberation movement.

The explosion of the AIDS epidemic tested the growing security of this urban network. New needs, political fights, and movement coalitions changed the landscape of the movement as AIDS decimated the gay population in Los Angeles. Most importantly, factions within the community sought to create new alliances across the social divisions, reversing the previous decade's move to self-segregate. Activists also turned to institutions, funders, and political supporters outside the movement, reaching out to the medical establishment and national and local politics in a way that previously had not been a priority. New institutions like AIDS Project Los Angeles (APLA) offered a new model for gay organizing, drawing strength and direction from within the traditional strongholds of gay and lesbian community but offering services to new groups, both gay and straight.

Despite the slow progress of a civil rights agenda in the movement and the election of a few openly gay candidates to public office, most gay and lesbian politicians remained closeted and most of the movement was generally focused inward. The enormity of the AIDS epidemic required that the gay and lesbian movement come to terms with its isolation, its divisiveness, and, as AIDS spread into other communities, its need for coalitions with other communities and with the people of color within its ranks. AIDS Coalition to Unleash Power (ACT UP) and AIDS activism in general reflected these changes, as activists targeted the White House, the National Institutes of Health, and the Supreme Court. In Los Angeles, ACT UP became a presence in local county politics and a very visible part of alternative politics, marching with labor unions, pro-choice activists, and others.

These new challenges, however, drew significant strength in Los Angeles from the new status of West Hollywood as an independent city. Although the creation of the city was not a gay victory alone, the city's commitment to gay and lesbian community issues—particularly AIDS and fair access to housing and employment—instantly transformed Los Angeles from a city without an obviously recognizable gay movement to one with national importance. In addition, the centrality of West Hollywood ensured that the gay economic presence, rather than the gay activist presence (in the familiar sense), defined the public face of the gay and lesbian communities.

The politics of place claiming for gays and lesbians in Los Angeles have been about the fundamental shifts in the movements themselves over the past twenty years. Attempts to find places for community building, both permanent (like creating a social services center) and temporary (like taking over a street for a political funeral), reflect the politics of the time. It is in these processes of place claiming—appropriating public spaces, developing neighborhoods, protesting, and being visible—where we see most clearly the politics of the movement itself. Conflicts over ideology, including the direction of the movement and the short-term and long-term agendas, are translated into conflicts over place and different strategies for claiming place. The gay and lesbian movement, which has struggled over the past twenty-five years with questions of difference and inclusion, reveals this intricate connection between politics, ideology, and place.

From the overtly gay and lesbian environment of West Hollywood to the more subtle presence of gays and lesbians in neighborhoods across the city, the strategic practices of gay and lesbian activists have redrawn the map of Los Angeles, creating a rich landscape accessible to all. Whether one constructs a pattern of daily life solely within these spaces, or travels through them inadvertently, the experiences of gays and lesbians struggling for visibility are apparent. This change is felt not only by gay and lesbians, but also by the entire city.

On the other hand, street protests are not specifically about the permanent claiming of gay or lesbian space, but the encoding of all space with sexual identity. Hollywood Boulevard, Santa Monica Boulevard, or Wilshire Boulevard—all sites of gay and lesbian protests—create the city's fabric and retain much more than a specific gay or lesbian meaning. Instead, as gays and lesbians claim these spaces, the city itself evolves into one more open and more politicized. When gays and lesbians claim their identities in public, they enter a particular relationship with the city. The everyday practice of moving through the city means an encounter with the boundaries between safety and fear. Each new place must be negotiated and evaluated with careful attention to the norms of behavior. For gays and lesbians, each encounter with the city requires radical decision making about performing and acknowledging their identity.

What then are the strategies against which the Los Angeles experience is compared, against which local activists test their accomplishments? Analyses of gay and lesbian community focus on the connection between visibility and community identity. The performative aspects of gay and lesbian life—public displays of certain types—require and support public claims on space. Analysis of the geography of the movement, then, understood here as the place-claiming strategies of individuals and groups, reveals a variety of ways gays and lesbians define a public identity. Their interventions into public space structure the development of community, the conditions for social and political change and affirmation, and a more realistic picture of their community beyond its boundaries.

The experience of the gay movement has been particularly about participating in public life and blurring traditional boundaries between public and private space. Although it looks at a largely preactivist era in gay community development, George Chauncey's book, *Gay New York,* has best investigated this defining characteristic of the gay experience in America. Charting the essential role of public places in the development of a gay culture in New York, Chauncey drew the important connections between community identity and the particular geographies within which the identity operates. Mapping the shifting geography of gay male life in New York before liberation, he pointed out, as one chapter title makes clear, "Privacy Could Only Be Had in Public." The activism that was to emerge in the 1960s had its roots in the assertion of the right to gather in semipublic, mostly commercial spaces. Although gays were increasingly tolerated in public places (even when public space meant sex), the regulation of more private spaces, including commercial establishments, remained a challenge to sexual freedom. Getting arrested in public posed less of a threat to gay men, reports Chauncey, than getting thrown out of a place of business:

> Gay men claimed their right to enjoy the city's public spaces. It was in such open spaces, less easily regulated than a residential or commercial venue, that much of the gay world took shape. The city's streets and parks served as vital meeting grounds for men who lived with their families or in cramped quarters with few amenities, and the vitality and diversity of the gay street scene attracted many other men as well. Streets and parks were where many men—"queer" and "normal" alike went to socialize, and where many men went for sex and ended up being socialized into the gay world.[6]

Although gay sex took place in Los Angeles's parks, such as downtown's Pershing Square Park and Griffith Park, or, as described by John Rechy in *City of Night,* the back streets of Hollywood, and because there was little street life in Los Angeles, even in the 1950s, opportunities were limited. Chauncey argued that the greater tolerance for gays in public space was connected to the largely working-class nature of New York street culture. Gay culture inserted itself into this space, which was already marginalized by its use by poorer residents. For a while, stated Chauncey, gay street life was "masked . . . by the bustle of street life in working-class neighborhoods." Eventually, however, both "came under attack . . . because they challenged bourgeois conceptions of public order, the proper boundaries between public and private space, and the social practices appropriate to each."[7]

In Los Angeles, by contrast, "street culture" was highly localized, restricted to less affluent areas of the city. The difference in Los Angeles, of course, is that these neighborhoods are hard to get to and out of because of the lack of public transportation. In addition, compared with other American cities, Los Angeles has fewer parks per capita and those that do exist are remote and relatively inaccessible, particularly for residents on the east side of the city, or tightly controlled by police and private security.

Given the particular nature of gay identity as one that, until expressed publicly by action or words, is not necessarily recognizable, the public performance is particularly crucial. The effects of Los Angeles's lack of public gathering places, however, affects activism in the city more generally. According to Mike Davis, author of *City of Quartz: Excavating the Future in Los Angeles,* the city has historically suffered the effects of a "dual architectural and police assault on public space." Access to the few public spaces designed in the late nineteenth and early twentieth centuries was restricted first by police and then by the privatization of public open space, a trend accelerated by downtown real estate speculation. Since the beginning of the century, then, activists trying to use public space for organizing have come up against both official prohibitions and the whims of an often-violent police force. The Los Angeles Police Department (LAPD), writes Davis, has been exceedingly vigilant in attempts to maintain order and control crowds:

> The LAPD, true to its class war background, has always hated certain kinds of public gatherings. Its early history was largely devoted to bludgeoning May Day demonstrators, arresting strikers and deporting Mexicans and Okies. In 1921 it arrested Upton Sinclair for reading the Declaration of Independence in public; in the 1960s it indiscriminately broke up love-ins and

> family picnics in battles to control Griffith and Elysian Park. Subconsciously it has probably never recovered from the humiliation of August 1965 when it temporarily was forced to surrender the streets to a rebellious ghetto.[8]

The inaccessibility of public space in Los Angeles can be understood, then, as both characteristic of the city's design and a result of city policies to control activism and gatherings in general. Gay activists have been no more and no less subject to these restrictions than other groups.

Los Angeles's geography required strategic decisions about where and how to protest that reached beyond the temporary needs of protesters and marchers. The location of community centers and businesses similarly required responding to the city's particular geography. Parking and public transportation, decentralized neighborhoods and boundaries based on color or culture, and the rising real estate costs in places where gays and lesbians felt safe were among the many issues affecting the strategies of activists. Depending on one's particular layering of identity, neighborhoods might be safe for some and hostile to others. The maps drawn by people of color, women, and the majority gay male population reflect conflicting notions of safety and comfort. Regardless of an area's attitude toward gays or lesbians specifically (if such an attitude could be discerned in such monolithic terms), other measures of crime and danger become sexually coded as well.

Although safety remained a central concern for activists and the community, the movement quickly adopted public strategies that reflected a need to protest outside the boundaries of the community's safety. With the exception of West Hollywood and, to a lesser extent, Silverlake, activists did not expect to march or gather in places where they were welcome or where there was a recognized gay and lesbian community. Instead, activists operated under the assumption that there was no optimal place to gather and that concessions were necessary. Gays and lesbians in Los Angeles acknowledged that they were not going to create a neighborhood, like the Castro in San Francisco or the Village in New York City, which would reflect the diversity of the city's gay and lesbian population.

Given the experience of those activists most engaged in street protest—particularly those connected with the GLF, ACT UP/LA, or the marches against the AB101 veto—the character of gay and lesbian activism in Los Angeles results not from the lack of political motivation in Los Angeles (as is often assumed), but from the difficult geography within which these activists must work. Despite a certain enthusiasm for protest in Los Angeles, and the persistence of this model in the face of enormous obstacles, most activists talked about Los Angeles as an impediment to organizing. As the ACT UP experience revealed, Los Angeles's size and low density limited the numbers of activists able to travel to action sites and virtually ensured that few Angelenos would notice any disruption. Only the most extravagant media events, carefully coordinated and professionally packaged, caught the public's attention. In choosing locations for protests, both ACT UP and the GLF evaluated potential sites for parking and public transportation accessibility as well as for size of the potential crowd.

Some activists, most typically those who emerged as leaders in the early days of liberation, are less likely to emphasize the differences between Los Angeles and other cities as inherently negative. For those who entered (and forged) the movement before a dominant model established itself, the character of the Los Angeles experience is more often seen in a positive light. As Morris Kight describes, with a typical and (given his longevity in the movement and in Los Angeles politics) understandable bravado, the geography and culture of Los Angeles offered a certain opportunity for activism not necessarily present elsewhere:

> I thought this was the ideal place in the world from whence to stage radical lesbian gay liberation. I came here in 1957 deliberately. . . . There were a whole variety of socioeconomic and

> geographic and sociopolitical reasons for coming here . . . lesbian and gay people escaping homophobia all over the world. That word hadn't been invented yet; but whatever that word, it existed.[9]

While concentrating on the public spaces of activism identifies a stronghold of movement power, one needs a wider understanding of who activists are and what they do. As the history of gay and lesbian activism attests, for social change to happen, those who do not march in the streets or have access to politicians must still get involved. Focusing on the connection between place and politics draws attention to the participation of those activists whose strategies constitute more subtle forms of place claiming: creating and staffing community centers, running bookstores and cafes that function as information clearinghouses. For many gays and lesbians, the simple but daring act of being out, on the streets, and as one wishes is the most revolutionary place-claiming act. For gays and lesbians, this notion of strategic visibility is an obvious survival strategy.

Not every gay or lesbian participates in the formation of gay and lesbian places, nor do they always consider themselves to be activists. There are many gays and lesbians who because of social strictures against their lives do not protest publicly and remain in the closet rendering them invisible. Similarly, there are those gays and lesbians who are out, but participate in the movement in ways not immediately recognizable. Most importantly, there are groups within the movement who remain invisible or unwelcome, including bisexuals, youth, seniors, and transgendered people. Just as the last twenty years has changed the face of the movement and the dimensions of place claiming in the movement, so will the continued efforts of gay and lesbian activists. The voices of gay and lesbian mothers and fathers, seniors, and teenagers are among those who are often silenced in public discussions or actions. At the same time, their presence in the city enlarges the boundaries of the gay and lesbian communities and will increasingly affect place claiming as well.

To complete the map of lesbian and gay Los Angeles, an emphasis on the home as a site of community building can no longer be interpreted as solely conservative or regressive. The gay and lesbian presence in the city remains primarily communal, but outside of West Hollywood and apart from the Gay and Lesbian Center (which now occupies three sites in the city) the most significant process of place claiming by gays and lesbians has been less public than the rhetoric about the movement would suggest. In part because of the successes of the more traditional activist strategies described earlier, there is a gay and lesbian landscape that is largely indistinguishable from its surrounding, built up through the accumulation of community in that most Southern Californian landmark, the single-family house. In fact, it is not easy to identify most Los Angeles neighborhoods with any significant concentration of gays and lesbians.

The gay and lesbian map is constructed of both tangible and symbolic space. Most observers point first to those obvious neighborhoods and institutions—West Hollywood, Silverlake, the Gay and Lesbian Center sites—as the core of the community, a constellation of points dispersed across the city. Other landmarks are those created by once-a-year events—marches, parades, ceremonies—and more occasional protests. Gays and lesbians can associate these events with particular places, adding resonance and meaning to otherwise unobtrusive sites. Thus, for a time, the Metropolitan Community Church gained significance after hundreds gathered outside to hear community leaders decry Matthew Shepard's murder. The building itself is hardly a landmark, blending in with the anonymous Southern California commercial architecture of West Hollywood. The intersection at San Vicente and Santa Monica in West Hollywood has become recognized as the place where the gay pride festival begins and where ACT UP protests culminated, and has drawn more attention as groups build on the corner's importance. Thus, when Queer Nation needed to create a political intervention in West Hollywood, they immediately chose this location.

One of the markers of a mature community, however, is the accumulation of space, the creation of a series of landmarks to stand in for the actions and evolutions that have taken place. Few markers of the history of gay and lesbian struggle in Los Angeles remain, with the past obliterated both by the mechanisms of gay and lesbian community building and by the development of the city as a whole. As each of the case studies has made clear, the process of community building in Los Angeles has been a fluid one, with successive waves of activists claiming space in subtly different ways.

In Los Angeles, known for its propensity for tearing down and building anew, many neighborhoods and intersections are marked as places left behind in the expansion of the movement. For many Angelenos, the abandoned storefront at Sunset Junction recalls (in its peeling pink paint) the first, and more independent, location of A Different Light bookstore. The first site of the Gay Services Center on Wilshire Boulevard is now an abandoned lot in a part of town where few gays would feel safe to walk hand-in-hand. The landmarks of the women's movement are mostly abandoned or used for vastly different purposes. For lesbian activists the claiming of physical refuges—both from the straight and gay male worlds—led to the occupation of spaces around the city. The fragility of their efforts, however, meant that ultimately each of these spaces has been abandoned and stripped of its historical identity. Connexxus is now just another office space; the Woman's Building has been vacant since it closed. In a city where there is not, truly, a constant activist presence, these hints of an activist past generate a sense of loss, of an era when activism was more public, more contested, and more necessary. Across the city, the memories of the gay and lesbian movement are marked more by the absence of a landmark.

Symbolic markers of community life link the more obvious spaces together and draw more hidden spaces into the map. And none is more recurrent in Los Angeles than the rainbow flag. Rainbow flags along the Santa Monica Boulevard in West Hollywood matched by rainbow banners above the Center's entrance and rainbow insignia on storefronts, churches, office buildings, and private homes allow otherwise generic locations to signal otherness. This use of the flag defines a territory that challenges the uncoded or heterosexually coded space of the rest of the city. And, of course, in a city where mobility is the surest emblem of status, displaying rainbow license plate holders and bumper stickers makes claiming space as gay or lesbian as easy as driving to the supermarket. Radical activists often belittle the flag as an accommodationist alternative to the more defiant pink triangle. Whereas the flag symbolizes a tolerance for diversity, carrying with it the potential for traitorous alliances, the pink triangle recalls and makes present the oppression of the gay community, most importantly, but not solely, under Nazi rule. But many gays and lesbians use the flag to calmly identify themselves. Thus, as one drives along the freeway, beyond the boundaries of safe territory, the rainbow flag bumper sticker attracts attention from friends, and only rarely from enemies. In affirmation of the importance of this symbol, the City of West Hollywood has recently begin to use the rainbow flag in its official city logo, a move that has occurred so quietly as to spark little or no reaction from city residents. Given the city's reputation for public engagement in design and development issues, this easy acquiescence reveals the degree to which gay and lesbian visibility continues to be synonymous with the city.

The distinction of these two symbols—the rainbow flag and the pink triangle—can, very broadly, serve as a metaphor for the conflict within and the external analysis of the movement in Los Angeles. Where the pink triangle is serious and confrontational, the rainbow flag is comfortable, and now commercialized. Whereas the pink triangle identifies one as an activist, the rainbow flag can be worn by anyone, or, in Los Angeles, can be applied to anyone's sports utility vehicle. Understanding this important distinction, on its own terms, is the key to the history and geography of the movement in Los Angeles. Too often, critics of the politics in Los Angeles deride those activist strategies that have allowed other, more obvious, actions to occur. This city's uniqueness lies in the opportunities for less radical gays and lesbians to participate in the place-claiming strategies.

The changing strategies of gay and lesbian activists in Los Angeles and the shifting boundaries of the community as a whole reveal multiple ways to map the intersection of sexuality and place. Just as there is little consensus on the meaning or dimensions of sexual identity or the relationship between sexual identity and other individual markers, so there is no definitive way of claiming place. Rather than search for a precise answer to such issues, I have been interested in the different ways groups choose to project their difference, in this case their sexuality, in the course of political organizing and action. Looking at the collective, rather than individual, expressions of sexuality in the city, I see that many of these differences tend to fade into the background, leaving at the foreground the specific ways sexuality comes into conflict with the norms of social conduct and social organization in the city today. These conflicts are articulated through the agendas of the movement, including the desire for safety and security, the right to participate in the public sphere, and access to heath care and other social services. The actual connections between these collective identities and city life include both the abstract and the specific.

Notes

Chapter 1

1. Allan Scott and Edward Soja, "Introduction," in Allan Scott and Edward Soja, eds., *The City: Los Angeles and Urban Theory at the End of the Twentieth Century* (Berkeley: University of California Press, 1996), 1. An emblematic moment in the writing of Los Angeles's history was the uproar over the second volume of Mike Davis's planned Los Angeles trilogy. The publication of *Ecology of Fear,* a book that examines the denial of Los Angeles's natural environment as imbedded in the city's psyche and development politics launched a torrent of criticism that alternately claimed the book to be hyperbolically anti-Los Angeles or the only truthful reading of the city's discriminatory past and present. This desire to use the city's history to bolster either celebratory or condemnatory rhetoric is by no means unique to Los Angeles, although the relative lack of analysis of the city's past does make us take a closer look at those histories that do exist.

2. This chapter in Los Angeles's gay history has so far only been told in piecemeal form, with certain episodes (such as formation of the Mattachine Society in the 1950s) more well known than others. See, for example, Stuart Timmons's biography of Harry Hay, *The Trouble with Harry Hay: Founder of the Modern Gay Movement* (Boston: Alyson, 1990).

3. Dale Jennings, "To Be Accused Is to Be Guilty," *ONE* 1:1 (January 1953).

4. Roger Downs and David Stea, eds., *Image and Environment* (Chicago: Aldine, 1973), 9.

5. For a general overview of ideas about place, see Irwin Altman and Ervin H. Zube, eds., *Public Places and Spaces* (New York: Plenum, 1989).

6. See the discussion in Chapter 5 of the Stonewall Riots and the first commemoration parade in Los Angeles.

7. Douglas Crimp with Adam Rolston, *AIDS demo graphics* (Seattle: Bay Press, 1990), 100.

8. For readers familiar with contemporary gay and lesbian activism, my choice of terms—gay, lesbian, and bisexual—rather than queer or gay (without lesbian) requires clarification. The time frame for this study (over thirty years) necessitates the more inclusive term. Few of the activists I interviewed,

in fact, would recognize the term queer to describe their movement, particularly those involved in gay liberation or lesbian feminism. I recognize it primarily as a temporally bound political strategy used by certain gay and lesbian activists. In this work, I use queer when activists claim this term (and their actions) as such, and do not use it to strategically locate my arguments within the queer theory debate. For an overview of this academic debate, see Diana Fuss, ed., *Inside/Out: Lesbian Theories, Gay Theories* (New York: Routledge, 1991). In addition, I include the term bisexual in the discussion when specifically appropriate.

9. Iris Marion Young, *Justice and the Politics of Difference* (Princeton, NJ: Princeton University Press, 1990), 227.

10. Ibid., 231.

11. State of California, Office of the Attorney General, "Hate Crime in California, 1999," 1999.

12. John M. Gonzales, "Hate Crime Reports Increase 25% Trends: Commission Says Rise Is a Reflection of Law Enforcement Efforts." *The Los Angeles Times,* 27 April 1997.

13. Martin Duberman, *Stonewall* (New York: Dutton, 1991), 242.

14. Kathy Sarachild, quoted in Alice Echols, *Daring to be Bad: Radical Feminism in America 1967–1975* (Minneapolis: University of Minnesota Press, 1989), 87.

15. Rosalyn Deutsche, "Boys Town," *Society and Space* 9 (1991), 55.

16. David Bell and Gill Valentine, eds., *Mapping Desire: Geographies of Sexuality* (New York: Routledge, 1995), 2.

17. Bell and Valentine's *Mapping Desire* includes a number of concrete attempts to map the dimensions of a queer spatiality. These essays address the question of sexualized places on several levels. Tamar Rothenberg's essay on the construction of lesbian space in Park Slope, Brooklyn, adds to the traditional literature on gay gentrification as an example of lesbians' contributions to the changing character of urban neighborhoods. She notes, however, that the impetus behind this development is less the desire to create lesbian-identified space through political or collective actions, than a household-based search for accommodation and sustenance. Similarly, Jerry Lee Kramer's essay on the lives of gays and lesbians in rural North Dakota emphasizes a social networking process that has no identifiable effect on the physical character of the area. Place, then, is irrelevant beyond that fact of its otherwise heterosexual character. On the other hand, Tim Davis's piece on the Boston St. Patrick's Day parade does deal with the intentional efforts of gays and lesbians to mark space, although their efforts were directed at the desire for recognition within a community, rather than a place.

18. Gordon Brent Ingram, Anne-Marie Bouthillette, and Yolanda Retter, eds., *Queers in Space: Communities, Public Places, Sites of Resistance*

(Seattle: Bay Press, 1997), 6.

19. Some of the key texts include Margaret Cruikshanks, *The Gay and Lesbian Liberation Movement* (New York: Routledge, 1992); John D'Emilio, *Sexual Politics/Sexual Communities* (Chicago: University of Chicago Press, 1983); and Dennis Altman, *Homosexual Oppression and Liberation* (New York: New York University Press, 1971). With the exception of D'Emilio's work, however, none of these texts probes the crucial connection between politics (the gay and lesbian movement) and the meaning of community. D'Emilio, focusing on the political economy of the gay and lesbian community and the link between growth of visible gay communities to urban development and changing employment opportunities, reconstructs the context for community formation and adds a crucial dimension to the discussion of place claiming.

20. Feminist political theory is useful here, particularly the discussions of public and private space and critiques of liberal democracy. See Carole Pateman, *The Sexual Contract* (Stanford: Stanford University Press, 1988); and Anne Phillips, *Engendering Democracy* (University Park: Pennsylvania State University Press, 1991).

Chapter 2

1. Interestingly, other businesses that flourished during the county years included animal hospitals and dry cleaning establishments. Both of these businesses are heavily regulated in incorporated sections of the county. As a result, West Hollywood now has more dry cleaners per square mile then anywhere else in Los Angeles. California Economic Development Department, *Los Angeles County Business Patterns 1992* (Sacramento, CA, 1992).

2. As discussed elsewhere, Manuel Castells's study of the Castro District in San Francisco argues that these enclaves emerge from the mismatch between increasing social acceptance and continued social repression. Through the development of "liberated zones," gays looked to create places where they could be "socialized in a new culture more suitable to their needs and behavior." Manuel Castells, *The City and the Grassroots* (Berkeley: University of California Press, 1983), 156.

3. Martin Levine, "Gay Ghetto," in Martin Levine, ed., *Gay Men: The Sociology of Male Homosexuality* (New York: Harper & Row, 1979), 201.

4. Esther Newton, *Cherry Grove, Fire Island* (Boston: Beacon Press, 1992), 9–10

5. Mickey Lauria and Lawrence Knopp, "Towards an Analysis of the Role of Gay Communities in the Urban Renaissance," *Urban Geography* 6 (1985), 159.

6. Ibid.

7. Castells, *The City and the Grassroots.*

8. See longer discussion in Chapter 3.

9. Sy Adler and Johanna Brenner, "Gender and Space: Lesbians and Gay Men in the City," *International Journal of Urban and Regional Research* 16:1 (1992), 31.

10. Edmund White, *States of Desire: Travels in Gay America* (New York: E. P. Dutton, 1980), 25–26.

11. Ibid., 11.

12. Ron Stone, "Gay Pride: Will Success Spoil West Hollywood?" *LA Weekly,* 30 June 1983, 27.

13. Benjamin Forrest, "Political Territory as Symbol" (M.A. Dissertation, University of California, Los Angeles, 1991).

14. Bob Craig, Presentation to the Lesbian and Gay Advisory Council, City of West Hollywood, 14 June 1994.

15. See Adam Moos, "The Grassroots in Action: Gays and Seniors Capture the Local State in West Hollywood, California," in Jennifer Wolch and Michael Dear, eds., *The Power of Geography* (Boston: Unwin Hyman, 1989), 351–369. In short, West Hollywood needed to show sufficient tax revenues to maintain the county's level of services.

16. Ibid., 357.

17. "The Post Supports Cityhood," *West Hollywood Post,* 20 September 1984.

18. Moos, "The Grassroots in Action," 359.

19. "The 'Gay Camelot' Grows Up," *Los Angeles Times,* 27 June 1994, A18.

20. West Hollywood Community Needs Assessment, 1998, 10.

21. West Hollywood Community Needs Assessment, 1994. Using both telephone interview and mail surveys, the study elicited 832 responses, approximately 3.6 percent of all households. The report also analyzed data from the 1980 and 1990 U.S. Censuses. Given that the U.S. Census does not ask questions about sexual orientation, the telephone interview and mail survey data were most useful in analysis of the city's lesbian and gay population.

22. West Hollywood Community Needs Assessment, 1994, xvi.

23. Milton Diamond, "Homosexuality and Bisexuality in Different Populations," *Archives of Sexual Behavior* 22:4 (August 1993), 291–311.

24. West Hollywood Community Needs Assessment, 1998, 16.

25. West Hollywood Community Needs Assessment,1998, 38.

26. Jodi Curlee, interview with author, 3 June 1994.

27. City of West Hollywood, California, "Final Report of the Gay and Lesbian Task Force" (21 November 1988), 3–4.

28. West Hollywood Community Needs Assessment, 1998, 1–7.

29. Curlee, interview.

30. Ibid.

31. Lesbian and Gay Advisory Council staffperson, interview with author, 27 May 1994.

32. Thomas Crail, interview with author, 2 June 1994.

33. Rita Boyadjian, interview with author, 8 July 1994.

34. Ibid.

35. Eric Reyes, "Queer Spaces: The Geography of Lesbians and Gay Men of Color in Los Angeles" (M.A. Thesis, University of California Los Angeles, 1993). Reyes's work is also valuable as an attempt to use cognitive mapping methods, including sketch maps by a selected group of gay men and lesbians of color.

36. SS, quoted in ibid., 99.

37. SL, quoted in ibid., 100.

38. BF, quoted in ibid., 102.

39. Ibid., 110.

40. EB, quoted in ibid., 99.

41. Crail, interview.

42. Ibid.

43. Carter Bravmann, interview with author, 31 May 1994.

44. "WeHo Lounge," *The Advocate,* 28 October 1997, 20.

45. Bravmann, interview.

46. Crail, interview.

47. Ibid.

48. *Los Angeles Times Magazine,* 15 December 1996, 24.

49. E. Michael Gorman, "The Pursuit of the Wish: An Anthropological Perspective on Gay Male Subculture in Los Angeles," in Gilbert Herdt, ed., *Gay Culture in America: Essays in the Field* (Boston: Beacon, 1992), 93.

50. West Hollywood Lesbian and Gay Advisory Committee member, interview with author.

Chapter 3

1. Frances Fox Piven and Richard A. Cloward, *Poor People's Movements: Why They Succeed, How They Fail* (New York: Vintage Books, 1979), xxi.

2. Bettina Boxall, "The New Gay Muscle," *Los Angeles Times Magazine,* 28 October 1993, 28.

3. Ibid., 28.

4. Ibid., 29.

5. Ibid.

6. For more on Stonewall and gay liberation protest in Los Angeles, see Chapter 5.

7. Their street protest activities will be detailed in Chapter 5.

8. Karla Jay, *Tales of the Lavender Menace: A Memoir of Liberation* (New York: Basic Books, 1999), 210.

9. Other early organizers in the GLF included Troy Perry, founder of the Metropolitan Community Church, and Greg Byrd, as an African American one of the few people of color involved in the GLF LA.

10. Morris Kight, interview with author, 3 June 1994.

11. John D'Emilio, "Forward," in Karla Jay and Allen Young, eds., *Out of the Closets: Voices of Gay Liberation,* 20th anniversary edition (New York: New York University Press, 1992), xxvii.

12. The Gay Survival Committee became institutionalized as the Gay Services Center, which, in the late 1970s, was finally renamed the Gay and Lesbian Community Services Center. The omission of the word *lesbian* was a source of great dispute within the agency throughout the 1970s and reflects the disproportionate representation of gay men within the agency, as well as the participation of lesbians in the women's movement rather than the gay movement (see Chapter 4).

13. Los Angeles Gay and Lesbian History Project interview, 1997.

14. Kight, interview.

15. Ibid.

16. Jodi Curlee, interview with author, 3 June 1994.

17. Ibid.

18. Ibid.

19. The AIDS epidemic is, obviously, very complex and created an array of shifts in the lesbian and gay community. In this section, I talk specifically about the connection between AIDS and the Center's role in the community. Later, in separate sections, I will talk about the rise of AIDS service organizations in the city (particularly APLA) and the effect of AIDS on lesbian organizing in the city.

20. APLA staffperson, interview with author, 25 May 1994.

21. Charles Perrow and Mauro Guilen, *The AIDS Disaster: The Failure of Organizations in New York and the Nation* (New Haven, CT: Yale University Press, 1990), 110–112.

22. APLA former Director of Operations, interview with author, 25 May 1994.

23. Ibid.

24. Ibid..

25. APLA staffperson, interview.

26. John R. Logan and Harvey L. Molotch, *Urban Fortunes: The Political Economy of Place* (Berkeley: University of California Press, 1987), 44.

27. Susan M. Ruddick, *Young and Homeless in Hollywood: Mapping Social Identities* (New York: Routledge, 1995). Ruddick explores the chang-

ing social policy toward runaways in Los Angeles, and the evolution of this policy in the context of Hollywood's redevelopment.

28. John Kaliski, interview with author, 24 May 1994.

29. Ed Gould, Board of Directors, Gay and Lesbian Community Services Center, interview with author, 18 May 1994.

30. CRA staffperson, interview with author, 23 May 1994.

31. "Gay Services Move to Hollywood," *Los Angeles Times,* 25 August 1991, J1.

32. Cooke Sunoo, CRA, quoted in "Gay Services Move to Hollywood," *Los Angeles Times,* 25 August 1991, J11.

33. Center Youth Services staffperson, interview with author, 20 May 1994.

34. Torie Osborn, quoted in "Gay Services Move to Hollywood."

35. Gould, interview.

36. APLA former Director of Operations, interview.

37. Phill Wilson, quoted in APLA, "1993 Annual Report" (Los Angeles, 1993).

38. Ferd Eggan, quoted in Doug Sadownick, "Victims of Success: As Treatment Improves, AIDS Clinics Shut Down," *LA Weekly,* 18 October 1996.

39. CRA staffperson, interview.

40. Center Youth Services staffperson, interview.

Chapter 4

1. This is not exclusive to Los Angeles or to my selection of interviewees, but has often been noted as a characteristic of lesbian activism. The role of lesbians in the women's movement is well documented, as is the role of lesbians in the labor movement—often to the exclusion of their participation in gay and lesbian issues per se. See Margaret Cruikshanks, *The Gay and Lesbian Liberation Movement* (New York: Routledge, 1992).

2. In an essay written early in the AIDS epidemic, Sarah Schulman described the presence of lesbians at the forefront of AIDS activism, propelled in part by their "more sophisticated analysis of the state and a clearer impetus towards direct action." Lesbians' exclusion from gay organizations in the years since liberation had, as Schulman suggested, emboldened activists and prepared them for the viciousness of the antigay rhetoric around AIDS. At the same time, however, Schulman acknowledged lesbians' "resentment towards gay men for the years of self-absorption and the pre-AIDS goal of trying to access the same power as straight men." Sarah Schulman, *My American History: Lesbian and Gay Life During the Reagan/Bush Years* (New York: Routledge 1994), 124.

3. Dolores Hayden, *Redesigning the American Dream: The Future of Housing, Work and Family Life* (New York: Norton, 1984).

4. Bonnie Zimmerman, *The Safe Sea of Women* (Boston: Beacon, 1990), 121–123.

5. Sy Adler and Johanna Brenner, "Gender and Space: Lesbians and Gay Men in the City," *International Journal of Urban and Regional Research* 16:1 (March 1992), 24–25.

6. Tamara Rothenberg, " 'And She Told Two Friends': Lesbians Creating Social Space," in David Bell and Gill Valentine, eds., *Mapping Desire: Geographies of Sexuality* (New York: Routledge, 1995), 165–181. Anne-Marie Bouthillette, "Queer and Gendered Housing," in Gordon Brent Ingram, Anne-Marie Bouthillette, and Yolanda Retter, eds., *Queer in Space: Communities, Public Places, Sites of Resistance* (Seattle: Bay Press, 1997).

7. Lillian Faderman, *Odd Girls and Twilight Lovers* (New York: Penguin Books 1992), 219.

8. Ibid., 276.

9. Much of this theorizing has concentrated on lesbian texts and critical theory. See, for example, Sally Munt, ed., *New Lesbian Criticism: Literary and Cultural Readings* (New York: Columbia University Press, 1992); Karla Jay and Joanne Glasgow, eds., *Lesbian Texts and Contexts: Radical Revisions* (London: Onlywomen, 1991); and Diana Fuss, ed., *Inside/Out: Lesbian Theories, Gay Theories* (New York: Routledge, 1992). Among more works highlighting lesbian politics beyond the text are Julia Penelope, *Call Me Lesbian: Lesbian Lives, Lesbian Theories* (Freedom, CA: The Crossing Press, 1992); and Shane Phelan, *Identity Politics: Lesbian Feminism and the Limits of Community* (Philadelphia: Temple University Press, 1989).

10. Penelope, *Call Me Lesbian,* 55.

11. Joan Nestle, "The Bathroom Line," in Joan Nestle, ed., *A Restricted County* (Ithaca, NY: Firebrand Books, 1987), 37. "Butch-femme" refers to the role-playing practices of prefeminist lesbian society, which was sharply segregated into masculine women, who dressed in drag, and more feminine women, who were their partners.

12. Jeanne Cordova, interview with author, 17 June 1994.

13. For an account of the break between the women's movement and the lesbian feminist movement, see Alice Echol's *Daring to Be Bad: Radical Feminism in America 1967–1975* (Minneapolis: University of Minnesota Press, 1989), in particular, her account of the infamous lesbian purges in the National Organization of Women. For an account of the lesbian tensions within the GLF, see the following selections in Karla Jay and Allen Young, eds., *Out of the Closets: Voices of Gay Liberation,* 20th anniversary edition (New York: New York University Press, 1992): "Leaving the Gay Men Behind"; "Take a Lesbian to

Lunch," Rita Mae Brown; and "Realesbians and Politicalesbians," Gay Revolution Women's Party Caucus.

14. Arlene Stein, "Sisters and Queers: The Decentering of Lesbian Feminism," *Socialist Review* 22:1 (1992), 32.

15. Cordova, interview.

16. Yolanda Retter, "Lesbian Spaces in Los Angeles, 1970–1990," in Ingram, et al., *Queers in Space*, 325–338.

17. Efforts to create an "artists district" in downtown Los Angeles have enjoyed public support for decades although the still very industrial character of Los Angeles's warehouse district and the inadequacy of social services for the large homeless population directly adjacent have jeopardized many city initiatives.

18. Los Angeles Woman's Building, *Fifteen Years and Growing: Celebrating the Fifteenth Anniversary of the Woman's Building* (Los Angeles, 1988), 6.

19. Sheila de Bretteville, in ibid.

20. Cheri Gaulke, interview with author, 8 June 1994.

21. Terry Wolverton, interview with author, 17 June 1994.

22. Gaulke, interview.

23. Ibid.

24. The Woman's Building participants, concerned that their role in the development of performance art and public art has been overlooked by art historians and artists, have begun an extensive project to document the history of the building. This project is ongoing and will, it is hoped, result in a more complete documentation of the types of projects I mention here.

25. Elizabeth Wilson's *The Sphinx in the City* (Los Angeles: University of California Press, 1992) addresses these issues of erasure and reclamation in a historical context.

26. Wolverton, interview.

27. Ibid.

28. Gaulke, interview.

29. Ibid.

30. Lauren Jardine, interview with author, 17 June 1994.

31. Ibid.

32. Ibid.

33. Del Martinez, interview with author, 14 June 1994.

34. Jardine, interview.

35. Carla Barboza, interview with author, 18 June 1994.

36. Ibid.

37. Ibid.

38. The June Mazer Archives, named for the community activist who had found a home for the archives in Los Angeles (bringing it to the city from

Oakland, California), remains the most enduring lesbian-only space in the city, housing a constantly growing collection of lesbian papers, nearly complete sets of numerous underground lesbian newspapers and magazines from the 1950s to the present, and posters, buttons, videos, and other memorabilia representing all aspects of lesbian culture in the United States.

39. Jardine, interview.
40. Ibid.
41. Barboza, interview.
42. Martinez, interview.
43. Julie Anderson, interview with author, 20 May 1994.
44. Schulman, *My American History,* 286.
45. Mary Pickert, interview with author, 26 May 1998.
46. Judy Sisneros, interview with author, 26 May 1998.
47. Pickert, interview.
48. Marsha Schwemer, interview with author, 26 May 1998.
49. Jeri Deitrick, interview with author, 26 May 1998.
50. Pickert, interview.
51. Bunnie Meyer, interview with author, 26 May 1998.
52. Dyke march activist, interview with author, 26 May 1998.
53. Pickert, interview.
54. Meyer, interview.
55. Pickert, interview.

Chapter 5

1. Iris Marion Young, *Justice and the Politics of Difference* (Princeton, NJ: Princeton University Press, 1990), 96ff.
2. Lauren Berlant and Elizabeth Freeman, "Queer Nationality," in Michael Warner, ed., *Fear of a Queer Planet: Queer Politics and Social Theory* (Minneapolis, University of Minnesota Press, 1993), 196.
3. Robin Podolsky, "Stretching the World," *LA Weekly,* 15 November 1991, 15.
4. Doug Sadownick, "The Center Moves West," *LA Weekly,* 15 November 1991, 14.
5. Ibid.
6. Ibid., 24.
7. Joel Barraquiel Tan, interview with author, 8 June 1994.
8. Vanessa Place, quoted in Sadownick, "The Center Moves West," 25.
9. Tan, interview.
10. Colors United, *Shades,* 1:1 (Spring 1992).
11. Tan, interview.
12. Sadownick, "The Center Moves West," 25.

13. John D'Emilio, *Sexual Politics/Sexual Communities* (Chicago: University of Chicago Press, 1983), 57–58.

14. Ibid., 59.

15. John Bryan, "Police Outrages Help Create L.A. Homosexual Rights Drive," *Los Angeles Free Press,* 10 March 1967, 5.

16. D'Emilio, *Sexual Politics/Sexual Communities,* 233.

17. Ibid., 234.

18. "A Gay Manifesto," in "I'm Gay and I'm Proud: Los Angeles Free Press Gay Liberation Supplement," *Los Angeles Free Press,* 14 August 1970.

19. Morris Kight, interview with author, 3 June 1994.

20. Kight recalls 1,850 marchers with 35,000 onlookers.

21. Angela Douglas, "Gays March on Hollywood Boulevard," *Los Angeles Free Press,* 3 July 1970, 5.

22. Ibid.

23. Morris Kight, "The Great Christopher Street West," in "I'm Gay and I'm Proud: Los Angeles Free Press Gay Liberation Supplement," *Los Angeles Free Press,* 14 August 1970, 62.

24. As discussed in Chapter 3, the Los Angeles GLF disappeared earlier than chapters in other cities, in part because it shifted into a mode of providing social service.

25. Kight, interview.

26. Ibid.

27. Jeanne Cordova, interview with author, 17 June 1994.

28. Kight, interview.

29. Ibid.

30. Paul Daniels, interview with author, 7 June 1994.

31. For an excellent and detailed account of the struggle for AIDS funding and care in Los Angeles County and, in particular, the conservative health care politics of the County Board of Supervisors, see Ty Geltmaker, "The Queer Nation Acts Up: Health Care, Politics, and Sexual Diversity in the County of Angels," *Society and Space* 10:6 (1992), 609–650. Geltmaker, an ACT UP veteran, reviewed the protracted battle to establish an AIDS budget in the county (finally realized in the 1989–1990 fiscal year) and the particularly homophobic nature of the health care debate in Los Angeles. Geltmaker explored the AIDS struggle in Los Angeles against the backdrop of the racial politics of the county and the recent emergence of Latino power bases to challenge the white conservatives on the board.

32. Statement quoted in ACT UP archive records, 16 May 1989.

33. Geltmaker, "The Queer Nation Acts Up," 625.

34. Daniels, interview.

35. Walt Walker, personal interview, 10 June 1994.

36. Daniels, interview.

37. Geltmaker, "The Queer Nation Acts Up," 633.

38. The first cases of AIDS were identified in Los Angeles in 1979 and 1980.

39. Daniels, interview.

40. Ibid.

41. Geltmaker, "The Queer Nation Acts Up," 610.

42. Daniels, interview.

43. *ACT UP/LA News,* 4:2 April/May 1991.

44. Geltmaker, "The Queer Nation Acts Up," 637.

45. Daniels, interview.

Chapter 6

1. Doug Sadownick, "Jim Kepner: 1923–1997," *LA Weekly,* 12 December 1997, 20.

2. Essex Hemphill, *Ceremonies: Prose and Poetry* (New York: Plume, 1992), 41–42.

3. LAAPIS activist, interview with author, 6 June 1994.

4. Ibid.

5. "LAAPIS is in Hibernation" [on-line], 15 March 2000. Available: www.geocities.com/WestHollywood/8878/#status.

6. George Chauncey, *Gay New York: Gender, Urban Culture, and the Making of the Gay Male World, 1890–1940* (New York: Basic Books, 1994), 180.

7. Ibid.

8. Mike Davis, *City of Quartz: Excavating the Future in Los Angeles* (New York: Verso, 1990), 258.

9. Morris Kight, interview with author, 3 June 1994.

Index